About this book

The Pinochet Affair is the epic story of the events that surrounded the dramatic arrest of General Augusto Pinochet in London in October 1998. Based on interviews and intimate sketches of the leading protagonists, Roger Burbach begins this narrative with the violent military coup that Pinochet led against the democratically elected government of Salvador Allende on September 11, 1973.

To understand what drove Chile's strong man, a profile is constructed, discussing the sociopathic, paranoid and authoritarian tendencies that led the dictator to murder thousands of his own people while authorizing acts of international terrorism in Argentina, Italy and Washington DC. In response to his brutal reign, a human rights movement was forged in Chile and abroad that played a critical role in finally ousting the dictator in 1990. But even out of office, his power was such that he suppressed all efforts to prosecute him, until his detention in London.

The final part of *The Pinochet Affair* describes the global clash that then took place – in Spain, Britain and Chile – between the politicians who sought to cover up and wash their hands of Pinochet, and the efforts of a number of brave judges, lawyers and human rights organizations determined to see justice prevail. Roger Burbach concludes by discussing the impact of the Pinochet Affair around the world, as the global human rights community seeks to establish an international regime of justice that stands in direct opposition to cynical politicians such as George W. Bush and Tony Blair who mouth the slogans of justice a   acts of state terrorism.

About the author

ROGER BURBACH is Director of Research and Publication at the Center for the Study of the Americas (CENSA) in Berkeley, California. A historian by training, he was for a number of years a staff member and writer with NACLA, the North American Congress on Latin America. During the 1990s he was Visiting Scholar in Peace and Conflict Studies, and subsequently at the Institute of International Studies, University of California, Berkeley. He is the author of numerous books, including most recently *Globalization and Postmodern Politics: Zapatistas versus High Tech Robber Barons* (London, Pluto Press, 2001) and *Globalize This! The Battle against the World Trade Organization* (Monroe, ME, Common Courage Press, 2000; edited with Kevin Danaher). He coauthored with Orlando Núñez *Fire in the Americas* (London, Verso, 1987).

The Pinochet Affair

State terrorism and global justice

ROGER BURBACH

ZED BOOKS
London & New York

in association with

THE TRANSNATIONAL INSTITUTE

The Pinochet Affair was first published by
Zed Books Ltd, 7 Cynthia Street, London N1 9JF, UK,
and Room 400, 175 Fifth Avenue, New York, NY 10010, USA

www.zedbooks.demon.co.uk

in association with
The Transnational Institute, Paulus Potterstraat 20,
1071 DA Amsterdam, The Netherlands

www.tni.org

Designed and typeset in Monotype Bembo by Illuminati, Grosmont
Cover designed by Andrew Corbett
Printed and bound in Malta by Gutenberg Ltd

Distributed in the USA exclusively by Palgrave, a division of
St Martin's Press, LLC, 175 Fifth Avenue, New York, NY 10010

A catalogue record for this book is available from the British Library
Library of Congress Cataloging-in-Publication Data available

ISBN 1 84277 434 4 (Hb)
ISBN 1 84277 435 2 (Pb)

Contents

Dedicated to the
human rights activists,
lawyers and judges
who persevered

The Transnational Institute was founded in 1974 as a worldwide network of committed scholar–activists coordinated from Amsterdam. In the spirit of public scholarship, and aligned to no political party, TNI seeks to create and promote transnational cooperation in analysing and finding possible solutions to the global problems of today and tomorrow. Much of its work is geared to providing intellectual support to those movements concerned to steer the world in a democratic, equitable and environmentally sustainable direction.

In the context of the co-publication of this book, TNI would like to honour the memory of Orlando Letelier, who served as a minister in the Allende government until the Pinochet coup. He was director of TNI at the time he was assassinated by Pinochet's secret services in a car bomb in Washington DC on September 21, 1976, which also killed Ronni Karpen-Moffitt of the Institute for Policy Studies.

Preface

The origins of this book go back to the years 1971–73 that I spent in Chile working on my doctoral dissertation. Like many Americans who went to Chile at that time I became fascinated with the experiment in democratic socialism that was taking place under President Salvador Allende. This was a period unlike any other in my life, before or since. It felt like a political paradise as the people of Chile at the grassroots stood up and mobilized to make a better life for themselves and all the disadvantaged of the country. Authentic democracy was palpable as the popular classes took control of their food distribution systems and worked through unions and political organizations to take over and run factories, farms and mines that legitimately belonged to them.

Even in the waning days of the Popular Unity government, when the economy was in shambles and virtually everyone believed a confrontation was imminent, one still felt the popular impulse and the drive of the people from below. I'll never forget the last major demonstration on September 4, 1973, when the Alameda, the major avenue of downtown Santiago, was packed with tens of thousands of marchers, all intent on passing by the presidential palace where Allende stood on a balcony waving to the crowd. This was no government-orchestrated demonstration in which people were trucked in from the barrios and countryside. These people came out of a deep sense of commitment, a belief that this was their government and that they would defend it to the end.

Exactly one week later the presidential palace was in flames. A coup led by General Augusto Pinochet brutally smashed the dreams of Chileans, as well as the hopes of many foreigners in Chile and abroad who for three years had watched in awe and solidarity as the Popular Unity government attempted to build a new socialism with a humane and democratic face. Like other foreign supporters of the Chilean process, I had to abandon the country, leaving on October 9 by crossing over the Andes into Argentina. Before I left, two friends of mine from the United States, Charles Horman and Frank Teruggi, were picked up and murdered by the junta, most likely with the acquiescence of US covert operatives in Chile.

My first acknowledgement in this book is to Jim Williams, a Peace Corps volunteer in Chile at the time who allowed me and my companion, Elizabeth Patelke, to reside in his 'safe house' in downtown Santiago until we left the country. When the Peace Corps officials in Chile found out that I was at Jim's place, they ordered him to throw me out because I was an 'undesirable element who endangered the Peace Corps mission'. Jim refused and resigned his position as a volunteer.

After leaving Chile I went to work for NACLA, the North American Congress on Latin America, which put out one of the few publications where one could write about the Chilean dictatorship and continue a commitment to left politics in Latin America and the United States. Then when the Sandinista revolution occurred in Nicaragua in 1979, I instinctively felt the need to become involved. It was inevitable that the US government would intervene covertly and overtly to destroy the revolution, just as it had in Chile, and I was intent on doing what little I could as a writer and international activist to counteract US intervention. But as we now know the Nicaraguan revolution was also destined to fail. The complex factors that led to the Sandinista government's defeat in the elections in 1990 are too extensive to go into here, but US intervention and the bloody Contra war were decisive.

Even while working in Nicaragua, my gaze was continually drawn
to the south, to Chile where the first signs of crisis for the dictatorship began to appear in the early 1980s. In 1985 I took the first of
several trips back to Chile and was there on October 5, 1988 when
Pinochet was defeated in a plebiscite. Unfortunately, it immediately
became clear that the new political class that took over had no
intention of continuing any of the policies and programmes of the
Popular Unity era. Pinochet himself, even though ousted from office,
largely dominated the transition process, preventing the prosecution
of those who had engaged in systematic human rights violations,
while ensuring that the conservative social and economic classes of
Chile would exercise a decisive influence over the country.

Like millions of others in Chile and around the world, I was
ecstatic when I heard of Pinochet's arrest in London on October 16,
1998. Perhaps now there could be justice after a quarter-century of
the general's rule and pervasive influence. For the first time a dictator
had been apprehended in another country and was being charged
with crimes for which the courts of his own nation were unable to
prosecute him. These events inspired me to begin work on *The
Pinochet Affair*. At last a story could be written that would hark back
to Allende's last speech in the presidential palace when he prophesied
that 'the cowardice, treachery and treason' of the coup leaders would
be punished.

My acknowledgements for assistance on this book begin in
Europe. In the summer of 1999 I went to Spain and Britain to talk
with people who were involved in the Pinochet case. Fiona Dove
and the Transnational Institute in Amsterdam graciously helped
finance this trip. In London I'd like to thank my long-time friend
Hermione Harris for putting me up at her house and helping me
out with contacts and information. Also Andy McEntee of Amnesty
International, Jeremy Corbyn of the House of Commons, and
Vicente Alegría of the local Chilean exile community graciously
recounted their own experiences in the Pinochet affair and helped
me get in touch with others who had information.

When I went to Spain, Mario Aguirre assisted me in setting up
contacts and interviews. In Madrid I met Joan Garcés for the first

time. A close advisor to Allende from 1970 to 1973, he was also the attorney who first brought charges against Pinochet in Spain. If there is an unsung hero in this book it is Garcés, who committed his life to pursuing Pinochet after leaving the besieged presidential palace.

My work in Chile on the Pinochet affair began in early March 2000, several days after the general returned to Chile upon being released from house arrest in London. The first person I met at the airport in Santiago was Elias Padilla, a former president of Amnesty International in Chile, who had also investigated and written on the crimes of the dictatorship. During the next two and a half years as I returned to Chile on different occasions, Elias was inevitably there to greet me, to recount the latest events in the Pinochet affair, and to help me set up interviews. Without Elias's help, this would be a very different and inferior work.

Aside from the generally obnoxious and socially conservative upper class, the Chileans are a very gracious people, willing to share their lives and experiences with outsiders like me. Some old friends like Fernando Zegers, Juan Pablo Cardenas, José Bengoa and Alvaro Díaz talked with me and related information as they had in bygone days. Eduardo Deves's assistance was critical as he gave me a copy of his unedited manuscript on Pinochet and helped me shape my initial thoughts on writing the socio-psychological profile of Pinochet. During my second trip to Chile for this book in January 2001, I met Cecilia Bottai, who helped me in many uncountable ways to get around Santiago, to set up interviews, and to secure lodging. As a dentist she even took care of my dental problems, expecting nothing in return.

Francisco Coloane, who wrote a book on Pinochet in London, was also very helpful in sharing his thoughts and ideas. Tomas Moulían, perhaps the most prominent writer on the left in Chile, also shared his thoughts with me. It was delightful to meet and interview Carmen Hertz and Roberto Garretón, both human rights lawyers who have been directly involved in the pursuit of Pinochet for his crimes against humanity. Juan Guzmán, the judge prosecuting Pinochet, also proved to be exceptionally helpful. After our first rather formal meeting in his chambers, we were able to meet in more relaxed settings on several different occasions and to have extensive personable conversations, parts of which will remain off the record until he retires from his judicial responsibilities.

In the final stages of the book I met Francesco Jara, a reporter and seminar student of mine at the University of Santiago, who was helpful in setting up some final interviews as well as in just talking about the book. Linessett Toro, who works in the doctoral programme at the university, also provided me with research assistance in the libraries of Santiago. Nelson Osorio, the director of the doctoral programme, discussed some of the ideas of the book with me at critical moments. Pascale Bonnefoy of Chile also provided assistance in the final stages of the manuscript.

In New York, my long-time friend Karen Judd was particularly helpful, as were Robert Armstrong and Hank Frundt. Paul Cantor and Joyce Horman provided support and encouragement. Cathy Schneider on the East Coast also provided assistance. John Dinges and Peter Kornbluh helped out with some key documentation in understanding the United States' relationship to the Pinochet regime. Finally I appreciated the help and companionship of Marcela Coutinho in Rio de Janeiro, where I finished working on the final editorial details of this book.

Regarding the book itself I want to thank Marny Requa for writing Chapter 5 on 'The Bitter Democratic Transition'. When I met her and found out she was working on the transition from 1990 to 1998, I was delighted because it meant that I did not have to investigate systematically yet another period of Chilean history that was dominated by the dark figure of Augusto Pinochet.

As readers will see, in the notes to Chapters 1 and 6 I thank Claudio Duran for his involvement in helping me work on the initial drafts of these chapters in 1999. Our different work commitments and agendas unfortunately made it impossible to continue this collaboration. However, Claudio's spirit is present throughout the book as he showed me how to write in a more popular, less academic style than I was accustomed to.

In northern California, where I try to reside, I would like to thank my life-long friends Marilyn and Glenn Borchardt for having me over for dinner on innumerable occasions just to relax from the travails of the book. David Parkhurst as usual kept my laptop running and helped me advance my use of the Internet. Cecile Earle was a source of friendship as I worked on the book. Eric Leenson and Monica Marini, two 'Chilean veterans', also kept up my morale and helped out in many different ways. Elizabeth Farnsworth also provided support and some thoughts on the manuscript. My two children, Matthew and Alexandra, were supportive and a joy to be with as I worked on the book.

The first September 11
that shook the world

A common refrain heard in the United States after September 11, 2001 was: 'The world has changed; nothing will ever be the same again.' In another corner of the world, exactly twenty-eight years earlier, a military coup led by Augusto Pinochet on September 11, 1973 transformed the lives of the Chilean people. It marked an upheaval in some ways even more profound than that which occurred in the aftermath of the destruction of the World Trade Center towers. To this day, tens of thousands of Chileans are still dealing with the consequences of the bloody overthrow of the democratically elected government of Salvador Allende in 1973.

Although it was not clear on September 11, 1973, that date also marked the beginning of the end of one historical epoch and the start of another. On hindsight we can see that the overthrow of the first and only democratically elected socialist government marked the inevitable decline of 'actually existing socialism'. Salvador Allende and the Popular Unity coalition had come to power in 1970 on a platform that promised to transform Chile into a socialist country by using democratic principles. It was called 'the Chilean road to socialism'.

For the next three years millions of people in Chile, and un-countable numbers abroad, hoped and believed that it was more than a dream, that this type of revolutionary transformation was possible. The Popular Unity government upon taking office launched a profound agrarian reform programme, recognized the right of workers to take over factories and run them collectively, took control of most of the country's financial institutions, and expropriated multinational corporations such as Kennecott Corporation and ITT.

From the start virtually all of the Chilean business clans, backed by multinational corporations and the US government, moved to undermine and destroy this experiment in democratic socialism. By 1973 it was clear to many, including this writer, that there would be a confrontation and that the democratic institutions of Chile would not hold. The opposition was openly calling on the military to violently overthrow the government so they could retake control of the country. And on the left, some argued that the existing constitutional system and many democratic liberties had to be suspended or tossed out, that it was necessary for the workers and the popular classes to unite with loyalist sectors of the military in an attempt to establish a new political regime in Chile.

But one man, Salvador Allende, refused to violate the democratic institutions that brought him and the Popular Unity coalition to power. He would not install a new regime by violent means. On the day of the coup Allende intended to announce a plebiscite in which the people of Chile would vote on whether or not he and the Popular Unity coalition should continue to lead the country. Allende is probably the most tragic figure in the twentieth-century political history of the Americas. He was caught in a bitter dilemma: if he seized power and ruled by decree he would be violating the fundamental democratic principles he believed in, and yet by not abandoning these principles he risked subjecting the country to rule by reactionary forces.[1] Authentic democratic socialism died with Allende in the presidential palace of Chile on September 11, 1973. His quest for a peaceful democratic socialist revolution proved to be a contradiction in terms.

The end of democratic socialism meant that there was no viable alternative to the existing state socialist model – a system in which governments controlled the means of production and distributed their countries' resources in a relatively equitable manner but did not practice authentic democracy. As we now know this meant that state socialism was headed for an implosion in the late 1980s and early 1990s. It proved impossible for rigid, top-down state-directed economies to sustain themselves. State socialist anomalies, like North Korea and Cuba, would continue to exist, but they no longer represented the wave of the future.[2]

Yet out of the ashes of Chile, a new concept of a different world began to materialize. In the aftermath of September 11 the bitter struggle of Chileans to survive the brutal dictatorship led to the emergence of a human rights movement. This new social movement drew broad support from the diverse sectors of Chile that were disarticulated by the coup. They soon forged a network with international human rights organizations, including many in other southern cone countries that were also confronting repressive dictatorships.

The rise of the human rights movement proved to be a harbinger of a new global movement that would sink deep roots in civil society over the next three decades. Specific political ideologies, which for so long had divided and fragmented the left, would now become less important as people at the grassroots level fought to resist the rule of dictators, global capital and the dominant imperial nations.

The Pinochet affair is a case study of how these two global forces – the new social movements and the dominant global interests – have evolved and confronted each other over the past thirty years in the arena of human rights. The demand for basic human rights now extends beyond the cry for freedom from torture and repression. It includes the right to a decent life, to be free from hunger and to have access to the basic amenities, including shelter, education and medical care. Those who mobilize behind these demands are engaged in a confrontation with the corporate and state interests that are currently traumatizing the world. This alternative global movement first surfaced visibly in Seattle in 1999 and today finds its broadest expression in the World Social Forum of Porto Alegre, Brazil, along with the popular mobilizations that have taken place in cities as diverse as Quebec City, Prague and Genoa.

This book lays out the specific evolution of the global human rights movement in relation to the Pinochet affair. It traces the quest to bring Pinochet to justice in three countries, Chile, Spain

and Great Britain. Much of the book focuses on what happened in
Chile, since this is where the Pinochet dictatorship imposed its reign
of evil.

The first chapter discusses the political and social terrain of the
people who lived on this long narrow strip of land on the South
American coast at the time of Allende and the Popular Unity government. It then looks at the forces that came together to overthrow
Allende, and the tragic events of September 11, 1973.

The next two chapters are a study of the man who led the coup,
Augusto Pinochet. First his formation in the years leading up to
1973 is analysed, looking in particular at his psychological and
personal profile during the first fifty-seven years of his life. Then the
succeeding chapter discusses the early years of his regime, depicting
the personal and institutional forces he mobilized to consolidate his
tyrannical rule over the country for seventeen years.

The next chapter describes the emergence of the human rights
movement in Chile and abroad, the different social and political
forces that joined together to challenge the regime with growing
intensity in the late 1970s and 1980s. Its biggest success occurred
with the plebiscite on October 5, 1988, when the Chilean people
voted to oust the dictatorship. But its very success led to a crisis as
traditional political forces conspired to control and contain the popular movement so they could seize the spoils of political office.

The period from 1990 to 1998 was a bitter period, referred to by
mainstream political scientists as the 'democratic transition'. It was a
period in which the civilian politicians made a pact with Pinochet
and the forces he represented, committing themselves to forgo
prosecuting the gross violators of human rights in exchange for
being allowed to exercise formal political power. The families of the
victims of the military regime were expected to bury the past, to be
'reconciled' with a brave new world in which they would have the
right to vote in a controlled democracy, but no justice for the atrocities that had been inflicted on them.

But the human rights movement never abandoned hope. For
years, both in Chile and abroad, it insisted on maintaining the
memory of what had happened. Human rights activists and lawyers,
in the name of this movement, launched numerous campaigns and

legal assaults on the torturers and murderers of the military regime. Then on October 16 they shocked the world with the arrest of Augusto Pinochet in London.

The last part of the book describes the global clash that took place – in Spain, Britain and then Chile – between the politicians who sought to cover up and wash their hands of Pinochet, and the efforts of a number of brave judges and human rights lawyers who were determined to see that justice prevailed. The Conclusion then discusses the impact of the Pinochet affair around the world, as the global human rights community seeks to establish an international regime of justice. Today it confronts cynical politicians like Bush and Blair, who mouth some of the words and slogans of justice and liberty while seeking to impose a new reign of terror on the world.

I

The dictator's prelude:
Allende, Chile and the coup

The genesis of Augusto Pinochet's entrapment in London begins on July 4, 1996. In the middle of the Spanish summer, when most people have abandoned the hot cities and flocked to the beaches, Joan Garcés, a 52-year-old Spanish lawyer, went to court in Valencia to file criminal charges against Pinochet. Garcés, an adviser to President Salvador Allende during the Popular Unity government, had been waiting for this occasion for a long time, twenty-three years to be exact. His filing was part of a personal commitment he made to Allende in the Chilean presidential palace on the day Allende died in the military coup led by General Pinochet.

Joan Garcés' case was in a certain sense simple and straightforward; he wanted to know what happened to Antoni Llido, a Spanish Catholic priest who went to Chile in 1969. Llido, who joined the underground resistance after the coup, was picked up by the military secret police in October 1974, brutally tortured, and last seen in a detention centre in December of the same year.[1] He became a *desaparecido*, or 'disappeared', a sinister word that became all too familiar during the Pinochet regime.

From this almost innocuous beginning has ensued one of the most intriguing international human rights cases of the past half-century. The historic setting of this case begins in Chile, a thin sliver of land on the west side of the Andean mountain range at the end of the South American continent. It is a spectacularly beautiful country with deserts, mountains, volcanoes, archipelagos and one of the few surviving ancient redwood forests on the planet. The country is more than 2,600 miles long, north to south, and only an average of 250 miles wide. Chileans thus either come from the north, the centre or the south. To say that one comes from the east or west of the country is not in the Chilean lexicon. The central valley, where most of the population is concentrated, enjoys benign Mediterranean weather and possesses rich soils, thus accounting for the cornucopia of fruit and wines that Chile produces for the world market. To position Chile in relation to the United States, one needs to imagine a thin piece of land that runs from Baja California, Mexico, across the entire US West Coast to the Northwest Territories of Canada. The difference is that the seasons are reversed, so that Chile produces its fruit for export when the northern hemisphere is locked in winter.

The 15 million people who live in Chile have a rich blend of diverse racial origins. Many are mestizo, a mixture of Indian and European blood, although the Indian presence is much less prominent than in other Latin American societies like Peru and Bolivia. Although upwards of a million Chileans consider themselves Mapuche Indians, Chileans by and large hark back to their Spanish origins with the celebration of *Día de la Raza*, on October 12. Others of European descent are also solidly represented in Chile. During the late nineteenth and early twentieth centuries, a large number of French, Italian and German immigrants arrived on Chile's shores, many setting up their own settlement colonies, some of which survive to this day. Into this mix one must add a lesser number of English, Jewish, Arab and Slavic immigrants, along with Gypsy communities, making Chile a unique and fascinating pot-pourri of peoples for such a small country.

The first Spaniards settled in Chile in 1541. Led by Spanish conqueror Pedro de Valdivia, who had arrived late to the looting of Peru, they ventured southward down the Andes in search of precious metals. But the Spaniards found little gold or silver in Chile, and the inhabitants, the Mapuche Indians, never welcomed them, fighting a war against the intruders that lasted more than three centuries.[2] So fierce was the Mapuche resistance that Spanish soldiers often refused to go to Chile. In colonial times Chile became known as the 'Spanish Cemetery'.

In 1818, when the Spaniards were defeated by the local elites that rebelled against the Spanish Crown, at least a third of the country had not been conquered. The continuance of the 'Indians Wars' created a stratified society where the military became the backbone of social stability, particularly during the first decades of the new republic. While most of the new Latin American nations slipped into total chaos as a result of the wars of liberation from the Spanish Crown, Chile was an island of stability in South America. The military exerted a strong influence over the society, supporting a civilian elite that set up a constitutional regime in which only about 2 per cent of the nation's population was able to vote. Since then, the military leaders have thought of themselves as the guarantors of social order, even though their direct intervention in politics has been limited.[3]

In the late nineteenth century an important sector of the Chilean elite, who viewed themselves as followers of the enlightened French *philosophes*, opened the state's coffers to provide comprehensive support for education. By the turn of the twentieth century Chile had a free compulsory educational system with two national universities. Many leaders of other Latin American countries attended Chilean universities. Chile became known for its world-calibre artists and two Nobel laureate poets, Pablo Neruda, and the first woman, Gabriela Mistral. In art and painting Chile has given the world the surrealist Roberto Matta and the expressionist Guillermo Nuñez.

Yet, at the same time, Chile produced one of the most ruthless regimes of the twentieth century. From 1973 to 1990, the country lived under the iron hand of Augusto Pinochet Ugarte. This societal calamity has spurred endless debates by Chileans about the nature and role of the armed forces in a country of relative civic tranquillity.

The Chilean road to socialism

To understand the origins of this traumatic experience we must go back to the 1960s, when Latin America was experiencing widespread social turmoil. The Cuban Revolution of 1959 had a dramatic impact on progressive Latin Americans, who saw in practice how a small country could defy the hemispheric order, especially the United States. Armed revolution and insurrection spread rapidly across the continent. By the late 1960s, revolutionary movements had a strong presence in countries like Guatemala, Nicaragua, Colombia, Peru, Uruguay and Argentina. In 1967, one of the main figures of the Cuban Revolution, the heroic and iconoclastic Ernesto 'Che' Guevara, went to Bolivia to try to spark a revolutionary upheaval in the heart of South America. One of his main aides was the French writer and intellectual, Régis Debray. European youth had also become contaminated by the call of revolution.

In Chile, the excitement of the times was not captured by armed revolutionaries, but by a charismatic family doctor, who had been trying to achieve social reform by the ballot box for decades. Salvador Allende was a socialist and a Marxist who began his political career in the Chilean Congress representing Valparaíso, the country's largest port city. There the doctor went from house to house with his stethoscope, curing poor people while campaigning for office. Allende wanted to rectify a social and economic order in which the bottom 28 per cent of the population received less than 5 per cent of the national income, while the top 2 per cent took in almost 46 per cent.[4] He believed that, given the strong democratic traditions of the country, Chile could become a more equitable society by playing by the rules of the democratic game. He also insisted that the country should have economic independence by taking control of its natural resources and key industries. This aroused the hostility of multinational corporations, which controlled most of the critical natural resources of the country, especially copper, Chile's largest export.

This political agenda and platform were called the 'Chilean Road to Socialism'. Supported by a broad alliance of political parties from the Communists to progressive Christians grouped together in the Popular Unity coalition, Allende embarked on his fourth quest for the presidency in the late 1960s. It was at this time that a 24-year-old Spaniard of Régis Debray's generation, Joan Garcés, arrived in Chile to finish his research on a political science dissertation for the University of Sorbonne in Paris. In 1968, two years before the presidential elections, he met Allende, then the president of the Chilean Senate.[5] The young man and the socialist politician hit it off well together, and Garcés, who travelled between Europe and Chile, became one of Allende's advisers on European affairs.

After defending his dissertation in political science at the Sorbonne in July 1970, Garcés departed immediately for Chile, this time to become a personal adviser to Allende at a low point in his presidential election campaign. In an interview in July 1999, Garcés stated that when he arrived 'Allende and I were the only ones who believed victory was possible.' The strong will and determination of both men in the face of adversity help explain much of what transpired in subsequent years, particularly in their historic encounters with Pinochet.

The imperial adversary

Allende's most formidable adversary in his quest for the Chilean presidency in 1970 was not another presidential candidate, but the hemispheric colossus that lay more than 5,000 miles to the north – the United States. In the 1964 elections, the United States had intervened heavily in Chilean politics, backing Eduardo Frei against Allende with over $20 million in covert funding. This represented more than half of Frei's campaign budget and was equal to $8 per voter, more than the Republican and Democratic parties spent that same year on each voter in the US presidential elections.[6]

As the September 1970 elections approached in Chile, the Nixon administration, which had taken office the year before, embarked on a determined campaign to stop Allende. In June 1970, Henry Kissinger, then Nixon's National Security Adviser, made one of the most cynical and arrogant statements ever attributed to an American leader. In a special meeting of US policy and intelligence planners called the 40 Committee, Kissinger declared: 'I don't see why we need to stand idly by and watch a country go Communist due to the irresponsibility of its own people.'[7]

In the run-up to the elections, the US intelligence community engaged in what are called 'spoiling operations', the spreading of propaganda and false information about Allende and his Popular

Unity coalition.[8] The CIA paid for newsletters, booklets, posters, and even wall paintings. Some of this propaganda equated an Allende election with Cuban firing squads and the 1968 Soviet invasion of Czechoslovakia. The CIA also heavily subsidized two wire services as well as the largest Chilean media conglomerate, run by right-wing Chilean business scion Agustín Edwards Eastman.

US corporations, which held a stake of $1.1 billion in Chile, also kicked into the anti-Allende campaign. ITT, the International Telephone and Telegraph Company, then the ninth largest corporation in the United States with investments of $200 million in Chile, headed up the US corporate effort to stop Allende. John A. McCone, a director of ITT and a former head of the CIA, served as the go-between with the Nixon administration and the CIA, channelling over $350,000 from the company's coffers into Chile.[9]

All these efforts came to naught when Allende won a relative majority of votes on September 4. Shocked by this unexpected victory, Kissinger in his memoirs says, 'Nixon was beside himself.' Four days later Kissinger ordered the US ambassador in Chile, Edward Korry, to prepare a 'cold-blooded assessment' of 'the pros and cons and problems and prospects involved should a Chilean military coup be organized now with US assistance'. Korry responded that the chances of a coup were 'non-existent', but this did not prevent Richard Nixon from meeting on September 15 with Kissinger, Attorney General George Mitchell, and CIA director Richard Helms to discuss ways to block Allende. According to notes given by Helms to the US Senate Intelligence Committee in 1975, Nixon in the meeting endorsed a coup against Allende, making remarks like '$10,000,000 available, more if necessary'; 'full-time job – best men we have'; and 'make the economy scream'. Helms told the committee, 'If I ever carried the marshal's baton in my knapsack out of the oval office, it was that day.'[10]

Since Allende in a three-man contest had received only a relative majority in the elections with 36.3 per cent of the votes, he had to be confirmed as president by the Chilean Congress on October 24. In past elections, the Congress had always confirmed the largest vote getter. But the Nixon administration was determined to block Allende in Congress or to provoke a coup during the days leading up to the congressional vote.[11] Money was offered to members of Congress to support Arturo Alessandri, the runner-up in the general election. If chosen by Congress, Alessandri agreed to resign immediately after being sworn in and call for new elections. The US lobbied Frei to assist in this scheme by having him run again for president. Even more menacingly, the CIA dispatched special operatives, money and weapons to assist extreme right-wing army officers to carry out a military coup.

The efforts to turn the vote against Allende in Congress failed abysmally, with Frei refusing to cooperate, possibly because it was not clear he could count on his own party to nominate him for new presidential elections. The military coup conspirators did succeed in assassinating the pro-constitutionalist head of the military, General René Schneider, just a few days before the congressional vote, but his death, rather than provoking a coup, led to a backlash as even right-wing politicians denounced the assassination.

These terribly botched conspiracies did not stop Nixon, who had become obsessed with Allende. When Ambassador Korry was summoned to the White House from Chile he entered the Oval Office to see Nixon smacking his fist into his hand and declaring 'that S.O.B., that S.O.B.'. Korry was startled, not sure whom the president was referring to until Nixon said, 'it's that son-of-a-bitch Allende'.[12]

A CIA study in September 1970 stated: 'The US has no vital national interests within Chile', and 'the world military balance of power would not be significantly altered by an Allende government'. However, Nixon, who had built his political career on anti-communism, may have focused on another point of the report: 'An Allende victory would represent a definite psychological set-back to the U.S. and a definite psychological advantage for the Marxist idea.'[13]

In spite of all the US machinations, Allende assumed office on November 4, 1970. It was an unbelievable event, a real 'people's' inauguration, with hundreds of thousands flooding into the streets of Santiago around La Moneda, the presidential palace. The international press also turned out in droves, for this was the first time in the twentieth century that an explicitly socialist government had been voted into office.

The Nixon administration hardly waited until the streets were cleaned up after the inauguration before embarking on a strategy of destabilizing the new government. Ambassador Korry, even before Allende took office, had delineated the administration's approach: 'Once Allende comes to power we shall do all within our power to condemn Chile and the Chileans to utmost deprivation and poverty.' This strategy was spelled out in detail in National Security Decision Memorandum No. 93 on November 9 and Kissinger took charge of orchestrating it. The US cut off virtually all bilateral funding, pressured international agencies like the World Bank to make no loans to Chile, and in general worked with US corporations to strangle the economy. The CIA was authorized to spend $3.5 million on coup plotting in Chile in 1971, and a total of at least $8 million by the time of the coup in September 1973. Right-wing terrorist groups like Patria y Libertad were funded, and by late 1971 the CIA was making almost daily contacts with the Chilean military. In October 1972 the CIA helped finance a truckers' strike that severely crippled the Chilean economy.[14] The Chilean military was the only government organization to receive increased US funding under Allende, rising from $5.7 million in 1971 to $15 million in 1973.[15]

A thousand days of drama

Virtually every one of the thousand days that the Popular Unity government remained in power could be turned into a book of high drama. It was an exciting period, one filled with social, cultural and political turbulence, unlike anything the country had experienced in its century and a half as a republic. As promised, Allende nationalized the US copper companies, Anaconda, Kennecott and Cerro de Pasco. He expropriated eighty strategic industries, including ITT. There were educational reforms, labour and health legislation – such as the provision of one litre of free milk for every child – all of them aimed at creating a more egalitarian and democratic society.[16]

The Chilean elite and business classes quickly closed ranks against Allende. From 1970 to 1973 Chile became a country in which the historical roles of the different social classes were reversed. In the past it had been the trade unions, the working poor and the leftist parties that had demonstrated against governments and gone out on picket lines. Now it was the powerful who decided to go on strike. Large commercial houses and shopkeepers closed their doors, making goods unavailable. The *latifundistas*, the large landowners, refused to plant their fields, creating food shortages. The owners of the means of transportation, mainly trucks and buses, stopped their vehicles, while some industries curtailed or halted production.

But these actions by the wealthy and well-to-do only infuriated the popular classes, generating even more support for Allende and the Popular Unity coalition. Workers, in the face of the transportation strike, went to their jobs on foot and organized worker brigades to keep products and essential commodities flowing to consumers and key industries. Peasants seized control of *latifundios*, and workers took over scores of factories when the owners sabotaged or stopped production.[17] A virtual civil war was fought over the country's commerce and means of production. The Nixon administration, to foment domestic discontent, cut off the flow of US and international financing for Chile, erecting what some called an 'invisible blockade'.[18]

It was the right-wing and business classes that resorted to violence in this conflict. Backed by the CIA, terrorist groups bombed and destroyed state railroads, power plants and key highway arteries in order to create chaos and stop the country from functioning. In the midst of this struggle for control of Chile, Allende insisted, almost stubbornly, on maintaining the country's democratic institutions, and the Popular Unity coalition went to the polls in March 1973 for congressional elections. Both the opposition and the ruling coalition agreed that these elections would test the popularity of the government. To the surprise of many, Allende's coalition increased its percentage of votes from 36.3 per cent in the 1970 presidential elections to 43.4 per cent in the congressional elections. It was clear that the social and paramilitary insurrection of the elite was not working. They needed a bigger and more deadly assault on the government, and it was right after the elections that many of the top military leaders decided to begin preparations for a *coup d'état*.[19]

To encourage the military to intervene, women from the upper-class neighbourhoods of Santiago marched in front of military garrisons and threw grain and corn kernels, chanting 'You are a bunch of chickens, you are not defending the honour of the women of Chile.' And just weeks before the coup, many of these same women, this time led by wives of conspiring military officers, demonstrated violently in front of the house of the head of the military who was loyal to Allende, General Carlos Prats González. Days later, Prats resigned and Augusto Pinochet became the commander in chief of Chile's armed forces.

Although there is no doubt that the US government worked incessantly to overthrow Allende during his three years in office, the precise role of the CIA at the time of the coup is still shrouded in mystery. The CIA of course destroys records or does not even record its decisions and activities at the time of coups and assassinations. About all that a Senate Intelligence Committee report in 1975 could come up with is that 'the CIA received intelligence reports on the coup planning of the group which carried out the successful September 11 coup throughout the months of July, August and September 1973.' On the day of the coup the US Navy was present offshore, ostensibly to participate in joint manoeuvres with the Chilean Navy, and thirty-two American observation and fighter planes arrived at the US air base in Mendoza, Argentina, just across the border from Chile. A US WB-575 plane, an airborne communications control system, was spotted flying in Chilean air space, probably to assist in the coordination and communications of the coup conspirators.[20]

We do, however, have a clear record of what transpired on the ground in Chile. A week before the coup, Allende and his cabinet began meeting daily as they suspected that the armed forces might not respect the constitution. Joan Garcés, who had become one of the most trusted advisers of Allende during the three years of his presidency, was constantly at Allende's side during these deliberations.[21] On September 8, the cabinet learned that the armed forces were being mobilized without presidential authorization. A critical part of this mobilization was the strike of Chile's commercial airline pilots. At the order of the commander of the air force, General Gustavo Leigh Guzmán, all passenger airlines had been moved to the main airport in Santiago, which was also a military base.

The day before the coup, on September 10, Garcés participated in tense and heated discussions with the cabinet about pressuring Leigh to demobilize the air force and to tell Allende why the planes were at the base. Allende also made calls to Pinochet asking him about possible actions by the military against the constitutional government. Pinochet bluntly denied any extraordinary actions or mobilizations by the military.

Then, late at night on the 10th, while meeting with his cabinet, the president learned that naval troops were leaving the port of Valparaíso for Santiago. Military officials would not respond to calls about this troop movement, and at 2.30 a.m. on the 11th, with the cabinet members exhausted, Allende adjourned the meeting. Some of them, including Garcés, went with Allende to his personal residence, Tomas Moro, located in the foothills of the Andes, a 45-minute drive from the La Moneda presidential palace in central Santiago. Exhausted, they went to sleep. Unbeknown to them the coup had already started.

The battle of La Moneda on September 11

At five o'clock in the morning Allende received a call informing him that the navy had rebelled and taken control of Valparaíso, the second largest city, 120 kilometres west of Santiago.[22] Allende and his closest advisers, including Garcés, sped through the streets of Santiago in an escorted convoy for the presidential palace. Allende's two daughters decided to accompany him. At 7.20 a.m. they entered the palace. The entire cabinet has been summoned. At the palace, Allende immediately placed phone calls to the military leaders, but they did not respond. At the same time Allende was informed by his advisers that the military had taken control of Santiago, throwing up roadblocks at the country's major arteries, taking over radio and television stations, bombing the transmitters, and slowly moving tanks to surround the presidential palace. The battle of La Moneda had begun.

Allende soon realized that virtually the entire military had rebelled and it would be impossible for his government to survive. Determined not to abandon his democratic constitutional mandate, he would not entertain resignation or exile. At 9.15 in a broadcast over the last free radio station, Magallanes, Allende made his final address to the nation.[23] Garcés was in the same room listening.

> This is the last time I will address you.... My words are not spoken in bitterness, but in disappointment.... Foreign capital and imperialism united with the internal reactionary forces to create a climate so that the armed forces would break with tradition.... There will be a moral judgment against those who betrayed the oath they took as soldiers of Chile....They have the strength; they can subjugate us, but they cannot halt social advances by either crime or force. History is ours and the people will make it.... Long live Chile! Long live the people! Long live the workers! These are my last words. I am convinced my sacrifice will not be in vain. I am certain that this sacrifice will be a moral lesson that will punish cowardice, treachery and treason.[24]

As he spoke, the military had begun to move on the palace.

To coordinate this attack and the coup, the military conspirators set up a secret short-wave communications system. But someone was listening and recording, probably a low-ranking military officer involved in communications; his identity remains unknown to this day. In 1998, Patricia Verdugo released a CD of these secret communications, along with a book, *Secret Interference of September 11, 1973*. From this recording, we see how Pinochet quickly became the dominant and most vitriolic of the coup conspirators.

Debate and intense discussions occurred among Pinochet and the other military leaders about what to do with Allende, who refused to resign. When contacted by the military early in the day, Allende yelled over the phone: 'A president elected by the people does not surrender.' He slammed the phone down with such fury that it cracked.[25] Allende's advisers and family also refused to leave the presidential palace. In conversations with those in the palace, Allende made it clear that he would not leave La Moneda alive, that he would die fighting or commit suicide rather than surrender.

When Pinochet was told that Allende was resisting and carrying a machine gun, he responded: 'The fucker doesn't even know how to shoot rubber bullets.' As to the advisers and cabinet members who were with Allende, Pinochet declared: 'We need to coordinate with the military police. We'll put all these guys in prison. They should be hidden like snakes.' In fact Allende was himself defending the presidential palace from a window in his main office, using a machine gun – given to him by Fidel Castro – to resist the surrounding troops. An intimate member of his personal staff, Miria Contreras or 'Payita', who would remain with him until the last, yelled at him to stop shooting, to get away from the window. He refused. Finally Payita persuaded another member of Allende's entourage to drag him from the office window.[26]

Later, when Pinochet thought Allende was trying to negotiate to buy time or to secure a more favourable outcome, he shouted over the radio: 'Unconditional surrender, we don't want to talk! Unconditional surrender! [Tell Allende] we will take him prisoner, and respect his physical integrity.' A few moments later Pinochet proclaimed: 'Offer to take him out of the country, in a plane … but have the plane explode in mid-air.'[27] Until the release of this tape transcript Pinochet had always insisted he intended no harm to Allende or his family.

Faced with Allende's rejection of the military ultimatum to resign and go into exile, Pinochet pressured General Leigh of the air force to bomb the presidential palace. Pinochet shouted: 'Look this guy is buying time! We are looking weak! Listen to me, do not negotiate with him. Unconditional surrender! We must bomb [the palace] as soon as possible.' By this time it was clear that Pinochet had become the leader among his comrades-in-arms. Not only was he commander of the army, but he was also giving orders to the generals of the air force, the navy and the police.

The military informed Allende that unless he and everyone in the palace abandoned the building immediately, the air force would bomb them. Allende, his cabinet, advisers and personal guards met for the last time. The president insisted that everyone should leave the palace and that only his guards were to remain with him. Most of the cabinet, including Garcés, and Allende's daughters refused to leave. Allende insisted they must go, and turned to Garcés with a personal charge: 'Someone has to relate what has happened here, and only you can do that.' They left. A few minutes later at 11.52 in the morning, the first rocket struck La Moneda from a British Hawker Hunter warplane.[28] The palace was quickly engulfed in flames as other planes strafed and bombed the building. The palace was assaulted by troops at about one in the afternoon, and at two o'clock they finally moved into the palace and Allende's office.[29] In one of the more bizarre moments of the coup, revealed by the tapes, Pinochet was informed in English: 'They say that Allende committed suicide and is dead now.'

Along with Allende's two daughters, Garcés had departed earlier from the palace undetected by the military. The new junta, led by Pinochet, took control of the country and placed Garcés on the most wanted list, knowing that in the days prior to the coup he had proposed the purging of top military officers who might be disloyal to Allende. His name was printed in the national newspapers as one of the junta's most wanted men. Garcés, however, managed to hide in Santiago for a couple of weeks until acquaintances had negotiated with the Spanish embassy and he was given the green light to seek asylum there. In disguise, hunted as prey by the military, Garcés made it into the embassy. He eventually flew to Spain. Pinochet's reign of terror had begun, but so had the numbering of the years until Garcés would bring him before the courts for his crimes against humanity.

2

The formation of a dictator

A dramatic photograph of the Chilean military junta was sent over the international wire services immediately after the coup. It showed four stern officers, with a scowling Pinochet sitting in the middle with dark sunglasses. This foreboding and austere picture communicated to the world that this would be no routine or bloodless seizure of power. General Leigh, as the commander of the Chilean Air Force on the junta, called for 'the elimination of the Marxist cancer'.[1] As the photograph was taken, thousands were being rounded up in the cities and countryside, while scores were summarily executed in the days following the coup.

What the photo could not tell, and what no one imagined, was that Augusto Pinochet would dominate the junta and rule over Chile as a dictator for almost seventeen years. One week after the coup, Pinochet, as president of the junta, told the press: 'I do not intend to remain as head of the junta. We will rotate the position. For now it is me, tomorrow it will be Admiral Merino, next General Leigh, and later General Mendoza.'[2] But nothing of the sort happened. Nine months later, in June 1974, Pinochet, still head of the junta, proclaimed himself the 'Supreme Leader of the Nation'. Then, in December, believing that this title made him sound like the leader of a 'tropical country', he forced the other members of the junta to sign a declaration making him president of Chile.

What explains Pinochet's ascent and determination to consolidate power in his hands? The general's long reign clearly violated the norms and traditions of Chilean history. Since Chilean independence no figure had ruled over Chile for as long as a decade, and no other leader was so ruthless in his determination to hold on to power. And until Pinochet, Chilean rulers generally treated their political opponents in a relatively civil manner. A bloody civil war did break out in 1891 among the aristocracy, but after the incumbent president, José Manuel Balmaceda, committed suicide the conflict ended and relative harmony was restored among the political elites. Then, in the early twentieth century, the government and the military harshly repressed strikes and uprisings by the new working class, particularly in the mining areas. But even these actions pale in comparison with the seventeen years of outright brutality by the Pinochet regime.

The figure of Pinochet is an anomaly when compared to other strongmen and dictators in Latin America and twentieth-century Europe. Pinochet was not a particularly charismatic figure like the historic caudillos of many Latin American countries. Nor did he possess the messianic and redemptionist visions of a Mussolini or a Hitler before he became president of the junta. Pinochet was 57 years old at the time of the coup; there was little in his public life prior to September 11 to indicate that he thirsted for absolute power, or that he was capable of methodically eliminating all potential contenders for supremacy within the military while torturing and murdering those in the political opposition.

Born on November 25, 1915, in the port city of Valparaíso, Augusto José Ramon Pinochet Ugarte enjoyed what could be considered a relatively normal childhood. His family lineage in Chile dates back to the early eighteenth century, when the first Pinochet migrated to the Spanish colony from France. Most of Augusto's paternal ancestors were small or medium-size landowners who raised cattle in the part of central Chile renowned for its cheese production. His mother's family, the Ugartes, also had roots in the countryside. Neither side of his family numbered among the elites or well-to-do. As a young man Pinochet's father moved to Valparaíso, where he worked as a customs official in the port while selling insurance in his spare time. His mother, Avelina Ugarte Martínez, was a house-keeper; Augusto, as the oldest of six children, was lavished with attention.[3] To the end of her days, his mother would proclaim that Augusto was her favourite, her 'special love'.[4]

One interesting biographical quirk is that Hitler, like Pinochet, was the son of a customs official. And they both had mothers who adored and spoiled them. However, the behaviour of their fathers was vastly different. Pinochet's father was hardly present at home and played a largely benign role in the family. He worked long hours in the customs office and selling insurance, allowing his wife to run the family. Hitler's father Alois, on the other hand, was very domineering and authoritarian. A leading biographer believes that Alois often beat his children and his wife.[5] Hitler deeply resented, even hated, his father, while Pinochet harboured no strong anti-pathies towards his father. As Pinochet himself proclaimed, 'my father was a very good man, loved by his family. I was never punished by my father.'[6]

Some students of Hitler point out that he had little or no personal life or relations outside his public and political persona.[7] The reverse can be said of Pinochet – until 1973. He clearly had a personal life, about which much is known, but he had virtually no political persona that the world knew of before September 11. His writings prior to 1973 are largely devoid of political discussion. Even when one reads his most autobiographical work, *El Camino*, written in 1983, one finds little discussion of politics or political events that shaped his life before 1970. Pinochet in essence appeared to be a shallow political vassal when he seized power, open to being shaped by the political needs that he perceived once he proclaimed himself president of Chile.

Eduardo Deves, in an unpublished biography, argues that Pinochet had a particular ability to morph his political thinking or orientation during the different stages of his life. It is certainly true that Pinochet, like many other political figures, adapted to political and ideological necessities when he confronted new realities. However, it is also important to recognize that even in Pinochet's early years he displayed certain personal and psychological characteristics that contributed to his emergence as a ruthless dictator of Chile.

The neighbourhood bully

It is known that the young Augusto was something of a bully in his Valparaíso neighbourhood, perhaps because he was the oldest child and pampered by his mother. After school he and a small group of cohorts would often chase after children from the poorer barrios, swinging their belts at them, forcing them to run home. He also bullied his younger brothers and sisters; as Pinochet himself later confessed, 'They were afraid of me because I acted liked an ogre.'[8] Perhaps in line with this need to be domineering, he took up boxing at a young age as his major sport.

A trait in Pinochet's childhood that foretold his rise as a military ruler was his obsession with military games. At a very young age he would make believe he was a soldier, marching around, beating on a tambour and blowing a trumpet. He had toy soldiers that he would play war games with, often changing the guard in the evenings before he went to bed. While his father wanted him to become a doctor, his mother encouraged Augusto's military proclivities.

Perhaps in part due to his rambunctious and rancorous youth, Augusto performed poorly in the Catholic schools he attended, even having to repeat grades and classes that he failed. At the age of 14 he had had enough of Catholic schooling and applied to the Bernardo O'Higgins Military School to become an army officer. He was rejected. Pinochet asserts that this was due to his age and height, but in fact his grades were not good enough for entry. He applied the next year, but again was refused entry. Reflecting his singular determination to pursue a military career, he applied a third time in 1932, and this time was accepted, apparently due to the intercession of one of the priests from his school.[9]

When he entered military school in 1933 for four years of study he was 17 years old. Pinochet relates that he was so excited that 'in the days before school started, I counted the hours until March 11'. Once in military school his life changed dramatically. Pinochet himself states: 'At home I was accustomed to everyone paying attention to me. They took care of me, I could go to bed at any hour. I could do whatever I wanted. But when I attended the military school my life changed. I became a man who assumed a strict regime of living.' Perhaps more importantly for later life, his military schooling meant that 'I knew no other way of life. I only recognized discipline: obedience as a soldier, or respect as a commander.'[10] The discipline of military school also led to the complete organization of his life around the clock and the time of day. Years later his schedule would be so regimented that on every Sunday he would set aside exactly the same hour in the early afternoon to interact with his children and grandchildren.[11]

During the years that Pinochet aspired to enter military school Chile was ruled by the government of Carlos Ibáñez del Campo. A military officer who had served as interior minister and vice-president, General Ibáñez assumed power in 1927 when the president was forced to resign. Ibáñez ruled imperiously, suppressing the opposition, particularly the left and the Communist Party.[12] However, just before Pinochet was accepted at the military academy Ibáñez was forced out of office when the Great Depression of the 1930s hit Chile with a particular vehemence, due to its dependence on mining exports. In the wake of Ibáñez's departure, broad sectors of the Chilean population repudiated his rule and the Chilean army as well.

It was probably in part due to the adverse legacy of Ibáñez that the military was largely marginalized from politics in the 1930s. In fact while Pinochet was in the military academy, politics as a topic of conversation was virtually forbidden. As Pinochet himself recollects: 'When someone wanted to discuss our political thinking, we would evade the theme with this simple statement to end the discussion: "Excuse me, we are apolitical and we don't like to discuss the issue".'[13] This ability to negate any political tendencies served him well in the years to come. It lends credence to Deves's thesis that Pinochet was able to reflect and assume different political postures during the different stages of his life, depending on the ideological currents that swirled around him.

Pinochet's infatuation with strongmen and authoritarianism

Even in his early life Pinochet manifested certain personal views and characteristics that would one day lend themselves to his assumption of dictatorial powers. One of these was his identification with the strongmen of history. In the early 1980s when he ruled Chile, Pinochet admitted in a lengthy interview that he had definite opinions about the global protagonists that were shaping the world in the late 1930s. At the beginning of World War II, Pinochet flatly states, 'I sided with the Germans.' He adds: 'we followed the battles on a wall map, putting up flags to follow their movements.' In particular Pinochet was 'enchanted by Rommel. We watched as this man defended himself when they tried to defeat him in Africa.'[14] This fascination with Nazi Germany lasted a lifetime; years later, just before he was arrested in London, he visited a bookstore in Piccadilly and was seen purchasing a biography of Hitler.[15]

Even before the war Pinochet had an infatuation with the strong leaders of history. Napoleon was his most admired figure. Pinochet lauded Napoleon's achievements 'not only because he was a great strategist, but also because he was an analyst. He was a patriot. Napoleon had many virtues.'[16] Not once does Pinochet mention that Napoleon ruled as a despot or that the Napoleonic wars inflicted horrendous suffering and destruction on all of Europe. When he was placed under house arrest in London, Pinochet's favourite reading included the memoirs of Napoleon.[17]

Pinochet's favourable views of Hitler found a particular resonance in the Chile of the late 1930s. A Nazi movement was founded in 1932 in Chile that was anti-liberal, anti-Marxist and anti-Semite. It had the support of many of the youth. In 1938 a large group of these Nazi sympathizers took over the social security building opposite the presidential palace, killing one police officer in the process. They were surrounded, forced to surrender, and then the police, in revenge for their fallen comrade, took sixty captives and executed them. Between 1938 and 1940, a fascist political organization, the Vanguardia Obrera Nacionalista, emerged which tried to penetrate the armed forces to carry out a coup. But it, too, had little success. However, within the Chilean military, Hitler and Germany enjoyed significant support among the officer corps, in part because Prussian officers had trained the Chilean army in the nineteenth century. It was not until 1943 that Chile broke relations with Nazi Germany.[18]

Rather than the Nazis or the right wing, it was the left that proved to be the ascendant political force in Chile in the 1930s.

After the fall of Ibáñez, a period of political upheaval gripped Chile. In 1932, a 'Socialist Republic' was proclaimed by General Marmaduke Grove of the air force, which lasted for twelve days. One year later, Salvador Allende along with other Marxists founded the Chilean Socialist Party. In 1938, the Socialists along with the Communist Party (founded in 1922) called for the formation of a Popular Front to resist the Nazis and the fascists in Chile and abroad.[19] They backed Pedro Aguirre Cerda of the reformist Radical Party as their presidential candidate and won the elections in 1938. The Popular Front under Aguirre Cerda proceeded to implement a series of reforms that strengthened the role of the state in advancing the economic and social development of Chile.

If Pinochet ever had any thoughts of becoming involved with the Nazi movement after the victory of the Popular Front, they were surely quashed by his subsequent romance with the daughter of a prominent senator from the Radical Party who also served as Minister of the Interior in the Popular Front government. Pinochet had met Lucia Hiriart in 1940. The young lieutenant married Lucia, ten years his junior, in 1943 when he was 27 years old. Like Pinochet's mother, Lucia was a very strong woman, determined to advance the career of her husband. She drove his ambitions. She once noted sarcastically that her husband 'was only a soldier' (in contrast to her father); on another occasion she told him that he should aspire to be more than just a general, perhaps Minister of Defence.[20] It is common knowledge that at home Pinochet was henpecked and de-graded by Lucia. He hardly spoke around the house, playing a secondary role much like that of his father. But the pent-up feelings of resentment that he felt at home found an outlet when he went to the army barracks. Those under him often experienced his anger as he shouted at them, abusing them verbally and demanding com-plete submissiveness and obedience.[21]

When Pinochet became dictator of Chile, Lucia was the classic power behind the throne, a woman who was feared by other military officers almost as much as Pinochet himself.[22] This did not, how-ever, stop Pinochet from having affairs. He had relationships with at least two women of prominence.[23] He took extreme precautions to make sure that Lucia would not find out about them, in one of the affairs having a bodyguard rent an apartment under his name where Pinochet and one of the women, a well-known journalist, carried on their relationship.

A sociopath in constitutional drag

While Pinochet's mother and wife played decisive roles in his life, he had virtually no consistent male confidants or advisers that he relied on during his long military career. Patricia Lutz, who worked as a baby-sitter for the Pinochets in Antofagasta while her father was posted to the same city as a more junior officer, states that Pinochet 'had no friends in whom he confided.[24] Even as dictator, there was a constant turnover of the people around him. Federico Willoughby, a key civilian adviser during Pinochet's early years on the junta, attributes this distance and estrangement to a tendency towards cruelty and the need to dominate others that Pinochet had manifested in his youth.

> One way Pinochet's cruelty and perversity manifested itself was in his constant manipulation of his aides and subordinates as president, playing them off against each other. He would shunt subordinates aside, and then months or even years later, bring them back, making it clear that they were completely at his mercy. Pinochet got a perverse enjoyment out of doing this.[25]

What Willoughby did not specifically mention in the interview was that Pinochet's cruelty and distrust of others also meant that he had no scruples about eliminating competitors who had once befriended him. Patricia Lutz, who consulted four psychiatrists who knew Pinochet, asserts that he displays 'no emotional commitment or empathy with others' outside of his immediate family. 'He believed only in himself, this justified everything, and enabled him to make the argument "If we don't get them, they will get us".'[26] Lutz describes these tendencies as 'psychopathic'. In strict psychological terminology, however, what she is actually describing is a sociopath with paranoid tendencies, someone who is overly suspicious of others, who has no social or moral values, and who believes he can do whatever is necessary to advance their personal interests and objectives.[27]

This capacity to coldly eliminate opponents was never manifested before 1973. It was suppressed or controlled by the norms and regulations of the military hierarchy that Pinochet adhered to. This interpretation of his early life coincides with Eduardo Deves's belief that Pinochet's life prior to the coup can be divided into two stages. The first, that of a young man aspiring to a military career, ended with his marriage in 1943; this marked the advent of the second stage, which would last for three decades, and which Deves characterizes as that of the 'Constitutional Officer', the period when Pinochet would remain loyal to the elected civilian leaders. He even favoured some social reforms, including those of the Popular Front in the 1930s and 1940s, and of the Christian Democrats under Eduardo Frei in the 1960s.[28]

This view is formally correct in that Pinochet did not violate the constitution or engage in any rebellious acts. But it does not take into account certain adverse psychological and political tendencies that manifested themselves during this period and would become transparent during his dictatorial reign. The mid- and late 1940s, for example, exposed Pinochet to emergent political conflicts between leftists and conservative interests that would be decisive in the 1970s. In 1947–48 Gabriel González Videla, after being elected president in a coalition with the Communists in 1946, came under intense pressure from the US government to turn against the Communists with the onset of the Cold War. In 1947 he dismissed the Communists from his cabinet, and then in 1948 the Communist Party was banned.

Now a captain, Pinochet was posted to the northern port city of Iquique in 1946, and then with the crackdown on the Communists in 1948 he was placed in charge of a prison camp in the nearby town of Pisagua where members of the Communist Party were being held. A book sympathetic to Pinochet published in 1984 asserts that Pinochet did the prisoners no harm, that he even invited several who had been municipal officials 'to dine at his table' in the officers' mess hall.[29] This account could be true, but one would hardly expect a young captain whose father-in-law had served in a government with the Communists to go out and torture or abuse mayors who might one day again emerge as important political figures. In fact Pinochet's treatment of the more common prisoners provided early evidence of his sadistic tendencies. According to several of Pinochet's military peers he boasted to them that he cut the hair off some of the prisoners, mixed it in with noodles, and then made them eat the foul concoction.[30]

In his memoirs Pinochet relates that his first direct encounter with Salvador Allende occurred in Pisagua. The anti-Communist law did not proscribe the Socialist Party, and Allende as part of a congressional delegation travelled to northern Chile to investigate the prison conditions of the Communists. When Allende asked to talk to the prisoners under Pinochet's control, Pinochet told Allende 'there is no authorization from the proper authorities of Iquique to see the prisoners.' Allende insisted, and Pinochet then let the delegation pass, saying: 'You don't have permission, but if you do enter, you're responsible for the consequences.' Pinochet goes on to recount that by the time Allende became president he did not remember this incident, or that Allende might have confused him with another, more right-wing officer who also had the name Pinochet.[31]

Not long after this, Pinochet was sent to southern Chile to deal with a labour dispute in the mining town of Coronel where the workers were on strike. Here again Araya Villegas relates a largely sympathetic account of Pinochet's activities, asserting that Pinochet after talking to the miners went to the owners and convinced them to take back the workers. But a few months later the workers held a new meeting to vote on further strike action. Araya Villegas states that Pinochet had soldiers posted around the union hall. The workers voted against the strike. However, the president of the union, Enrique Perez Valdés, a Communist, refused to accept the election results and called for a new vote. Pinochet then terminated the meeting, claiming, 'any effort to push further [for a strike] had to be considered subversive'.[32]

Pinochet himself, in his memoirs of the 1980s, provides a slightly different account of the effort to break the strike. He says that prior to the meeting to call a strike he met with some of the workers who he had helped get their jobs back, and told them to station themselves at key points in the union hall to begin chanting 'No strike' at the beginning of the meeting to undermine the union's Communist leadership. According to Pinochet this strategy worked and succeeded in disrupting the meeting. When Perez Valdés pleaded with Pinochet to allow a vote, Pinochet told him that he would be reported to higher authorities in the provincial capital of Concepción, whereupon the head of the union 'gave up', according to Pinochet.[33]

In 1949 Pinochet was admitted to the main school for military officers in Santiago: the Academia de Guerra, the War Academy. This was a key posting for Pinochet, since virtually no one could expect to advance to the highest ranks of the Chilean military without attending the Academy. All accounts indicate that Pinochet was by no means an outstanding student, but he applied himself doggedly to his studies. Some sources suggest that in lieu of his lack of intellectual talents, he would fawn over his professors and portray himself as a young 'patriotic' officer, eternally loyal to the academy's military traditions.[34]

Carlos Ibáñez returned to power as the elected president of Chile from 1952 to 1958. His new tenure favoured the military and officer advancements, and in 1953 after Pinochet had completed his studies at the War Academy he was promoted to major and placed in charge of an army regiment in the northern port city of Arica, near the frontier with Peru. According to Pinochet, this was one of the best times of his military career.[35] He enjoyed mingling socially with other military and civilian officials, particularly on Chilean national holidays when he represented the army in parades and commemorative events.

Several years later he was briefly dispatched to Washington DC as part of a military mission and visited other parts of the United States. In April 1956 he was posted to Ecuador for three years, where he helped set up the Escuela Superior de Guerra and taught basic courses at the school. In 1959 he went on a prolonged tour of the United States with some of his Ecuadorian students, visiting US military bases and institutions.[36] He returned to Chile and was sent to another port city in the north, Antofagasta, where he once again mixed with the upper crust of the city's municipal and military officials.

During the late 1950s and 1960s Pinochet dedicated himself to writing texts, which were published by the military press. None of the books displayed any particular insights or genius. They were largely compilations, as the title of his first book indicated, *Geographical Synthesis of the Republic of Chile*, which totalled all of 120 pages.[37] Then in 1968 he published what some of his apologists consider his *magnus obra*, *Geopolítica*. On the surface it appeared to be something of an advance in his intellectual aptitude. In it he draws upon the thinking of the major figure who consolidated the Chilean nation in the early nineteenth century, Diego Portales, as well as contemporary theorists of political–military affairs.

Returning in this book to his earlier fascination with Hitler and fascism, Pinochet lauds the role of Karl Haushofer in developing the field of Geopolitics. Haushofer was an early collaborator of Hitler's, contributing the concept of *Lebensraum* to *Mein Kampf*. Pinochet notes that the 'German school' of geopolitics was repudiated after World War II, but 'twenty years later we see that many of its concepts are being implemented'.[38] But the most damning aspect of this work is that Pinochet apparently plagiarized parts of it. Pablo Azócar demonstrates in his biography of Pinochet that major sections of *Geopolítica* are copied verbatim from conferences and lectures given by one of his professors at the War Academy back in 1950.[39]

In 1969 Pinochet rose to the rank of General and was placed in charge of an army division headquartered in the northern port city of Iquique. He used this posting in the province of Tarapacá to begin writing *The War of the Pacific: The Tarapacá Campaign*. It deals with a decisive battle in 1879 in which Chile triumphed over Peru and Bolivia, annexing territories from these countries, including the province of Tarapacá. Araya Villegas, Pinochet's earliest biographical apologist, claims that this work reveals Pinochet's 'talents as a narrator, historian and strategist' along with his 'patriotism and love of his military profession'. The truth is that Pinochet did little of the research or writing that went into the book. One officer under Pinochet's command in Iquique testifies that Pinochet 'asked me and others to undertake the research' for the book. 'We did it'; Pinochet then simply 'organized' the material, putting 'his name on it and passing it over to the Department of Publications of the Army for editing'.[40]

The plodding opportunistic officer

Clearly Pinochet had little aptitude for research and analysis. He published mainly to gain notoriety and to further his military career. From the 1950s to 1970 Pinochet's advance in the military ranks, like his publications, show that he was largely a plodding, opportunistic officer, not very imaginative, and not given to questioning his commanding officials or the civilian authorities. There were dissident military movements during these years, one a grouping of officers called PUMA that mobilized behind Ibáñez to advance his presidency in the 1950s. Then in 1969 General Roberto Viaux led a rebellion within the ranks of the army against the Christian Democratic government of Eduardo Frei. Pinochet had nothing to do with these movements, hewing to the straight and narrow, intent on proving his subservience to his superiors and advancing as a 'constitutionalist' officer.

However, during these years Pinochet's authoritarian tendencies and lack of tolerance for dissent continued to manifest themselves. In Iquique in 1969 Pinochet, in his post as an army general, was also placed in charge of maintaining public order. In that position he had to deal with the growing social mobilizations and student protest movements that were becoming prominent in Chile. When the students of a large technical college in Iquique went out on strike in June 1969 to demand more resources for their school, Pinochet, after meeting with student representatives and their parents, declared that 'the strike was being manipulated … in order to stir up the situation' in the city.[41] Pinochet claims in his memoirs that 'the youth of the Communist Party' were the primary instigators of the strike.[42] After the students met again with Pinochet, he promised to deal with their demands within thirty days.

The students' demands were not met and in August they again went out on strike. This time, Pinochet notes, he ordered the school to be surrounded, 'cutting off water, electricity and telephones'. Pinochet refused to meet the student leaders, and instead ordered the police to arrest a number of students demonstrating in the streets for 'violating public order'.[43] Eventually the national government and the Ministry of Education intervened, agreeing to meet the students' demands, and ordering Pinochet to release the imprisoned students. Pinochet proclaimed in disgust that if the government 'wanted to solve the problem in this manner, it will have to assume responsibility for the consequences, I'm going home.'[44]

Salvador Allende's victory in the presidential elections of September 4, 1970 occurred while the recently appointed general was still posted in Iquique. Nothing is known about his opinions regarding Allende's election, or even whom he favoured in the three-way presidential contest between Allende, Radomiro Tomic of the Christian Democrats and Jorge Alessandri of the conservative National Party.

The month of October 1970, however, was to mark a turning point in the history of the Chilean military. Because Allende did not win an absolute majority of the vote, the Chilean Congress had to select the president from the top two contenders, the other being Alessandri. Historically, the Congress had always chosen the canditate who had won the most votes; however, a number of conspiracies were afoot to stop Allende's assumption of the presidency, involving the CIA, the Chilean right wing and sectors of the Chilean military. The immediate strategy of the right was to try to persuade the Christian Democrats in Congress to vote for Alessandri. Their votes along with those of the conservative parties would comprise a majority. Alessandri, in return, agreed that after being sworn in as president he would quickly resign, opening the way for new popular elections. This would enable Eduardo Frei to run for president once again while technically not violating the provision of the Chilean constitution that prevented a president from directly succeeding himself.

This strategy collapsed, however, when most of the Christian Democrats in Congress made it known that they would support Salvador Allende after he agreed to an amendment to the Chilean constitution that reinforced its democratic principles. But just two days before Congress was formally to elect Allende president, General Viaux, who had led a military rebellion in 1969, orchestrated a plot with CIA support to prevent Allende from taking power.

After Viaux had failed in his 1969 rebellion, the incumbent head of the army resigned in disgrace, and was replaced by General René

Schneider, a brilliant officer committed to democracy and the Chilean constitution. Schneider, concerned with the growing attempts to politicize the Chilean armed forces, issued a statement during the 1970 presidential campaign known as the 'Schneider Doctrine'. It declared: 'The army is the guarantee of a normal election in which the President of the Republic will be the candidate who receives the absolute majority of the popular vote. If none of the candidates receives more than 50 per cent of the vote, then Congress will select the president.' Asked by the press what he would do if Congress picked Allende as the president, Schneider responded: 'I insist that our doctrine and mission is to back and respect the political constitution of the state. In accordance with it, the Congress is sovereign. Our mission is to respect its decision.'[45]

It was this doctrine that provoked Viaux and the CIA to orchestrate a plot to kidnap Schneider on October 22, 1970 in order to trigger a coup by the military and/or to force the Chilean Congress to back off from its selection of Allende.[46] The kidnapping went awry, however: Schneider was gravely wounded when his car was stopped, and he died several days later. Instead of disrupting the presidential selection process, the assassination caused a popular revulsion against the right. Carlos Prats, another highly regarded general committed to democratic institutions, became commander in chief of the army, declaring he would follow the Schneider Doctrine. The Chilean Congress subsequently elected Allende president on October 24, 1970.

After the assassination of Schneider, a general state of emergency was declared throughout Chile; Pinochet was placed in charge of enforcing the emergency in the province of Tarapacá. Once again Pinochet became embroiled in a dispute with students from the Iquique schools. They called a strike, this time to show their support for Allende's election and to protest the right-wing conspiracy. Pinochet denounced the students, proclaiming that while the rest of Iquique was respecting 'the laws and providing an example for the country', the students 'were not showing loyalty'. Instead of 'continuing to work' they 'were acting idiotically'.[47]

In January 1971, Pinochet was transferred to Santiago to serve directly under General Carlos Prats and placed in charge of the

troops in the army barracks of the capital. This marked the beginning of what became a seemingly close relationship between Prats
and Pinochet. From then until August 1973, when Prats resigned,
Pinochet was absolutely loyal to Prats and there is no indication that
he collaborated with the right wing or any of the sectors of the
army in their early conspiracies against Allende and the Chilean
constitution.

In June 1971, an ultra-leftist organization, Vanguardia Organizada
del Pueblo, which was possibly infiltrated by the CIA, assassinated
the former Minister of Interior of the Frei government. (This
assassination was instrumental in turning the Christian Democrats
against the Popular Unity government as many party leaders believed that leftist sectors of the government were involved in the
assassination.) A state of emergency was declared, and Pinochet was
appointed by Prats to enforce it in Santiago. There were no public
incidents or 'protesting students' for Pinochet to rant about this
time.

By the end of 1971 Chile was becoming politically polarized,
particularly by the offensive of the right wing. It was determined to
make Chile ungovernable under Allende and intent on turning the
military against the elected government. Officers of the most conservative branch of the Chilean armed forces, the Navy, began to
conspire against the government along with business and trade associations in the port city of Valparaíso.[48]

In early December 1971 Fidel Castro began a historic trip to
Chile at the invitation of Salvador Allende, which lasted until just
before Christmas. Simultaneously, the right wing in Santiago initiated the 'march of the pots and pans'. It was led principally by
upper-class women in the well-to-do barrios of Providencia and Las
Condes in Santiago. The women took to the streets in their barrios
banging on pots and pans, supposedly symbolizing that they were
empty because of the politics of the Allende government.

In response, a state of emergency was declared, with Pinochet
once again placed in charge. This time he issued strict guidelines. All
public demonstrations were prohibited. The printed media, the radio
and the television stations were proscribed from broadcasting any
news that would provoke alarm or turbulence. Pinochet subsequently

shut down two right-wing radio stations, Radio Agricultura and Radio Balmaceda, for violating this decree.

Then on December 4 the right-wing newspaper *La Tribuna* published a political jingle, which read in part:

> Our struggle is just beginning,
> The armed forces are selling out
> For a new automobile
> For a house,
> For a salary increase.

General Pinochet was furious. He ordered all the editors of the newspapers in Santiago to meet with him. He announced that a suit would be filed against *La Tribuna* for defaming the Chilean armed forces. He confronted the director of *La Tribuna*, saying: 'I have not sold myself for thirty pieces of gold. I will undertake a military suit against *La Tribuna*.' In closing the meeting, Pinochet asked rhetorically: 'What do you want? A civil war? Coups d'état do not happen in Chile.'[49]

What is clear from this incident is Pinochet's determination to maintain order in Chile and to punish those who criticized the military. His guiding star was not support for one political tendency or another, but rather the absolute rule of law and order. In this instance it was clear that the right, rather than the left, was challenging Pinochet's determination to impose order on the country, and they accordingly felt his wrath.

Shortly thereafter, in January 1972, Pinochet was appointed head of the Joint Chiefs of Staff of the Army, a position second only to General Prats in the army chain of command. From then on Pinochet paid the utmost attention to the orders and needs of Prats, even fawning over him, according to some observers. He would inform Prats of any actions by subordinates in the army or elsewhere that seemed to question the authority of the commander in chief. In April 1972 Pinochet was the first to inform Prats that Senator Duran of the conservative National Party had dared to question Prats' declaration that leftist armed groups did not exist in Chile. Shortly thereafter Pinochet told Prats that an ex-major who had been forced to resign was organizing a conspiracy against the army's leadership and the government.[50]

Deceit, treachery and the 'crucial day'

Pinochet, in his book *The Crucial Day*, written after he had seized power, claims that he began conspiring against the Allende government shortly after his appointment as Chief of Staff of the army in 1972.[51] He asserts that, although 'it was extremely dangerous', he drew up an 'Internal Security Plan' to begin preparing for a military takeover of the country. According to Pinochet, his own intelligence reports concluded that a conflict was inevitable 'between the Executive and the Legislative branches', and that there would not be a constitutional solution. 'The Armed Forces which have traditionally acted as arbiters' would have to abandon this position and adopt a more forceful role to stop Allende and 'the paramilitary forces' of the left.[52]

In *The Crucial Day*, Pinochet goes on to claim that he became more intensively involved in the coup plotting during the course of 1972 and 1973. The historical record does not back any of these claims. Mónica González concludes in her study of the conspiracy leading up to the 1973 coup, based on extensive interviews with military and civilian officials, that there is absolutely no evidence to support Pinochet's assertions that he ordered such an intelligence report or that he began to consider military intervention at this early date.[53]

Pinochet's plagiarist writings in the 1950s and 1960s apparently enabled him to believe that he could get away with rewriting history in any way he chose, regardless of memoirs, interviews and the actual historical record. *The Crucial Day* is largely an effort to justify Pinochet's assumption of absolute power as dictator and his elimination of all contenders. Pinochet was actually the last army general to join the plot to overthrow Allende, just days before the coup took place. As the principal beneficiary of the coup, he wanted to make it appear that he was its major instigator and to justify his subsequent dominance over the other conspirators.

After the pots-and-pans demonstrations of December 1971, the next major crisis of the Popular Unity government erupted in October 1972 when the business and transportation sectors called for a shutdown of all economic activity in the country. It initially paralysed Chile. But then the trade unions and popular community organizations, with the backing of the government, stepped into the breach and began to move critical agricultural commodities and industrial supplies. Many factories shut down by their owners were seized by the workers and reopened.

Allende finally succeeded in defusing the crisis in early November by calling upon the heads of the distinct branches of the armed forces to assume cabinet positions. General Prats became Minister of the Interior and Pinochet became his interim replacement as head of the army. Pinochet retained this position until March 1973, when Prats stepped down as Minister of the Interior after congressional elections. These elections were a moral defeat for the right wing and appeared to stabilize the Allende government.

However, the congressional elections of March proved critical in the decision of the right wing and sectors of the military to violently overthrow the Popular Unity government. Because Allende had only won 36.3 per cent of the vote in the three-way presidential contest of 1970, the right-wing political parties in alliance with the Christian Democrats had believed they would win two-thirds of the congressional vote in the 1973 elections, given the economic turmoil they had sown in the country at large. This, they calculated, would enable them to impeach and remove Allende from office. But instead of a decline in support for the governing coalition, the Popular Unity parties actually won 43.4 per cent of the popular vote in 1973. Whereas the left was euphoric on the day after the elections, the right wing and the Christian Democrats became more desperate and intent on overthrowing Allende by any means possible. The conspiracy against the government gained more adherents among the military due to the adverse election results.[54]

According to all accounts, except his own, Pinochet had no relations with or involvement in these conspiracies. Of particular interest during 1972 and 1973 was his relation with the Minister of Defence, José Toha, a close confidant of Allende and a member of the Socialist Party. Pinochet and his wife Lucia were frequent dinner guests of Toha and his wife Moy. According to Moy de Toha, Pinochet would show up at their house frequently, sometimes on a daily basis. In one instance, after José Toha was savaged by a right-wing newspaper, Pinochet came to his house, threw the newspaper on the table and angrily proclaimed: 'This cannot be tolerated: it shows a lack of respect.'[55]

This supposed friendship with the Tohas, however, like most of Pinochet's social relationships, was largely opportunistic, an attempt to ingratiate himself with those in power. Immediately after the coup, José Toha, along with other high-ranking members of the Popular Unity government, was seized and imprisoned in harsh conditions on Dawson Island in southern Chile. Moy de Toha attempted to intervene with Pinochet to secure her husband's release, but her petition was denied. José Toha subsequently died in prison, allegedly committing suicide.[56]

The first military uprising against the Popular Unity government occurred on June 29, 1973, when the right-wing paramilitary organization Patria y Libertad collaborated with a tank division in Santiago to launch an assault on the presidential palace. The coup attempt was put down by armed units led by Prats and Pinochet. But the growing political polarization of Chile only emboldened other generals in the army to begin plotting their own coup in earnest with air force and navy officers. Prats remained loyal to the government, to the consternation of the right wing and many military officers. In late August, the wives of the treacherous army officers assembled in front of Prats' house, shouting insults at the general and his wife, and demanding his immediate resignation.[57]

Prats now realized he had lost the confidence of most of the generals of the army and tendered his resignation on August 22. Allende initially rejected it, but Prats insisted; they then jointly decided that Pinochet should become head of the army, believing he would remain steadfastly loyal to the government. Pinochet formally assumed charge of the army on August 23. One of Pinochet's first acts as commander in chief was to insist in a meeting with army officials that the removal of Prats 'would be washed with the blood of other generals', meaning that the officers who had not supported Prats and whose wives had demonstrated in front of his house would be forced to resign.[58] However, after conversations with the officer corps, Pinochet quickly backed off from his declaration, realizing that it would be difficult to enforce.

After Prats' resignation the military conspirators accelerated their plans. With the support of the head of the air force, General Gustavo Leigh Guzmán; of the second highest-ranking commander of the navy, of Vice-Admiral José Toribio Merino; and of a group of generals in the army, the coup plotters decided to approach Pinochet on September 8, 1973. One of the leading army conspirators, Brigadier General Sergio Arellano Stark, visited Pinochet's house that night and informed him of the plans for a coup. He gave Pinochet two choices: he could resign and step aside, or he could join the coup and lead the army. Visibly agitated, Pinochet finally brought his fist down on the arm of the chair in which he was seated and proclaimed: 'Shit, I'm not a Marxist.'[59] Arellano Stark then told Pinochet that he should call General Leigh, head of the air force, to inform him of his decision to join the coup, planned for September 11.

However, Pinochet did not call Leigh, or communicate with any other coup conspirator regarding his plans. The military plotters became distraught, worrying about what Pinochet would do. In fact at noon on September 9, Pinochet had a meeting with Allende and his closest advisors, including Joan Garcés. However, Pinochet mentioned not a word about his conversations with Arellano Stark. He assured Allende that measures were being taken by the army to neutralize any coup attempt.[60] This was Pinochet's final face-to-face meeting with Allende. It marked his decision to betray the man who had appointed him head of the Army just sixteen days earlier, when Pinochet swore to uphold the constitution of Chile with his life.

Anxious about what Pinochet was up to, Leigh went to Pinochet's home on the afternoon of Sunday, September 9. Two high-ranking naval officers subsequently joined them, carrying a declaration signed by Vice-Admiral Merino endorsing the coup. At the end of the declaration Merino added a personal note to Pinochet: 'Augusto, if you don't put all the forces of Santiago [behind the coup] we will not live to see the future.' The naval officers asked Leigh and Pinochet to sign the declaration. Leigh, of course, immediately placed his signature on it. Pinochet demurred for a few minutes, saying he had to look for his official seal to stamp the document. No one at the meeting understood why he needed his seal. Nonetheless he finally added his signature at 7 o'clock that evening.

According to Pinochet, he hardly slept that night and rose the next morning 'greatly preoccupied and anxious'. His main concern was how to cover up from the government the confinement of the troops in their barracks on the night of the 10th so they would be ready to attack the next day. Pinochet first went to the Ministry of Defence to present a pretext for his decision regarding the troop confinement, saying that they might be provoked by leftist agitators led by the head of the Socialist Party, Carlos Altamirano. Then, in the afternoon, Pinochet met with the leading army conspirators to plan the details of the coup. In *The Crucial Day* he relates that he called together in his office a number of the leading army officers backing the coup, 'took a replica of the sword of General O'Higgins', and made the other officers 'swear, as soldiers' that all that they had talked about 'would be kept absolutely secret'.[61] Pinochet says he then surprised the assembled officers, including Brigadier General Arellano, with the announcement that the coup was to take place the following day. No other military officer has ever testified to this scene; it was sheer fabrication by Pinochet. What they do remember are a series of meetings on the 10th, some involving Pinochet, in which they drew up the final details for the coup the next day.

On the night before the coup Pinochet once again had difficulty sleeping. In his memoirs he says that he was preoccupied with planning for the coup. More likely he was concerned that the coup would go awry and his military career would be ruined. On September 10, Pinochet had his wife and family sent to a military base near the frontier with Argentina, believing that if the coup failed they could take exile in the neighbouring country and that he would be able to follow them.[62]

The hours leading up to the coup were surely traumatic for Pinochet. Here was a general who had been very cautious, intent on advancing his military career in a subservient, obeisant and opportunistic manner. His decision to join the coup plotters was most likely based on a straightforward understanding of the realities of power that were at play. The navy, the air force and a large number of the officer corps of the army were intent on carrying out a coup. If Pinochet had decided to remain loyal to the government, there would have been a split in the army, and he would be in a minority position, forced to side with the popular sectors that had no singular organization to resist the bulk of the military forces. Aside from believing that the rebellious officers probably had the best chance of coming out on top, his previous anti-Communist stance, particularly against students and labour leaders, also probably reinforced the realpolitik behind his decision to back the coup.

At 5.30 in the morning on September 11 Pinochet rose to shower, dressed in his combat uniform and put on his dark sunglasses. An hour later he went to a communications centre in a suburb of Santiago to help coordinate the coup. At 8.00 a.m. the declaration of the armed forces that they were overthrowing the government of Salvador Allende was read on the country's radio stations. The bloody rebellion by the military that would lead to a seventeen-year dictatorship under General Augusto Pinochet had begun.

3

The quest for absolute power

As with all pivotal events, the coup in Chile and the rise of the Pinochet dictatorship reflected a confluence of particular historic factors as well as the attributes and personalities of its leaders. Forces much larger than Pinochet predetermined the immediate repression that began on September 11. Chile had been polarized under the Popular Unity government, and now with the coup those who had seen their interests menaced by the social reforms and the takeover of their lands and factories were bent on vengeance.

The left had virtually no armed or military capacity to resist the coup, but it had sunk deep roots in Chilean society. The strong trade unions, the popular base of the Socialists, Communists and other parties of the left; their control of newspapers, magazines and radio stations; and the support of El Nuevo Chile among artists, musicians and writers – these were the reasons why the right wing, along with the military conspirators, were determined to wage a total war against those who had led and participated in the popular movement that backed Salvador Allende.

For decades the right had been stirring up anti-Communist hysteria against the left, but it became particularly shrill during the three years of the Popular Unity government. Comments by Pinochet's wife, Lucia Hiriart, reveal the tenor of this campaign.

One evening, just before the coup, when two of Pinochet's grand-children were asleep at his residence, Lucia took her husband into the bedroom and said: 'Look at your grandchildren. These children are going to be condemned to be slaves of communism and you are doing nothing.' Pinochet, who had not discussed the plans for a coup with his wife, said 'Be patient. Have faith in God.'[1]

This conversation reflected the twisted and distorted propaganda war the right wing had mounted. No party in the Popular Unity coalition ever called for the establishment of a communist regime even vaguely similar to those existing in Eastern Europe or the Soviet Union. Indeed the Chilean Communist Party, more than the other parties of the governing coalition, was constantly searching for an accommodation with the Christian Democrats, even if it meant abandoning some of the social and economic planks of the Popular Unity platform. But the right wing insisted that the left was intent on creating a totalitarian order, and among the conservative rank and file many actually came to believe this anti-communist propaganda.

It was this campaign to paint the left as evil and intent on enslav-ing the people of Chile that provided the social milieu for the military junta to imprison and execute Popular Unity leaders and their supporters. Any individual or group that questioned the regime was viewed as an enemy and part of the 'international Marxist con-spiracy' that had to be confronted and eradicated in Chile. This obviously meant that Pinochet, on the day of the coup, was by no means the only figure bent on terrorizing the country and destroy-ing the political and social forces that had backed the Popular Unity government. Every member of the junta supported the crackdown, the suspension of civil liberties, the roundup and imprisonment of tens of thousands of people, and the summary executions.

In addition the wealthy business establishment, the National Party and the right wing of the Christian Democrats all joined in the vitriolic campaign that strove to silence and eliminate those who had challenged their right to dominate and rule the country. Neo-fascist groups like Patria y Libertad also numbered among the junta supporters. In the days after the coup, these organizations and move-ments provided the junta with a hardcore social base to wage its bloody war of repression.

At the grassroots level, those who had banged on their pots and pans in the protests against the Allende government now constituted the neighbourhood 'eyes and ears' of the junta. Thousands of them called into police and military posts to report the names of neighbours who had supported the Popular Unity government. Many of the foreigners who had come to study and work in Chile under Allende were also fingered by neighbours as 'communist sympathizers'. One of the two Americans murdered by the junta, Frank Teruggi, was arrested along with his roommate, David Hathaway, after a neighbour reported them to the military.[2]

Mónica González, who has studied the relationship of the military and civilian forces at the time of the coup, notes 'the right wing business groups were iron willed. They knew that a quick return to democracy would hinder their ability to take control of the country's economy. They were determined to reverse the agrarian reform and the state takeover of factories.'[3] At the highest level, the nearly total support of the business clans of Chile for the overthrow of Allende was reflected by the appointment of Fernando Leniz to the Ministry of Economy less than a month after the coup.[4] Leniz had served as director of the country's dominant newspaper, the right-wing El Mercurio, which also put out two more yellow journalistic tabloids, Clarín and Últimas Noticias. These papers were owned by the Edwards family, which also had extensive interests in other areas of the Chilean economy, including the powerful Agustín Edwards Bank. The Edwardses and associates like Leniz had conspired to topple the Popular Unity government since the very day Allende won the elections in 1970. It is a matter of public record that the head of the Edwards family had extensive relations with the CIA.[5]

Pinochet's 'total war'

While the initial repression obviously cannot be attributed to Pinochet, the direction it soon took and its continuation for seventeen years depended on the role of the general who came to head up the military junta. Once the coup had succeeded, Pinochet's admiration for the strongmen of history and his severe authoritarian bent were characteristics that drove him to consolidate absolute power in his own hands. From the moment the junta seized power, Pinochet began manoeuvring to become more than *primus inter pares*.

Gonzalo Vial, who served as Minister of Education during the military regime, has written a two-volume, largely sympathetic study of the dictator. In describing the consistency in Pinochet's character before and after the coup, Vial aptly portrays the central role of military discipline and authoritarianism in his subject's personal evolution: 'There is a logical continuum between the "second man" [Pinochet] ... who rose through the ranks of the army, and the "first man" who emerged on September 11, 1973.' According to Vial, 'the second man was a follower of orders without rival', a soldier 'who was absolutely obedient' and acted 'as a slave to the chain of command'. Once in power, 'the first Pinochet demanded of his subordinates an equal discipline and respect, and upon civilians he imposed the same rigorous principles.'[6]

Patricia Lutz describes the impact of Pinochet's military training in a somewhat harsher light, bringing into play the psychological traits he had manifested in his career before the coup. By temperament and training, she argues, Pinochet 'was a military strategist, and his warrior philosophy led him to see an internal enemy.' Pinochet was 'fighting international Marxism', and this meant 'total war, in which all moral values are alterable. His military formation meant a discipline that distanced him from the enemy. It is a position that assumes no feelings and no sensitivity.'[7] These traits explain in large part why Pinochet's brutal violation of human rights continued for years after the early anti-communist hysteria had spent itself.

In his quest for absolute power in this war, Pinochet had one critical advantage over all potential adversaries: he was commander in chief of the army. The military potential of the air force, the navy and the national police of Chile paled in comparison to the strength and firepower of the army. According to Gonzalo Vial, Pinochet once commented to a close civilian adviser: 'the navy cannot advance beyond Casablanca' (the closest sea access to Santiago), and 'the air force pilots have to land for fuel'.[8]

It was this type of crude power analysis that Pinochet used repeatedly to outmanoeuvre or eliminate all adversaries. It also enables us to understand why Pinochet was the only military leader among the southern cone military regimes that emerged in the 1960s and 1970s who refused to rotate power with his military counterparts. Gustavo Leigh, the head of the air force, confronted this base reality before the swearing in of the junta. Leigh suggested that as the senior commander among the members of the junta he should be the first president. Pinochet quickly replied that the commander of the oldest military institution of the country, the army, would become the first head of the junta. The other two members of the junta supported this stance, and Pinochet became president.[9]

Transcripts of the tapes that were secretly recorded on September 11 of communications among the military commanders revealed that Pinochet's more visceral impulses quickly came to the fore following the coup. Paz Rojas, a psychiatrist who works for CODEPU, a human rights organization in Chile, has used the transcripts to analyse Pinochet's behaviour and character. She notes that among the coup leaders Pinochet used the most vulgar and vehement language. Almost immediately he began dehumanizing Allende and the people resisting in the presidential palace, describing them in animalistic terms as *gallos* (cocks), *pericos*[10] (parrots) and *culebras* (snakes). He never said 'President Allende', only on one occasion using the letters, 'S.E.' in a deprecating manner, meaning 'Su Excelencia', or 'His Excellency'. Aside from referring to them as animals, Pinochet often calls Allende and others in the presidential palace *hijo de puta* (son of a bitch), *carajos* (fuck-heads), *mugrientos* (dirty bastards) and *jetones* (fools).[11]

Paz Rojas also notes from the transcripts Pinochet's paranoid tendencies. In one communication, he fears that Allende 'will ride a tank' out of the presidential palace, and take command of the opposition to the junta. In another, he depicts 'the *poblaciones* [shantytowns] rising up' and mounting an assault to rescue Allende. In yet another, he sees thousands of foreign combatants from within Chile leading an assault on the military.[12] None of these scenarios had any basis in reality. What they do reveal is a man who for the next seventeen years would everywhere see enemies to be eliminated.

It was this limited capacity of Pinochet to assess events in the real world objectively that leads Paz Rojas to describe him in psychological terms as 'débil mental superior', meaning that he has limited cognitive mental capacity to interpret and articulate events, but an excessive belief in his own capabilities.[13] Pinochet, in his language on September 11, and in his subsequent public speeches for seventeen years, is a man who is 'extremely stiff, harsh, has a limited vocabulary and difficulty in communicating and resonating with a broader public.'[14] Patricia Lutz puts it correctly: 'Pinochet, as president of Chile was in over his head. He achieved a post far beyond his capabilities.'[15] Both women agree that Pinochet had an almost primordial understanding of how to use power to serve his own interests and needs. 'He was a crude Machiavellian', says Lutz. 'He may not have possessed the finesse and sophistication the original Machiavelli urged upon the "Prince", but Pinochet had a capacity to move deliberately and obsessively to eliminate all antagonists of his regime.' Lutz adds: 'He had no moral qualms about torturing or getting rid of anyone. He probably slept like a lamb at night, not worrying at all about the death and pain he inflicted.'[16] This reinforces the view of Pinochet as a sociopath, someone who holds no moral principles, who believes he can do as he pleases to advance his self-interest.

In the bloody aftermath of the coup, the first major acts of terror instigated directly by Augusto Pinochet took place at the end of September when he appointed Brigadier General Sergio Arellano Stark, one of the leading conspirators of the coup, 'Official Delegate of the President of the Governmental Junta and the Commander in Chief of the Army.'[17] This appointment meant that Arellano Stark was in charge of a special military commission empowered to travel around Chile to administer military justice as it saw fit. By mid-October 1973, the commission, which became known as 'the Caravan of Death', had executed seventy-five people, many of whom had voluntarily presented themselves to local military commanders immediately after the coup. Some had already received light military sentences, but Arellano Stark, under orders from Pinochet, was determined to impose a draconian rule on all of Chile and ordered summary executions of selected prisoners.

Some of the victims were brutally tortured. Many of the bodies of the executed were dumped in mines and wells or buried in unknown sites and number among the first 'disappeared' of the Pinochet regime, meaning their deaths have never been officially accounted for because their bodies were not found. Brigadier General Joaquín Lagos, the commander of a military district in northern Chile visited by Arellano Stark, disagreed with many of the executions and notified Pinochet. The next year Pinochet had Lagos relieved of his command. Twenty-five years later Pinochet was charged with responsibility for the Caravan of Death, and it led to his first and only indictment for the crimes he committed as dictator of Chile.

DINA and the consolidation of state terrorism

At about the same time that the Caravan of Death began executing prisoners, Pinochet requested that Lieutenant Colonel Manuel Contreras present plans for a special intelligence unit to act against opponents of the military regime. Contreras, thirteen years younger than Pinochet, would act as the General's alter ego in the consolidation of his rule, despite the fact that the two men were quite dissimilar in their backgrounds and talents.

Before the coup, Contreras was the head of the army's Tejas Verdes Engineering School in Santiago, where he was known as a brilliant instructor and strategist. In the late 1960s he studied at the Fort Benning US army school in Georgia, where it is reported that he bested a computer in his final exams in drawing up alternative military strategies.[18] He was also unlike Pinochet in that he backed early military conspiracies against civilian governments. He supported General Viaux in 1969 and 1970, and he numbered among the early conspirators against Allende. The Popular Unity government requested the expulsion of Contreras from the army on one occasion, but his superior, General Guillermo Pickering, who remained loyal to Allende to the very end, refused to relieve Contreras of his position, arguing that he, Pickering, assumed personal responsibility for Contreras.

With the coup, two jail cells at Tejas Verdes, one for men and the other for women, were immediately filled with prisoners. It was then that Contreras began drawing up plans for a special unit to search out opponents of the new regime; this quickly came to the attention of Pinochet. In late September Pinochet asked Contreras to lay out his proposals before the four members of the junta and the heads of the intelligence agencies of the distinct branches of the Chilean armed forces. Contreras began by pointing out that the country was in an 'internal war', and that the main enemy was 'the subversive'. In order to combat this enemy, Contreras argued, a new organization was necessary to centralize the intelligence work of the different military services. Since the elimination of all subversive elements was of the highest priority, this new agency would require its own separate staff and material resources.[19]

There were immediate objections by members of the junta and lengthy arguments, but in the end it was decided to give Contreras the green light to begin forming a special intelligence unit. The exact nature of its relation to the rest of the military intelligence units would be determined later. Immediately after the meeting Contreras began assembling a group of officials and soldiers to work in the unit and started giving them special training at Tejas Verdes. Within days they were operating on the streets of Santiago, arresting, torturing and eliminating 'subversives'.[20]

Contreras's clout grew so rapidly that on November 12, 1973, a special session of the junta was convened. With the ardent backing of Pinochet, Contreras was named head of DINA, the National Directorate of Intelligence, and authorized to select 500 officers and staff members from the distinct branches of the armed forces.[21] Interestingly, all the high-ranking members of the commission that had served with Arellano Stark on the Caravan of Death were selected by Contreras to work with DINA. The new agency also developed an extensive network of civilian collaborators, including members of the neo-fascist organization Patria y Libertad. Within the different government ministries and agencies, DINA also counted on an extensive network of informants and conspirators.[22] DINA would also quickly develop an international network, particularly through Operation Condor, which collaborated with other military dictatorships in South America in hunting down opponents of these regimes. At its height, Contreras boasted that DINA had 50,000 functionaries, collaborators and agents![23]

For four long years, DINA terrorized Chile. Like Pinochet, Contreras and many of the people he assembled around him were undoubtedly sociopaths, with mixtures of sadism and other psychological disorders. They had no qualms about savagely torturing the men and women they picked up, and when they were finished with them, many would be executed and their bodies 'disappeared'. The official symbol of DINA was an iron fist. Contreras met with Pinochet on a daily basis to plot DINA's activities. Militants of political parties, along with members of social movements and church organizations, were placed on the hit lists of DINA. To help fund its activities, some of the state enterprises of the Allende years were privatized and turned over to DINA.[24] In the case of the disappeared victims alone, it is estimated that between January 1974 and the end of 1989 DINA was responsible for 324 of 562 disappeared.[25]

The horrors of repressive institutions like DINA have unfortunately been inflicted on other Latin American countries like Haiti, the Dominican Republic and El Salvador. But what was so appalling about DINA was that until Pinochet the Chilean leaders dating back to independence had never engaged in such barbaric practices on such a massive scale. Certainly the Chilean claim to a 'long democratic tradition' is of questionable validity, but until Pinochet leaders who engaged in repressive acts – like Diego Portales and José Balmaceda in the nineteenth century, and Carlos Ibáñez and Gabriel González Videla in the twentieth – did not come even close to the horrific crimes committed by the regime of Augusto Pinochet.[26]

DINA became the bedrock of the Pinochet regime from 1973 to 1978, empowered not only to deal with adversaries on the left but also to search out and keep tabs on members of the military who displayed questionable loyalty to the dictator. It was undoubtedly DINA's operations that enabled Pinochet to declare once that in Chile 'not a leaf moves if I don't move it, let that be clear'.[27] One of the early clashes between DINA and the other sectors of the military occurred over the pursuit of the militants of the MIR, the Left Revolutionary Movement. It was the first political organization that DINA targeted. The air force intelligence unit also set up the Comando Conjunto to pursue the MIR and other selected political targets. In mid-1974, the air force sent signals that it was interested in negotiating with the MIR, offering to end the savage repression of the organization if its leaders would accept exile.[28] The MIR leadership rejected the offer.

Eliminating military adversaries

These discussions came to the attention of Contreras, who was furious over this and other efforts by the air force unit to intrude on the operations of DINA. In a horrific act signalling to the air force that it could not negotiate behind the back of Contreras, Lumi Videla Moya, an imprisoned militant of the MIR, was murdered in a DINA facility and her bloody body tossed on top of the metal fence of the Italian embassy, where a number of Chileans, including MIR militants, had taken asylum.[29] Six months later, one of the two heads of air force intelligence, Colonel Horacio Otaiza, died in an aircraft accident. Everyone in the air force agency assumed Contreras was behind the crash.[30]

Other key military officials of the regime also ran afoul of DINA. Augusto Lutz, who was head of army intelligence at the time of the coup, and later became secretary to the military junta, complained directly to Pinochet about Contreras and DINA's operations. He was removed from his post in the government and assigned to head a regiment in Punto Arenas, the southernmost city of Chile next to the Straits of Magellan. In November 1974 he died in mysterious circumstances while he was being treated in a military hospital for food poisoning.[31]

General Oscar Bonilla was the highest-ranking military official to take on DINA. Appointed Minister of the Interior at the time of the coup, he soon became the number-two official in the army next to Pinochet, and his potential successor. Bonilla became known as something of a 'military populist' because of visits to the *poblaciones,* the working-class barrios around Santiago, and was close to the Christian Democratic Party, which was intent on a quick return to civilian rule so that it could once again enjoy the privileges of power. Concerned about reports of human rights violations, Bonilla made a surprise visit to Tejas Verdes in May 1974, virtually forcing entry into the facility. He was shocked by what he saw. 'Men tied up face down on the ground, some nude and bound, and others hanging by their arms, suspended in the air. You could see they had been beaten and tortured. The reality was more horrible that what I had been told.'[32] Bonilla ordered the immediate arrest of Contreras. But of course it never happened.

On June 18, just over a month later, the government's official newspaper published a decree formally establishing DINA with broad powers of arrest and detention. This was the first public statement of the existence of DINA. The day before the release of this decree, Pinochet convened a meeting of the junta in which he presented the other members with a document naming himself *El Jefe Supremo*, with presidential powers. The other members of the junta insisted on modifying the document so that they would retain veto powers over many of Pinochet's actions.

Nine days later Pinochet called another meeting of the junta, this time informing them that he was about to install himself in power with full presidential powers. The head of Chile's Supreme Court was waiting next door to place the tricolor presidential sash on Pinochet. The meeting quickly turned into a shouting match, particularly between Leigh and Pinochet. 'You think you are God', yelled Leigh; 'For how long?' An infuriated Pinochet replied: 'Here you can try to fuck around. If this uproar continues this [meeting] will be suspended, and we'll see how things are worked out. I won't let you toy with the country.' Pinochet then angrily smashed his fist down on the glass table in front of him, causing it to crack down the middle. Leigh and the others on the junta gave in to Pinochet. In the subsequent ceremony, Pinochet asserted, with seemingly misty eyes, 'I never thought of, nor sought' the presidency of Chile.[33]

Within days, Pinochet had reorganized the cabinet, removing General Bonilla as Interior Minister and assigning him to the post of Minister of Defence. On March 3, 1975 Bonilla died in a helicopter crash when he was returning from southern Chile, where he had gone to take a brief vacation to escape from the exhaustion and tension he faced in Santiago. A two-member French technical team sent to investigate the crash of the French-made helicopter also experienced a fatal air accident in which they died.[34]

Ultimately Contreras's undoing did not stem from his murderous internal activities against opponents of the regime, but from DINA's international operations, which began almost simultaneously with its founding. DINA sent operatives to Buenos Aires in late 1973 to monitor the movements of Carlos Prats, the general who had personally anointed Pinochet as his successor as head of the army just eighteen days before September 11. Forced into exile in Argentina after the coup, Prats was viewed as a potential threat by Pinochet because the former general was still much admired by certain sectors of the army. One plot in early 1974 to eliminate Prats failed, but on September 30, 1974 DINA carried out its first major international terrorist act when its operatives blew up the automobile of Prats and his wife as they returned home late at night from a theatre in Buenos Aires.

Emboldened by this cold-blooded assassination, DINA in June 1975 participated in an operation with the southern cone dictatorships of Argentina and Brazil in which news stories were planted in these countries claiming that 119 exiled 'extremists' had died in an internecine battle among leftist political organizations. In fact the dead had earlier been apprehended in Chile and 'disappeared' by DINA. Then, on October 5 of the same year, DINA operatives in Rome attempted to assassinate a progressive Christian Democratic leader, Bernardo Leighton, gravely wounding him and his wife.[35]

The most astounding international terrorist operation conducted by DINA occurred on September 21, 1976 when Orlando Letelier and his colleague at the Institute for Policy Studies, Ronni Moffitt, were killed by a car bomb in Washington DC, just blocks from the White House. Letelier had been the last Minister of Defence before the coup; in exile in the United States he had spoken out assertively against the crimes of the Pinochet regime, working with human rights advocates in the US Congress and travelling around the world to campaign for the suspension of international assistance to the dictatorship.

The crime occurred during the last months of the Ford administration when Henry Kissinger, who had backed the military coup in Chile, still served as Secretary of State. Appallingly, but not surprisingly, an initial FBI inquiry pursued a 'lead' that the assassination had been carried out by leftist elements.[36] The evidence, however, soon pointed to DINA, and with the accession of the Carter administration in January 1977 the US government began placing substantial diplomatic and legal pressure on the Pinochet regime to prosecute those responsible for the crime. This pressure, combined with the growing opposition within the regime to Contreras, finally forced Pinochet to dissolve DINA on August 13, 1977. It was replaced by a new intelligence agency, the National Information Centre (CNI) and headed up by a retired general, Odlanier Mena.

Pinochet made clear, however, that Contreras retained his confidence. Upon the dissolution of DINA, Contreras was elevated to the rank of General. Then, as if to flaunt his support for Contreras in front of the Carter administration, Pinochet placed the former head of DINA in charge of his security force when the dictator travelled officially to Washington in September 1977 to join the other presidents of the hemisphere to witness the signing of the new Panama Canal treaty. In a press conference in Washington Pinochet was asked about the assassination of Letelier. He responded: 'I can swear that no one in the Chilean government planned anything like that.'[37] Contreras, just a few paces from Pinochet, observed the scene with an inscrutable stare.

Contreras remained close to Pinochet and was a frequent visitor to his home for years afterwards. The dictator acknowledged his enormous debt to the man who had eliminated potential adversaries to his regime.

4

Globalization of the Chilean human rights movement

The military coup on September 11, 1973 and the initial unleashing of state terrorism in Chile provoked an international outcry. As would be expected, the Nixon administration did nothing to stop the killings and executions in Chile, as declassified intelligence documents reveal.[1] However, other governments allied with the United States, particularly those in Western Europe, took steps to assist those being pursued by the military junta. The Swedish and Italian ambassadors made heroic efforts to help victims of the regime flee the country. And even some Latin American governments, like Mexico and Panama, opened their embassy doors to Chileans seeking exile.

At the time of the coup, the most visible and prominent human rights organizations were intergovernmental in nature and linked to international organizations like the Organization of American States and the United Nations. There was, however, one major exception – Amnesty International. It launched an immediate campaign against the repression of the Pinochet regime, and soon sent a special delegation to investigate the conditions in Chile.

Founded in 1961, Amnesty International was the brainchild of Peter Benenson, a Catholic lawyer of Jewish descent, born of English and Russian parents. A barrister in London active around human rights issues, Benenson in early 1961 pulled together a group of like-minded individuals to start a campaign called 'Appeal for Amnesty, 1961'. Their opening salvo came on May 28 of that year, when the *Observer* newspaper carried an article entitled 'The Forgotten Prisoners'. It called for a letter-writing campaign for the release of eight political prisoners, among them Agostinho Neto, an Angolan poet, who would later become the first president of an independent Angola.[2]

The response to this appeal was overwhelming, with letters and donations coming in from around the world as the article was picked up by other newspapers and magazines. The genius of Amnesty from its inception was that many of these respondents were linked together in small groups that would 'adopt' individual prisoners. Letters were written by each of the groups to the respective governments holding the prisoners as well as to their families and the prisoners so that they would know that the world at large was concerned with their plight.

From the beginning Amnesty was notable for its efforts to be non-ideological in a world caught up in the throes of the Cold War. Each group of Amnesty supporters would adopt three prisoners, one from the West, one from the Third World, and one from the Communist bloc countries. By the end of 1961, Amnesty had become a permanent organization and its renowned icon had been devised, a candle with barbed wire encircling it.

Although Amnesty International underwent an internal crisis in the mid- and late 1960s over Benenson's personalistic leadership style and allegations that Amnesty had received funds from the British government, by the time of the coup in Chile it was a firmly established and highly respected organization. Events in Chile mobilized the organization as never before. Personal ties played an important role. Joan Jara, the British wife of renowned Chilean musician Victor Jara, who was tortured and executed in the days after the coup, worked with Amnesty to help galvanize British public opinion against the brutal repression in Chile. Aside from undertaking campaigns on behalf of political prisoners in Chile, Cosmas Desmond, an ex-priest from South Africa who headed up Amnesty International in London, helped launch a successful campaign to end British arms sales to the Chilean military government.[3]

Among intergovernmental organizations, the Inter-American Commission on Human Rights (IACHR), based in Washington DC, took the lead in pressuring the military junta. Founded in 1959 in Santiago, Chile, the commission returned to Chile in 1972 to hold its twenty-seventh meeting at the express invitation of President Salvador Allende. A year later, and six days after the overthrow of Allende, the commission cabled the Chilean Foreign Minister Admiral Ismael Huerta with its concerns over reports of mass arrests, executions and the junta's failure to respect the 'traditional right of political asylum granted to all political refugees in Latin American countries'.[4] Less than a month later, the head of the commission, Luis Reque, made an official visit to Santiago. After five days in Chile and a series of frustrating meetings with government officials over their failure to take steps to protect the rights of prisoners, Reque urged the commissioners of IACHR to establish an official subcommission to conduct an on-site investigation of human rights violations in Chile.

Two weeks after Reque's visit, Amnesty International sent a three-member delegation to Chile headed by Frank Newman, an American who also served as vice-chairman of the International Institute of Human Rights in France. Appalled by what he saw, Newman provided the first in-depth testimony on the human rights situation in Chile before the House Foreign Relations Committee of the US Congress in early December 1973. He reported to the committee that at least 15,000 detentions had occurred during the first month and a half following the coup, and that while the Ministry of Defence openly acknowledged the deaths of ninety-five people, he had no reliable information on the true number that were killed 'by warfare, death sentences after trial or summary execution'.[5]

The arduous birth of the Chilean human rights movement

While these and other reports galvanized international public opinion concerning the ongoing repression of the military junta led by Pinochet, Chileans within the country began the difficult task of trying to set up organizations to deal with the severe human rights violations. Among the first was the National Committee to Assist

Refugees (Comité Nacional de Ayuda a los Refugiados, or CONAR), an organization backed by the Chilean churches. It helped at least five thousand people leave Chile who were either imprisoned or threatened by the Pinochet regime.[6] The core of this committee in 1975 helped set up FASIC, La Fundación de Ayuda Social de las Iglesias Cristianas.

FASIC continued to help get prison sentences commuted to exile, and later it helped reunite exiles with their families in Chile and also became a centre for providing information on human rights issues to people in Chile and abroad.[7]

On October 6, 1973, the Comité de Cooperación para la Paz en Chile (Copachi) was founded to provide legal and material assistance to victims of the regime. Based mainly in the churches, the committee was initially directed by the Lutheran bishop in Chile, Helmut Frenz, and by Catholic bishop Fernando Asiztía. The suspension of the Chilean Congress and all political organizations in Chile meant that the churches were virtually the only functioning institutions that could openly engage in human rights work. Copachi itself comprised over three hundred lay and religious workers, the majority of whom were identified with political parties that had backed the Allende government.[8] The international support for human rights work in Chile was also evident at this early stage, as Copachi immediately received material assistance from foreign governments and the World Council of Churches.

Copachi helped search for and assist people who were arrested or detained by the regime, while also providing legal counsel to workers who were fired by their employers for political reasons. Reports on the work of the committee and other issues relating to human rights abuses were regularly published in the Jesuit magazine *Mensaje*, the only publication in Chile critical of the military regime that was not closed or heavily censored.[9] Petitions of habeas corpus were also filed by Copachi lawyers on behalf of missing persons, but the extreme subservience of the Chilean courts to the regime meant that virtually all of these petitions were rejected. The tragic role the Chilean courts played in supporting the new regime was signalled the morning after the coup, when the chief justice of the Supreme Court, Enrique Urrutia Manzano, sent a message of congratulations to the junta on behalf of the entire court.[10] For seventeen long years the courts of Chile abandoned any pretext of protecting even the most minimal human rights.

Cardinal Raúl Silva Henríquez of Santiago served as the driving force behind the Catholic Church's efforts to deal with the dictatorship's human rights abuses. Influenced by Vatican II and liberation theology, Cardinal Silva had enjoyed good relations with Salvador Allende; he had tried to prevent the coup, fearing its potentially bloody implications. There were two other major currents in the Church: the conservatives who had welcomed the coup and the dictatorship; and others, closer to the Christian Democrats, who were hopeful that the coup would lead to the quick installation of a moderate civilian regime.

Silva worked tirelessly on behalf of the victims of the coup, and as the ongoing abuses of the regime became more and more flagrant, he was able to persuade most of the Church hierarchy to take a more critical stance against the regime. In April 1974, the Church issued a declaration accusing the government of torture and stating that Chileans lived in 'a climate of insecurity and fear'.[11] The next month even many of those in the Church hierarchy close to the Christian Democrats who were initially open to the military's 'good intentions', endorsed a statement critical of the junta's human rights abuses. Pinochet, in turn, began to view Copachi as a hostile organization, even infiltrating Christian base communities that cooperated with Copachi.

As we saw in the previous chapter, in 1974 the Directorate for National Intelligence, or DINA, went on a rampage as it sought to eliminate all opposition to the regime by engaging in surveillance, abductions, torture and murder. Headed by Lieutenant Colonel Manuel Contreras, who reported directly to Pinochet, DINA focused much of its early efforts against the militant Left Revolutionary Movement, or MIR, which had gone underground to resist the regime. Many MIR members who were apprehended by DINA were tortured and 'disappeared', never to be heard from again. Antoni Llido, a Spanish priest in Chile since 1969 who went underground after the coup, became one of the more prominent cases of the disappeared. He was picked up by the secret police, brutally tortured at a detention centre, and never seen again. This method of repression was calculated to sow fear among political opponents and the friends and families of the disappeared, who never knew whether those apprehended were dead or alive.

In response to this insidious form of repression, a new human rights organization was set up in 1974, the Organization of the Families of the Detained and Disappeared (La Agrupación de Familiares de Detenidos Desaparecidos, or AFDD). Led principally by women – the wives, mothers and sisters of disappeared victims – the organization initially received assistance from Copachi and the Catholic Church, although it was primarily a secular organization. In 1975 and 1976, the membership of AFDD expanded to include families of victims from other political organizations, as DINA and the military government began targeting and disappearing members of the Socialist and Communist Parties.

Internationalizing the human rights struggle

The coup and subsequent repression also led to a proliferation of international non-governmental organizations concerned with the systematic violation of human rights. One of these, the Washington Office on Latin America, or WOLA, was established in 1974 in Washington DC. Joe Eldridge, a co-founder and early director of WOLA, had worked as a Methodist missionary in Chile until the coup in 1973. As Eldridge notes, 'Human rights entered my vocabulary on September 11, 1973, when it was suddenly denied to one-third of the Chilean population. That was a watershed. That defining moment has sustained my vision of what abuses of human rights are about. It has driven me.'[12] Eldridge and WOLA helped mobilize public opinion to lobby the US Congress and other governmental organizations to pressure the Chilean government to stop its flagrant human rights abuses. WOLA also collaborated with the National Council of Churches in New York, which set up an Office of Human Rights headed by William Wipfler.

Solidarity organizations, although not strictly defined as human rights organizations, also grew in importance in the 1970s. Non-Intervention in Chile, or NICH, was founded in 1972. After the coup it became, along with the Office for Political Prisoners and

Human Rights in Chile and Chile Democrático, one of the principal organizations in the United States supporting opposition to the Pinochet regime while publicizing information on repression in Chile and the collaboration of the Nixon administration with the military junta. The North American Congress on Latin America, or NACLA, a research organization based in Berkeley and New York, also produced reports and news stories on the Pinochet regime and the support it received from the Nixon administration.[13] Outside the United States, the solidarity network on behalf of Chile was also quite extensive. According to one source, in the aftermath of the military coup solidarity committees were organized in more than fifty countries.[14] In Western Europe, the solidarity organizations were especially active in protesting the abuses of the Pinochet regime and providing support to its beleaguered opponents.

The growth of solidarity and human rights organizations around the world reflected an increasingly vigorous human rights movement. Between 1973 and 1983, the number of formal international non-governmental organizations dedicated to human rights issues almost doubled, from 41 to 79.[15] A good number of these organizations focused their attention on the human rights abuses of the military and authoritarian governments in what is called the southern cone of Latin America. Along with Chile, the countries of Brazil, Argentina and Uruguay had also witnessed the displacement of democratic governments by authoritarian regimes that engaged in systematic violations of human rights.

Next to Chile, the human rights abuses of the Argentine military regime that seized power in 1976 drew the most attention. There, approximately 30,000 people were killed in what was called the 'dirty war'. The most prominent human rights group in Argentina, the Mothers of the Plaza de Mayo, organized marches in the main plaza of Buenos Aires, carrying placards of their sons and daughters who had been disappeared by the junta. In an effort to mute the growing criticism of the junta and to avoid the isolation faced by the Pinochet regime, the military leaders of Argentina invited Amnesty International to visit the country shortly after the coup. But the junta's strategy failed as the Amnesty delegation reported that Argentine jails held 6,000 political prisoners and that the military and police had abducted between 2,000 and 10,000 people.[16] Argentina, like Chile, had become a major focus of international human rights organizations. In the United States WOLA and the Argentine Commission on Human Rights became two of the major organizations pressuring the US Congress and the US executive branch to cut off military and economic aid to the Argentine regime.[17]

Thus by the mid-1970s an extensive human rights advocacy network had been established, both within Chile and internationally, comprising several distinct types of organizations: (1) inter-governmental organizations, like the Inter-American Commission on Human Rights; (2) international non-governmental organizations like Amnesty International and WOLA; and (3) domestic non-governmental organizations, like Copachi.

The successes of this network in drawing international attention to the ongoing violations of human rights in Chile drove the Pinochet regime to undertake an international campaign against the human rights organizations. In the United States, public relations firms like J. Walter Thompson were hired to refurbish the image of the regime. The Chilean government placed advertisements in newspapers like the *Washington Post* attacking organizations that were critical of Pinochet's government, claiming they were part of an 'international communist conspiracy'.[18] Then, in Chile in November 1975, Pinochet openly denounced Copachi, declaring that it should be dissolved, after some of its members helped several MIR militants escape into exile. As a result of this incident, some religious leaders withdrew their support from Copachi.

Cardinal Silva was forced to acquiesce to Pinochet's request, formally dissolving the committee in December. But the cardinal quickly outmanoeuvred the General. In January 1976 Silva set up the Vicaria de la Solidaridad, which, unlike Copachi, would be an official arm of the Catholic Church. Furious when he heard of the cardinal's plans, Pinochet summoned Silva to his office. The general declared: 'What's this about setting up a Vicaria, Cardinal. You aren't going to tell me that you are going to continue to fill the Church with Communists?' The cardinal replied: 'General, I have told you the Church cannot and will not abandon its defence of human rights.' Then Pinochet angrily stated: 'You mean that once again you are going to do the same thing. It appears the Church doesn't want to accept what I order.' The Cardinal brusquely replied in an assertive voice: 'You can't stop the Vicaria. And if you try to I'll put all the refugees under my bed if that's necessary.'[19]

The cardinal persevered, setting up the Vicaria, or Vicariate, in the historic centre of Santiago on the Plaza de Armas, right next to the Metropolitan Cathedral, the most important church in Chile. It was a far more secure site than Copachi's old offices in the barrio near Plaza Brasil. The entire staff of Copachi went to work in the Vicariate and carried on Copachi's basic mission of assisting the victims of the regime while documenting the ongoing human rights violations.[20] The Vicariate served as the principal centre of human rights activity in Chile, documenting abuses and waging a 'battle against terror' during the Pinochet regime.[21]

By the mid-1970s, the establishment of the Vicariate along with the rise and consolidation of a more potent human rights network – both in Chile and internationally – began to impact on the policies of Western governments, particularly on the United States. In June 1976, the US Congress voted to cut off arms sales to Chile. And in 1976, Jimmy Carter, as the Democratic Party's presidential candidate, called for a change in U.S policy towards dictatorial regimes. In a televised presidential debate with Gerald Ford, Carter reprimanded the Nixon/Ford administrations for not commenting 'on the prisons in Chile' where they 'overthrew an elected government and helped to establish a military dictatorship'.[22]

The contrast between the policies of Jimmy Carter and those of Henry Kissinger during the Nixon and Ford administrations was striking. Kissinger in his last year and a half as Secretary of State did feel compelled to pay lip service to the issue of human rights, as occurred at a meeting of the Organization of American States (OAS) in Chile in 1976 when he declared that 'the condition of human rights ... has impaired our relationship with Chile and will continue to do so'.[23] Yet documents uncovered in 1999 revealed that Kissinger in a personal meeting with the dictator before his speech to the OAS reassured Pinochet that his remarks were not meant 'to weaken your position', that they 'were designed to allow us to say to the Congress that we are talking to the Chileans and therefore Congress need not act'. Kissinger added: 'My evaluation is that you are a victim of all left-wing groups around the world, and that your greatest sin was that you overthrew a government which was going Communist.'[24] In contrast, Jimmy Carter when he took office declared that human rights were 'the soul of US foreign policy.'[25] In the State Department Carter created the position of Assistant Secretary of State for Human Rights, occupied by Patricia Derian. She proved to be a vigorous human rights advocate, maintaining close working ties with human rights organizations. While national security interests often led the Carter administration to override human rights issues in other parts of the world, in the western hemisphere, and particularly in the southern cone countries, human rights concerns were an integral part of US policy. This marked a transformation in the human rights movement. In effect, states and governments became a fourth leg in the international human rights network, joining domestic and international human rights NGOs along with intergovernmental organizations like the Inter-American Commission on Human Rights.

Partially in response to this growing international mobilization around human rights issues, the Pinochet regime abolished DINA, replacing it with the National Centre of Information (Central Nacional de Informaciones, or CNI). The dictatorship had largely failed in its efforts to eradicate domestic opposition or to mollify international critics, and, according to Hugo Fruhling, an analyst of the human rights movement in Chile, 'it became necessary to replace the policy of repression with a policy of containment'.[26] The instances of 'disappeared' dropped significantly, but systematic repression continued as selectively 'targeted' opponents of the regime were arrested and tortured. Instead of 'disappearing' prisoners, the regime now openly murdered them, often claiming that they had been killed in armed confrontations with military or police units.

Opposition to the regime continued to build, however. The year 1978 became known in Chile as 'El Año de los Derechos Humanos', or the year of human rights. In April, Pinochet issued an amnesty decree, which in effect meant that no one in the military could be prosecuted for human rights violations between 1973 and 1978. This was intended especially to cover the crimes of DINA, which had recently been dissolved. This infuriated the human rights organizations, especially the Organization of the Families of the Detained and Disappeared, which called on its members to organize hunger strikes to protest the decree. The most prominent strike occurred in the United Nations office in Santiago, where the strikers remained for weeks, calling on the Secretary General of the United Nations to demand that the Pinochet regime give an accounting of the disappeared prisoners.[27] The same year also witnessed the first public Symposium on Human Rights in Chile, attended by domestic and international groups concerned with human rights violations (particularly in the southern cone countries). Then in November 1978 the campaign around the disappeared received unprecedented attention and legitimacy when the remains of fifteen peasant union organizers abducted in 1973 were found in a kiln in an abandoned mine in southern Chile.[28] This discovery gave the lie to the regime's insistence that the disappeared had fled abroad or were murdered in internecine fighting within the left.

In 1978 a UN delegation visited Chile to assess the state of human rights. The United Nations Human Rights Commission had been one of the early intergovernmental organizations denouncing the dictatorship. Indeed Chile was the first case it took up that did not involve racially motivated violations of human rights. In 1974 the UN General Assembly, following a recommendation of the Human Rights Commission, established an Ad Hoc Working Group on Chile.[29] The Ad Hoc Group was repeatedly turned down in its requests to conduct an on-site investigation in Chile. After the UN General Assembly had overwhelmingly passed a resolution condemning the Chilean government, Pinochet staged a plebiscite in Chile on January 4, 1978 that asked the voters if they backed him or 'the international aggression against our country'. Those who voted 'Si' checked a box with a Chilean flag, while those who voted 'No' checked a black box. There were no voter registration roles for the plebiscite. Anyone with an identity card could cast a ballot, and the regime claimed a resounding victory – 75 per cent voted Yes, 20 per cent said No and almost 5 per cent abstained.[30]

After this 'mandate' the general decided to allow the Ad Hoc Working Group to visit Chile. Aware of the impending visit in July, the opposition held demonstrations and hunger strikes in Santiago timed to coincide with the delegation's arrival. Unbeknown to Pinochet, the UN team even managed to visit one of DINA's recently abandoned torture centres, Villa Grimaldi, accompanied by two men who had been held and tortured there. Photographs of the site with one of the two men were taken, which appeared even in right-wing Chilean newspapers. This and the Ad Hoc Group's formal report on human rights abuses in Chile incensed Pinochet. His government refused to attend future meetings of the UN Human Rights Commission. To the chagrin of the dictator, the Commission then replaced the Ad Hoc Group with a Special Rapporteur, who had more latitude in filing regular reports on the human rights violations in Chile.[31]

The Year of Human Rights also led to the rise of what can be called the second generation of human rights organizations in Chile. More overtly political than the Vicariate, they were closely linked to the growing political opposition to the regime. The AFDD was in many ways the forerunner of this new generation because of its ties to political organizations, ties that were strengthened from 1976 onward as its actions opposing the regime became more confrontational and its links with the Church more strained because of its political activities.

In 1978, the first major non-governmental human rights organization with no formal ties to the Catholic Church was founded, the Comisión Chilena de Derechos Humanos. Comprising figures identified with political parties from the centrist Christian Democrats to the Communist party on the left, the founding charter of the Commission called for the full restoration 'of civil, cultural, social and economic rights that are enshrined in the international charter of human rights'.[32] Two prominent left-of-centre Christian Democrats, Jaime Castillo Velasco, a member of the Christian Movement, and Andres Dominguez, were among the key founders of the Commission. To provide it with legitimacy and to help protect it from repression, the Chilean Commission established formal ties with international non-governmental organizations like the International

Commission of Jurists and the International League for Human Rights.[33]

The Chilean Commission in turn helped sponsor and set up other organizations like CODEJU, the Comisión de Derechos Juveniles, which provided an organizational base for youth and students in Chile. The junta had abolished virtually all student organizations with the coup, particularly in the universities where large numbers of students had been active in supporting the Popular Unity government and its political parties. CODEJU enabled the youth to begin organizing to demand the restoration of their basic civil and human rights.

The most militant of the human rights organizations in Chile, the Committee for the Defence of the Rights of the People, or CODEPU, was founded in 1980. It was directly linked to the Popular Democratic Movement, a political coalition that included the MIR, the Communist and the Socialist Parties. Fabiola Letelier, whose brother, Orlando Letelier, was assassinated in Washington DC in 1976, numbered among its principal founders and became its first president. CODEPU argued that authentic human rights depended on the establishment of a 'democratic regime ... based on popular sovereignty'. Moreover, it proclaimed 'the right of the people to engage in rebellion to free themselves from tyranny', a direct challenge to the Pinochet dictatorship. CODEPU provided legal defence for imprisoned members of leftist political parties and sent doctors to examine and treat those who had been tortured. Much of CODEPU's work was aimed at helping workers and young people 'create a Human Rights front that would promote the interests of the exploited and oppressed'.[34]

CODEPU, like the Vicariate, enjoyed extensive international support. Oxfam England and Bread for the World were among the early financial supporters. Later on, the European Community provided assistance to CODEPU, especially for its work with prisoners who were tortured. After François Mitterrand became president of France, his wife, Danielle, was especially helpful in securing international support for CODEPU. The National Lawyers Guild of the United States, the American Bar Association and Americas Watch also collaborated with CODEPU and other human rights organizations in publicity campaigns against the dictatorship's repression.[35]

By the early 1980s, the banner of human rights had become a powerful weapon in the formation of a much broader movement of opposition to the dictatorship. As Hugo Fruhling pointed out, the political opposition now felt strong enough to take on the goal 'of putting an end to the authoritarian order, instead of merely trying to contain its repressive activities'.[36] Furthermore, in the mounting struggle against the regime, the ties of the domestic organizations to international human rights networks played a critical role. All the major human rights organizations in Chile had links to a multiplicity of human rights agencies and advocates abroad. Patricio Orellana, a student of the human rights movement in Chile, notes that the international human rights movement 'provided moral and material support of incalculable value' to the Chilean opposition.[37]

In the early 1980s, a profound economic slump hit Chile, leading to an upsurge in demonstrations against the regime. Centred in the *poblaciones*, these protests became massive, leading to what became known as the 'national days of protest'. The first one was called for May 11, 1983; it was followed by similar protests on June 14 and July 12.[38] Hundreds were arrested during these demonstrations, many were tortured and at least eight people were killed. These protests were endorsed and led by renascent political organizations and human rights groups, particularly the Chilean Commission on Human Rights and CODEPU. When the regime responded with repression, these groups along with the Vicariate stepped in to provide legal assistance for those apprehended and undertook public campaigns to win their release.

The period from 1983 to late 1986 witnessed an expansion and radicalization of the opposition, as it called for the overthrow of the regime. The Commission and CODEPU stepped up their grassroots activities. Numerous local committees were founded, particularly in the major urban areas. Diversity and adaptability were the hallmarks of these local committees as they worked to assist those who had had their rights violated. They engaged in extensive educational campaigns in the communities, encouraging young people in particular to become politically active to resist the dictatorship.

The years 1983–86 also witnessed a resurgence of the political parties, particularly those on the left. The Communist Party was active in the shantytown protests along with the MIR, and the Communists stepped up their support of the Manuel Rodríquez Patriotic Front (FPMR), an armed guerrilla organization committed to overthrowing the regime.[39]

The United States: dictators and double standards

Two years before the mass protests erupted in 1983, the Reagan administration took office, determined to reverse the human rights policies of the Carter administration. Jeanne Kirkpatrick captured the outlines of Reagan's policy in an article that appeared in the conservative magazine *Commentary*, titled 'Dictatorships and Double Standards'. It argued that authoritarian governments allied with the US and the West were preferable to the 'totalitarian' regimes of the communist world.[38] If the US government undermined friendly authoritarian governments, as the Carter administration had done in the case of Anastasio Somoza in Nicaragua, then totalitarian regimes of the left would take their place. This approach became the bedrock of the Reagan administration's foreign policy towards the third world during its early years, as it engaged in what it called 'quiet diplomacy'. The US government continued to support Third World dictators, while supposedly working behind the scenes to get them to ameliorate their more flagrant human rights abuses. In accordance with this policy, the Reagan administration invited high-level Chilean officials to Washington, including a member of the military junta, reestablished US–Chilean joint naval exercises, and lifted the ban on military aid and arms sales to Chile.[41]

By the start of its second term in office, however, the Reagan administration was driven to begin rethinking its policy of collaborating with the Chilean dictatorship, as popular resistance to the regime grew more radical and the left gained ascendancy within the opposition movement. In November 1984 Pinochet declared a state of siege in an effort to control the deepening rebellion. Chilean human rights organizations, along with Amnesty International and more recently established human rights organizations, like Americas

Watch and the Lawyers Committee for Human Rights, reported on the stepped-up repression by the regime. The military employed massive military force to suppress popular demonstrations, in particular large-scale sweeps and raids in the shantytowns around Santiago.[42] Along with the poor in the shantytowns, the regime intimidated, arrested and tortured many student activists, priests and human rights workers. Thousands were rounded up and held in stadiums in scenes reminiscent of the junta's actions immediately after the coup when the National Stadium was the site of massive detentions. Even the US Department of State in its annual country report for 1984 noted the new repression, describing 'mass sweeps of neighbourhoods', 'remote detention camps' and 'internally exiled ... without charges or trial'.[43]

For the first time, the regime began using paramilitary units to eliminate opponents, aping the techniques employed by the Central American governments, particularly El Salvador. ACHA, the Chilean Anti-Communist Action group, was among the more notorious. It targeted CODEPU in particular, even raping and sexually abusing some of its workers while they were in or leaving their offices. A special clandestine unit of the police was also established to go after opponents of the dictatorship. It provoked a public outcry when it abducted and slit the throats of three leaders of the Communist party in 1985, including one who worked with the Vicariate.[44]

The intransigence and brutality of the Chilean dictatorship compelled the Reagan administration to change its policy of supporting Pinochet in late 1985. James Theberge, the US ambassador to Chile, often referred to as the 'fifth member' of the junta because of his unwavering support of Pinochet, was replaced by Harry Barnes, a professional diplomat known to be a moderate. Then, a month later, even the right-wing ideologue Elliot Abrams, the new Under-secretary of State for Inter-American Affairs, declared: 'The policy of the United States government toward Chile is direct and un-equivocal: we will cultivate the transition toward democracy.'[45] Abrams' statement reflected a fundamental shift in his own thinking as well as in US policy. Abrams was one of the early members of the Reagan foreign policy team who endorsed Kirkpatrick's approach to authoritarian regimes, and in his previous position as Assistant

Secretary of State for Human Rights, he often whitewashed the atrocities of authoritarian regimes in the State Department's human rights reports.

Abrams articulated the reasons for this change in policy in testimony before a congressional committee: 'Further delay in taking concrete steps to give the Chilean people confidence that their nation is headed for democracy and to restore full civil liberties can only benefit enemies of democracy on the extreme left and right.'[46] In other words, the Reagan administration, worried about the radicalization of the opposition in Chile, had begun to fear that Pinochet might be overthrown by an insurrectionary movement, much like that which occurred in Nicaragua when the Sandinistas toppled Somoza. The argument of Kirkpatrick was now reversed: instead of arguing that US opposition to authoritarian governments would facilitate revolutionary takeovers, the Reagan policymakers came to believe that the left would triumph if the US did not act to restrain or remove friendly dictators.

Furthermore, by the mid-1980s the United States had come to realize that many of the dictatorships established during the Cold War were no longer viable in the context of neoliberalism and the emergent process of globalization. Dictatorial regimes, of the right as well as the left, tended to exercise forms of authority over their societies and economies that were increasingly anathema to international capital. The expansion of Western interests required not only open international markets but also pliable political institutions. Accordingly, the United States shifted to a strategy of supporting what some call 'low intensity', or controlled democracies. As William Robinson argues in *Promoting Polyarchy*, the United States, in order to integrate the Third World into a global neoliberal economy, turned against many of the dictators it once nurtured and adopted a policy of supporting, and even imposing, controlled democracies.[47] This explains why the United States under Ronald Reagan moved against Ferdinand Marcos in the Philippines and 'Baby Doc' Duvalier in Haiti, as well as Augusto Pinochet, seeking to replace them with conservative or moderate governments that would accept the regime of international capital while containing social and political movements that advocated radical or nationalist policies.

US assault against the left

In Chile in the mid-1980s, the United States proceeded methodically in an effort to undermine both the left and the Pinochet regime, while working to build up centrist political organizations like the Christian Democrats. To advance this new policy, the Reagan administration had at its disposal an ideal instrument, the National Endowment for Democracy (NED). Founded in 1984 by an act of the US Congress as a bipartisan semi-public institution, the Endowment had interlocking activities with four other affiliates: the Center for International Enterprise, the Free Trade Union Institute, the National Republican Institute, and the National Democratic Institute. Representing US business, trade unions, and the Republican and Democratic parties respectively, all four of these institutions worked in coordination with NED to promote alternatives to the left in Chile.

Conscious of the growing radicalization of the popular sectors, NED in mid-1985 began funding and advising an organization dominated by the centrist Christian Democratic party, the Neighbourhood and Community Action group, known as AVEC. In a document titled 'Democratic Action in Slum Areas', NED stated that its support of AVEC was 'an effort to counter the predominance of the Communist party in the *poblaciones*'.[48] Through AVEC, NED funded and conducted leadership seminars for thousands of local activists from the *poblaciones*, encouraging them to abandon their sympathies for the left while getting them involved in moderate political projects.

Even earlier, the US trade-union affiliate of NED, FTUI, began funding a small group of Christian Democratic-led trade unionists who initially belonged to the leftist-led National Workers Command (CNT) that was set up in 1983. The CNT had brought together the remnants of the militant trade union movement that was decimated in the early years of the Pinochet regime. Soon after FTUI funding began, the Christian Democratic unionists broke away from the CNT to form the Democratic Workers Union, or UDT.[49]

Notably bypassed in any of the early funding initiatives of the NED and its affiliates were the human rights organizations, particularly the Chilean Commission and CODEPU. However, the Endowment and the National Democratic Institute in 1985 began to work with the Catholic Bishops Conference in Chile and Archbishop Francisco Fresno, who had replaced Cardinal Silva as head of the Church in Santiago. More conservative than Silva, Fresno and NED brokered an agreement in 1985 with eleven of Chile's moderate political parties on a 'democratic transition' that excluded the Chilean left.[50]

These manoeuvres by the moderates and the US government initially proved unable to contain the popular rebellion or to challenge the ascendancy of the leftist political parties. The year 1986 was even declared by the left to be the *Año decisivo*, the decisive year in which the popular movement combined with the armed organizations would topple the regime in a popular insurrection. But instead of overthrowing the regime, the left experienced a series of strategic setbacks. In August 1986, General John Galvin, the head of the US Southern Command based in Panama, visited Chile. His mission was to goad the regime to work with moderates while providing Pinochet with critical intelligence information to strike at the left. While he was there, the *arsenal del norte* was uncovered, a huge cache of weapons the FPMR had stored in the northern desert. Then, on September 7, 1986 the Front attempted to assassinate Pinochet in the Cajon del Maipo as he was returning to Santiago from his weekend retreat in the country. Using grenades, machine guns and even rocket launchers, the guerrilla unit took a heavy toll on the convoy escorting the general, but astonishingly Pinochet escaped unharmed, as one of the rockets that struck his vehicle failed to detonate.[51]

Initially the left took heart from this stunning event, but the Christian Democrats and the centrist forces were shocked by the discovery of the arsenal and the assassination attempt because these events appeared to indicate that the left had the armed capacity to seize power. The centrists redoubled their efforts to seek a *salida política*, or political solution, that would isolate the left. During the same period, the militant social movement entered a period of decline and demoralization. Taking revenge for the assassination attempt and the death of four bodyguards, the regime brutally assassinated four leaders of the left and stepped up its repression in the shantytowns. As one leader of the shantytown protests noted, 'The repression began to destroy the movement. People who left their homes were beaten, saw no clear purpose to endure the abuse.'[52]

As the *Año decisivo* drew to a close, it was clear that the centrist forces, and not the left, had seized the initiative. With US backing, they began to organize for the plebiscite that Pinochet had scheduled for 1988 on whether or not his regime would continue in power. Unlike the plebiscite in 1978 on the United Nations, this time there would be official electoral rolls with independent observers. Voters were to mark their ballots 'Si' if they wanted Pinochet to stay in power for another eight years, or they could vote no if they wanted new elections to decide who would be the next president of Chile. The moderate forces, led principally by the Christian Democrats, organized a coalition called the 'Comando de No.' Its adherents favoured a controlled political transition that would recognize the amnesty decrees and the authoritarian constitution established by the dictatorship in 1980.

The victory of this coalition in the plebiscite on October 5, 1988 and the relegation of the left to a secondary role were facilitated by the fractionalization of the human rights movement in Chile. From 1983 to 1986, the human rights organizations had grown by leaps and bounds as the left in general expanded its activities and actions against the regime. But from 1986 onward a crisis ensued in many of these organizations as sectors of the left began to adopt divergent political strategies, while the US-backed centrist organizations succeeded in winning over much of the opposition to a political programme that endorsed a transition to a controlled democracy in which the military would play a substantial role. CODEPU, for example, witnessed in the years 1983–86 a rapid growth in what it called 'Comités Anti-Represivos', or local anti-repression committees, but by 1987 most of these committees had ceased to function. The committees were short on resources, and many of their members had gone to work with more explicitly political organizations. Then, in 1987, the national leadership of CODEPU split into two groups, reflecting political divisions among the left over how much emphasis to put on supporting an armed rebellion against the dictatorship.[53]

By 1987, even the Chilean Human Rights Commission, which included members of the Communist Party, began to incorporate itself into more explicitly political activities linked to the Comando de No as it distributed leaflets and flyers for the plebiscite in 1988. This change was also reflected in the Communist Party's decision to break with the armed organization it had helped establish, the FPMR.

The Vicariate of Solidarity, under the leadership of the Catholic Church, remained intact, but its grassroots work became more distinct from the secular human rights organizations. The ascendancy of Cardinal Fresno meant a retreat from the days of liberation theology and a commitment to the oppressed. The Vicariate came to define human rights in a manner that focused on 'interpersonal relations of love and respect'.[54] Moreover, the Vicariate as well as the Church hierarchy joined the camp that supported the Comando de No and a gradual political transition from the dictatorship.

At the time of the plebiscite in October 1988, the human rights movement in Chile was clearly in crisis. For well over a decade after the coup it had spearheaded opposition to the regime, functioning when most of the political and social organizations had been decimated or moribund. To a large extent it was the very success of this movement in helping build a broad popular movement that caused the Reagan administration, along with many centrist political organizations, to step in and co-opt the opposition movement.

Yet the long and patient work of the human rights organizations, in Chile and abroad, would bear fruit in the years to come. In the 1990s the human rights movement fought a largely rearguard action, as Christian Democratic-led governments made only token efforts to deal with the massive human rights violations of the military regime. The year 1998 and Pinochet's arrest in London would reverse this process.

5

The bitter transition, 1990–1998

by Marny Requa

On October 5, 1988, Chileans went to the polls for the first time in more than fifteen years to vote in an unrigged plebiscite on whether or not Pinochet should remain in power. The dictator spent most of the day in the bunker below La Moneda, the presidential palace, telling reporters he had 'twenty-five thousand men ready'.[1] Hours after the polls closed, his election officials released the first results, which showed him winning by a significant margin. But the opposition knew the official figures were skewed. The 'Comando de No' camp, the coalition that opposed Pinochet, had set up a system to track the results at each polling station and began to publicize their own tallies. Pinochet had not anticipated defeat; he had even consulted with his fortune-teller, who told him to hold the plebiscite on the 5th of the month because it was his lucky number.[2] As defeat at the polls became more likely, Pinochet began blaming everyone else for the debacle, including his fortune-teller. He met with his cabinet ministers and demanded their resignations. He called for a meeting with the three other military commanders, including air force general Fernando Matthei. He had no intention of accepting the final election results, in which almost 55 per cent voted against him and 43 per cent supported him.

On his way to the meeting at La Moneda, General Matthei told reporters that it appeared the 'No' vote had won, a statement that was immediately broadcast over the radio. An outraged Pinochet proposed the enactment of emergency powers in order to nullify the plebiscite. The other military leaders, recognizing the crisis this would provoke, rejected the idea. For the first time since he took power in 1973 Pinochet faced the unified opposition of the other branches of the military. As a result he was compelled to accept the results of an election that had been stipulated in the 1980 constitution, which Pinochet himself had imposed on the country in a rigged plebiscite. According to the transitional measures of that constitution, a civilian president would take office no later than March 1990 after elections in 1989.

The day after the plebiscite, people flooded the streets of Santiago in their tens of thousands, demanding the immediate ousting of the dictator. He had lost, and the future belonged to those who opposed his regime. 'Que se vaya Pinochet', or 'Get out Pinochet', was the refrain heard throughout the streets. The crowds demanded that Pinochet and the junta resign immediately and that civilians take control until democratic elections could be held. In their euphoria, many stormed the presidential palace – and were met with brutal beatings by the police and army troops. At least three people in Santiago died in confrontations following the plebiscite.

Leaders of the 'Comando de No', a grouping of centrist and moderate political parties that excluded militant leftist parties like the Communists, were shocked by the demands of the crowd. They told protesters to disband and go home, that they had control of the political situation.[3] What they intended to do was negotiate a transition with Pinochet, one that would allow them to assume the reigns of formal political power while Pinochet would continue to exercise tremendous leverage over the country.

With almost a year and a half left of Pinochet's reign, a flurry of negotiations began. The struggle for control among those with political power – the right, centre and the military – would continue through the 1990s. Centrist political parties – including the Socialist Party, which had moderated its position dramatically since the days when it was led by Allende – banded together into the

'Concertación'. Pinochet appointed Carlos Cáceres as Interior Minister, charged with facilitating the discussions between the regime, the Concertación and the right-wing National Renovation Party. (The other main right-wing party, the Independent Democratic Union, did not participate in the discussions out of loyalty to Pinochet.) Cáceres had been a member of Pinochet's cabinet in the early 1980s and was an ardent neoliberal with close bonds to the dictator and the country's economic oligarchy, including the owners of *El Mercurio*.[4]

In the negotiations, Cáceres was intent on maintaining all the structures that guaranteed economic and political stability for his class, but was disposed to make some minor concessions in the political structures of the 1980 constitution. The Concertación tried to negotiate some semblance of independent governance, while the National Renovation Party played it both ways, distinguishing itself from the dictator while benefiting from its connections with him. The political left remained marginalized from the process but vocal, making a few inroads through demonstrations and unofficial channels.

During negotiations, Pinochet remained adamantly opposed to any concessions, intending to stick to the letter of 'his constitution'. He tried to ensure that even after he left office he would retain virtually all his powers. It was only after Cáceres threatened to resign, with the backing of the other junta and military leaders, that Pinochet finally agreed to any of the compromises proposed by the Concertación and the National Renovation Party.[5]

By June 1989, Pinochet had conceded reforms to the constitution, including an increase in the number of elected senators and a revocation of the ban on Marxist political parties. Other reforms made it easier to amend the constitution, although a two-thirds vote of Congress was still required, which meant that the right-wing parties would almost certainly have the power to block any changes. In a largely symbolic move, Article 5 of the constitution was altered. According to Pinochet's constitution, the article read: 'The sovereignty of the country resides in the nation. It is exercised by the people through plebiscites, periodic elections and, also, by the authorities that the constitution establishes.' A new clause was added stating that, 'the respect of essential rights ... emanate from human nature', which was later interpreted to mean that international human rights treaties ratified by Chile would have constitutional status in protecting citizens' rights.[6]

Protected democracy

Despite Pinochet's concessions, the 1980 constitution remained in force. Along with political appointments made by the dictator as he left office, the constitution ensured a protected democracy in the country. Pinochet encouraged Supreme Court justices to retire by offering them bonuses, allowing him to appoint younger judges to life terms. He thus appointed nine out of sixteen Supreme Court justices to life terms during his last 18 months in office.[7] After stepping down as president, the dictator would remain commander in chief of the army until 1998 and, having been a president for more than six years, would then become a 'senator-for-life'. Pinochet appointed nine senators, as well as the heads of the air force and navy and the general director of the police, posts which would not be revocable by the civilian government. The military would automatically receive a portion of the proceeds from the state-owned copper industry, the country's principal export, and the feared intelligence arm of the military regime would be incorporated into the army, instead of being disbanded.

The constitution ensured the military a role in the government by establishing the Council of National Security, designed to act as a guardian of the state. This body could make pronouncements if it perceived any serious discord in the political order. The Council comprised eight members: the four commanders in chief of the armed forces, the president of the country, the presidents of the Senate and the Supreme Court, and the comptroller general, a special auditing office peculiar to many Latin governments. The constitution also stipulated nine appointed senators, including four retired military officers, two Supreme Court judges, one former government minister, one former university rector, and one former comptroller of the republic, all for eight-year terms. In addition to those chosen by Pinochet, two appointed senators would be chosen by the president, three by the Supreme Court, and four by the Council of National

Security. Furthermore, 'senator-for-life' positions would be reserved for presidents who serve a full six-year term.

Chile's political landscape was fundamentally disfigured by the process of electing senators and deputies to Congress. To encourage a two-party system, which went against the grain of Chilean history, and to guarantee representation for the political right, the military regime established a 'binomial' process for electing both senators and deputies.[8] Each congressional voting district elected two representatives; to win both seats in a district, a party coalition needed to gain twice as many votes as their nearest competitor. Based on the plebiscite vote, it seemed unlikely that the centre/left coalition would garner more than two-thirds of the vote in most areas – which would be necessary to win both seats in a district. As a result, minority rightist parties were favoured. They could receive half of the seats with just over a third of the vote. This system, plus a gerrymandered electoral map and the existence of designated senators, allowed the right to be disproportionately represented in the legislature. In fact, after the 1989 elections – which the Concertación won with about 55 per cent of the vote – the right had a slight majority in the Senate and in the Chamber of Deputies.

In the 1989 elections, Patricio Aylwin, a Christian Democrat who in 1973 had supported military intervention against Allende, was the victorious presidential candidate of the Concertación. When he became president on March 11, 1990, his government had little legal space in which to manoeuvre. Pinochet's appointments were in place, the ex-dictator had created a lifetime role for himself, an amnesty law restricted investigations into human rights abuses, and the ability to amend the constitution was elusive, given the composition of the legislature. About the only arena where Aylwin had the ability to challenge the military was on symbolic issues. While Pinochet 'acted the statesman' just before the inauguration and 'bestowed "Mission Accomplished" awards' on his men, presumably for having saved the country from communism, Aylwin planned his inauguration address at the National Stadium, which had been used as a detention and torture facility during the regime.[9] Among the performances that night was a group of women whose spouses and relatives had disappeared under the regime. They did the national dance, the *cueca*, symbolically dancing alone.[10]

In response to human rights abuses of the Pinochet era, Aylwin called for 'truth and justice insofar as possible'.[11] This entailed an unwritten pact between the ex-dictator and the transitional government, allowing the transfer of power to occur if civilian leaders agreed not to prosecute Pinochet, his family, and high-ranking military leaders. Some Chileans refer to their protected democracy as the *jaula de hierro*, or iron cage.[12] The 1978 Amnesty Law, which amnestied crimes during the initial years of the coup, helped to uphold the pact, as did Pinochet's strong-arm references to protecting his men. Even so, the discovery of mass graves near Pisagua on former army land shortly after Aylwin's inauguration, as well as pressure from human rights groups and the left, lent weight to investigations into crimes of the previous regime.

Justice vs impunity

The first major move towards addressing human rights abuses was the formation of the National Truth and Reconciliation Commission (called the Rettig Commission, after its president, Raúl Rettig) in April 1990. Initiated by President Aylwin, who spoke out about the need to acknowledge human rights violations and seek justice and reparations for those crimes, the Commission was to investigate the most serious human rights violations, deaths and disappearances. A member of the centrist Radical Party, Rettig had supported Allende's Popular Unity government and served as ambassador to Brazil under Allende. He was a seasoned Chilean politician and lawyer, who had been a deputy Interior and a deputy Foreign Minister, Radical Party chairman, and a senator in 1949.[13] Although Rettig had actively opposed the dictatorship, the eight-person Commission was not universally anti-Pinochet. Three members were linked to the military regime, one of whom had founded a government-sponsored 'human rights commission' under Pinochet, and two were Christian Democrats.[14]

The Commission's report, released in February 1991 after nine months of investigation, detailed the death or disappearance of 2,025 individuals during the dictatorship, describing the political situation at the time of the coup as a 'climate favourable to civil war', a phrase that delighted the Pinochetistas, who claimed it justified the coup. In 1996, a follow-up investigation concluded that the correct number of those who died or disappeared was 3,197. The Commission provided an official forum for testimonies taken from families of victims, which led to the exhumation of unmarked graves. The information gathered was passed to the courts, presumably to initiate or support investigations of deaths and disappearances.

The report was widely criticized for its limited scope and uncritical treatment of the armed forces. In concentrating only on the dead and the disappeared, it avoided investigation of the hundreds of thousands of Chileans who were tortured, detained and/or forced into exile.[15] Most importantly, it failed to deal with questions of justice or any form of prosecution of past crimes. The document never mentioned the names of those who had participated in torture; nor did it advocate any trials in the Chilean courts. The main purpose of the document, it seemed, was to try and hastily close this sordid chapter of Chilean history, exchanging justice for stability.[16]

A number of ex-political prisoners and the relatives of the disappeared rejected the document, noting that even the words 'truth and reconciliation' undermined justice. An examination of the report and the discussions it spawned in the press suggest that it was intended to justify a choice made in agreements between Pinochet and those in charge of the transition: reconciliation without any recourse to justice. The report is also criticized for 're-constituting' Chilean history by describing the 1960s as spiralling towards inevitable political violence and for portraying a limited version of the truth, in not recognizing the institutional nature of the armed forces' role in human rights violations.[17]

In the courts, the Amnesty Law of 1978 ensured military impunity during the 1990s. Decreed by Pinochet's Minister of Justice, Monica Madariaga, the law stated that no one could be prosecuted for political crimes or human rights violations committed between 1973 and 1978. During the Pinochet years, judges repeatedly closed investigations of human rights crimes by citing the law.[18] Aylwin attempted to make one adjustment in this practice. When presenting the Rettig report, the president announced that judges should investigate crimes to ascertain circumstances and perpetrators before applying the Amnesty Law, an interpretation that came to be known as the Aylwin Doctrine. In theory this allowed for truth but not justice; in reality, judges seldom conducted more than cursory investigations into human rights crimes during most of the 1990s. Later in the decade, however, the legal concept of the doctrine became important.

Despite the lack of accountability, military demonstrations and outspokenness punctuated civilian governance throughout the 1990s, as the armed forces and Pinochet himself reacted to the threat of facing justice. The unspoken rule not to touch Pinochet or his family was tested in the first year of Aylwin's presidency, when a crisis surrounding Pinochet's son, Augusto Pinochet Hiriart, erupted. The 'Pinocheques' scandal involved army-issued cheques in Pinochet's son's name for the acquisition of an arms company. A congressional commission was formed to investigate the transfer of money, instigating the army to issue a statement of loyalty to Pinochet. The Pinocheques investigation, and attempts by members of the Aylwin administration to force Pinochet's resignation, led the ex-dictator to call army troops to their barracks, curtailing the government's efforts.[19]

Interest in the Pinocheques scandal resumed in 1993. Talk of investigations into those dealings and into human rights violations again spurred military reaction in May of that year, while President Aylwin was out of the country. Under orders from Pinochet, the army sent its special unit, the Black Berets, into the plaza in front of La Moneda armed with long knives and rocket launchers. He ordered the regular army troops confined to their barracks, so they could be called to action at a moment's notice, and he sent military vehicles out to patrol cities around the country.[20] Labelled the *boinazo* for the berets worn by the marching soldiers, this show of force is blamed by human rights groups for the subsequent closing of a number of human rights cases in the courts and also for the government allowing the army to monitor the investigation of Pinochet's son. Two years later, in 1995, President Frei ended the Pinocheques investigation, citing 'national interest' as the reason.[21] In the aftermath of the *boinazo*, calls by politicians for a *punto final*, or full stop, law – which would end the possibility of further investigations – and other solutions to ease tensions and appease the military were rejected by Congress, mainly because of demonstrations and resistance by the political left.[22]

Under pressure from the Carter administration in the late 1970s, one human rights case had been exempted from the Amnesty Law – the deaths of Orlando Letelier and Ronni Moffitt in a car-bomb explosion in Washington DC. Letelier had served as Minister of Foreign Relations and Minister of Defence under Allende, and Moffitt was his colleague at the Institute for Policy Studies in Washington, where both worked to publicize the crimes of the Pinochet regime. Investigation of the case led to the first and only high-profile convictions of ex-military officers in Chile before 1998. The trial took place in 1993, when General Manuel Contreras, the head of the Dirección de Inteligencia Nacional (DINA) intelligence unit during the dictatorship, and his aid, General Pedro Espinoza, were tried as the intellectual authors of the bombing. Long considered 'the worst act of state-sponsored terrorism' on US soil, Contreras and Espinoza were convicted of orchestrating the murders.[23] In light of the nature of their crimes, Contreras's and Espinoza's sentences of seven and six years respectively were absurdly light.

Contreras appealed against the sentence, but in May 1995 it was upheld by the Chilean Supreme Court. He refused incarceration, instead holing up in a military hospital surrounded by loyal troops. In a meeting with his generals, Pinochet also insisted that the general should not go to jail. With this, Contreras was emboldened to make the absurd declaration, 'I will not go to any jail as long as real justice doesn't exist.'[24] The Contreras affair dragged on for months, with Pinochet making numerous threats against the government and the courts if they dared to seize Contreras. In August, when someone asked Pinochet about Contreras's violation of human rights, the general responded, 'I don't know about human rights. What kind of question is this?' During military festivities on September 11 celebrating the coup, he lectured the government, saying, 'There has to be silence, we have to forget, the only thing left is to forget', referring to the human rights crimes of the past. He added: 'And you don't forget by opening new charges, by putting someone in jail.'[25]

The crisis abated somewhat at the end of September when Pinochet took an 'official' trip abroad to England, Malaysia and Brazil. On October 20, four months after he had been sentenced, Contreras agreed to abandon the military hospital and be confined to the Punta Peuco prison. There he had a special compound to himself, with all the amenities of a luxurious apartment, including his own cook, television, telephones and access to visitors at any time he pleased.

From 1994 to 1997, the first three years of the Frei presidency, about twenty-five lower-level retired military and police officers were convicted of human rights abuses that occurred under the dictatorship. Sentencing was light, and it was understood that the military would tolerate only a small number of convictions. One case after another kept human rights in the mind of the public, if only peripherally, but impunity continued to be the general rule. With the exception of Contreras and Espinoza, those high in the military ranks were not investigated. And no one was jailed for any of the estimated 1,200 disappearances that occurred during military rule, nor for the torture of countless citizens and the forced exile of thousands more.

Moreover, the military, with its virtual autonomy in the transitional order, continued to carry out some particularly egregious acts against its imprisoned opponents. The amnesty decrees did not apply to imprisoned opposition leaders, particularly the members of the Frente Patriótico Manuel Rodríguez (Manuel Rodríguez Patriotic Front, or FPMR). There were continual reports that these prisoners were abused, mistreated, and denied medical treatment. After four high-ranking members of the FPMR escaped from prison in late 1996 – in a sensational rescue operation in which a helicopter set down on the prison grounds – Amnesty International reported severe beatings of a number of political prisoners who remained in detention. On a broader scale, human rights abuses remained an issue in Chilean prisons during the transition. According to a 1999 report by the human rights group CODEPU, police officers and investigators had not ceased torturing prisoners. The officials responsible were rarely prosecuted for these crimes, because military courts still heard all cases involving the police.[26]

The military also exercised an iron hand within its own ranks. An 18-year-old military conscript, Pedro Javier Soto Tapia, was killed in 1996 after he told his parents he had been subjected to ill-treatment and excessive punishment. The military initially claimed his death was a suicide, but then blamed it on four conscripted soldiers, who were interrogated and tortured in order to extract confessions. They were subsequently released without charge, due to lack of evidence.

Thus Chilean citizens were confronted with many pressures in the 1990s: a partially democratic system that protected the previous repressive regime; a government that was accountable to groups much more powerful than the people; and few remedies for the human rights crimes of the dictatorship. The result was widespread political inertia – labelled *desencanto* or a disenchantment with political activity.

Some argue that the weakness of Chile's democracy had as much to do with the country's neoliberal economic policies as it did with the direct influence of the former military regime.[27] Like many Latin American countries that implemented neoliberal economic reforms, which Chile did under Pinochet and continued during the transition, Chile's social landscape was dramatically affected. Neoliberalism resulted in increased economic inequality, a large informal and marginalized workforce, and the atomization of citizens.[28] Voter turnout in Chile dropped significantly and linkages between political parties and voters weakened – a dramatic shift for a historically politically oriented country, where political affiliation was central to individuals' identities. In the 1997 congressional elections, for example, 17 per cent of voters deliberately spoiled their ballots to demonstrate the shallowness of the country's democracy.

There were some instances when the Concertación went out of its way to curtail political activity and consciousness, especially on the left. In the early years of Aylwin's presidency, the Dutch government offered to provide millions of dollars to help in 'the financial consolidation' of the leftist magazines *Análisis*, *Cauce*, *Apsi*, and the newspaper *Fortín Mapocho*. *Análisis*, which was headed by Juan Pablo Cárdenas and which had been closed down several times during the dictatorship for its scathing attacks on the regime, was to receive $500,000 in the first year. The Aylwin government told the Dutch that these donations would represent an interference in the country's internal affairs. As a result, the grants were withheld and all of the publications eventually folded.[29] The tragic irony is that Pinochet, in his last year in office, wiped out the debt of two leading right-wing dailies on the verge of bankruptcy, *El Mercurio* and *La Tercera*, and Aylwin continued to subsidize them while he was president.[30]

Judicial change

One of the more inspiring developments of the transition occurred in the judiciary, which became more independent as Pinochet appointees were gradually replaced and fear of reprisals waned. During the dictatorship, the judiciary was under the thumb of Pinochet – indeed many judges were vociferous advocates of the coup. Initially led by president Enrique Urrutia Manzano, Supreme Court justices supported the military regime, censuring lower courts in order to preserve their positions. In the few instances when judges challenged the political order, they were sanctioned – by being punished, investigated, or reassigned to remote jurisdictions – and their decisions overturned.

Pinochet appointees filled the courts during the Aylwin administration, and the Supreme Court 'continued to be the primary obstacle to the judicial defense of human rights' at the end of his term.[31] In a few short years, however, the judicial body that had allowed human rights abuses to go unpunished – dismissing thousands of habeas corpus petitions – would be pushing the civilian government to seek justice in the proper forum.

A constitutional amendment supported by President Frei in the late 1990s was a turning point. The bill, which Congress passed in 1997, increased the Supreme Court's size from seventeen to twenty-one and divided its chambers, gave the Senate a say in Court appointments, and effectively forced all judges over 75 to retire. An attempt to grandfather-clause the sitting justices failed, and in 1998 many of them retired, some of whom were enticed with severance pay to do so early. By March of the same year only three Pinochet appointees remained on the Supreme Court. Judges who were forced out claimed that the move was undemocratic, and the result of political pressure by the civilian government.

By 1998 the new Supreme Court was hearing cases and inter-preting the law less favourably for human rights violators, using arguments that overlapped with those in the local and international human rights community. A new criminal chamber, created as part of the 1997 bill, allowed for an increased focus on human rights cases in the Court and more consistency in decision-making. The new Court found that the military could be held responsible in some cases for crimes committed in the early 1970s despite the Amnesty Law, because Chile was party to the Geneva Conventions, which stipulate humane treatment of civilians during an internal state of war. This argument had previously been used by lower court judges, like those in the Santiago Court of Appeals, and by dissent-ing voices in the Supreme Court. Likewise, some justices found that disappearances could be considered kidnappings under domestic law, in that they were continuing crimes lasting beyond the 1978 Amnesty cut-off date.

Human rights lawyers had long argued that crimes committed during the period covered by the Amnesty Law, and the law itself, violated international law and the Chilean constitution, which was party to human rights treaties. Even under a state of siege, the military was obligated to respect the human rights of the opposition and to protect Chilean citizens. The first case in which this reason-ing was used by a Supreme Court majority was that of Enrique Poblete Córdova, an MIR militant who disappeared in 1974. On September 9, 1998, the Supreme Court revoked the use of the Amnesty Law in the case, ruling that the investigation of the case had to be completed before the law could be used and that the Geneva Conventions could be applied because a state of war had been declared by the Pinochet government.[32] While this case didn't implicate Pinochet, it represented a shifting interpretation of human rights by the new members of the Supreme Court. It also created the potential for convicting Pinochet or military personnel for crimes committed before 1978, and for reopening cases in which the Amnesty Law was applied before the case had reached the trial stage.

Despite continued political constraints, judicial change bolstered the position of human rights workers and the left, which had been struggling throughout the decade to force the Concertación to act on human rights issues. During the decade, the groups challenged impunity on many levels, by thoroughly documenting past and present human rights abuses, bringing cases in domestic courts and supporting international ones, publicizing the human rights situation and information about perpetrators, working with victims, fighting for institutional change, and maintaining ties to international human rights networks. Global ties and mass communication meant a broader awareness of human rights atrocities. For both passive viewers of television, and activists who used the Internet to spread information, government attempts to ignore human rights violations became more obvious.[33]

Chilean human rights organizations strengthened their position in the global community and their opposition to Concertación policies by hosting the Summit of the People of the Americas in April 1998, as an alternative to the official Summit of the Presidents of the Americas, which was simultaneously taking place in Chile. Although most of the participants were Chilean, representatives of organizations from the United States, Canada, Mexico, Peru and Nicaragua, among other countries, were also present. The purpose of the conference was to build a coalition of non-governmental organizations in the Americas and to examine the effects of globalization on economic, social and cultural rights in the hemisphere. Because economic agreements among the countries' elites and free-trade proposals were threatening state sovereignty and infringing social rights, participants outlined strategies to work together, challenge their governments, and spread information. Final resolutions of the summit included support for a permanent international criminal court and an acknowledgement that citizens should fight impunity on many levels – in international courts, domestic courts, and even third countries.[34]

As a result of their multifaceted efforts, human rights organizations and left parties were a vocal, if politically weak, counterbalance to the military in influencing the civilian government on human rights issues. They remained devoted to the pursuit of justice, as opposed to 'truth and reconciliation', and kept human rights issues in the minds of the public and politicians.

The eve of Pinochet's departure

On March 10, 1998, Pinochet's term as commander in chief of the army ended and the following day he assumed the first senator-for-life position, in accordance with the constitution he had imposed on the country. The step was significant in that he went from holding the top military post, keeping alive fear of military power in the government, to being a politician, albeit one who had profound influence over the political atmosphere.

Indeed, Pinochet was a pivotal figure in Chilean political life throughout 1998. A symbolic blow came on his first day as senator, as demonstrators clashed with the police outside the congressional building and hundreds were arrested. Deputies displayed photos of Allende and others killed during the coup; two were covered in signs reading 'Where are they?' with a list of 1,200 of those who disappeared.

Pinochet's new role allowed the civilian government technical control over the military. Although the president didn't have the authority to force commanders of the armed forces to resign, President Frei was able to pick Pinochet's successor from the top five army leaders. Frei chose the fifth in line of succession, General Ricardo Izurieta, a move that was against military norms and intended to herald a shift in civilian/military relations. Izurieta had not been accused of human rights violations; nor had he held an overtly political post in Pinochet's government. In the early months of the 'Izurieta era', older military generals continued to retire and the military was generally conciliatory toward the government. Between 1996 and late 2000, forty-six generals retired, most before Pinochet's detention in late 1998. At the same time the Frei government kept human rights issues outside the government's focus, avoiding provocation of the military and promoting its version of national stability.

Despite the government's stance, continued pressure by the left, factions of the Concertación and the international community began to weaken Pinochet's untouchable status in the late 1990s. In 1997, Judge Juan Guzmán of the Santiago Court of Appeals began investigating the former dictator's role in human rights violations. In January 1998, the Communist Party secretary, Gladys Marín, filed the first case against Pinochet for the 1976 disappearance of her husband, when DINA agents infiltrated the party and its leadership disappeared. At the time the case was brought there was little chance that Pinochet would be convicted, but the symbolism of a case pending against him was powerful. The ex-dictator was cautious enough to postpone stepping down as commander in chief until just before he took on his senatorial role, so there would be no gap in his immunity.

Also in early 1998, senators on the left challenged the constitutionality of Pinochet's senator-for-life post and put forward a bill to deny it to him. They accused him of having compromised the honour and security of the country. A debate in the Senate ensued, with the airing of many of the human rights violations of the Pinochet era. The measure failed by 62 votes to 52, with eleven members of Frei's Christian Democratic party voting against it. Despite the loss, the outcry against Pinochet demonstrated his vulnerability and strengthened claims of human rights violations. The international community added to the loss of Pinochet's stature, as the French government denied Pinochet a visa to visit the country, and advances in Spanish cases involving Pinochet's regime were publicized throughout 1998. The military–civilian pact was beginning to crack, as the left publicly questioned its validity and the stability it was supposed to bring. Even so, President Frei opposed the movement to deny Pinochet his new position as senator, stating, 'I want to maintain peace and coexistence among Chileans.'[35]

In his first months as a senator-for-life, Pinochet moved adeptly, positioning himself as a sort of senior statesman. He participated in public acts, discussed legislation in the Chilean Congress with his fellow senators, and made pronouncements that were closely scrutinized by the country's media and political analysts. He also acted as the patriarch of the country's two major right-wing political parties, which were gearing up to run in coalition in the presidential elections in 1999. Slowly but surely, Pinochet was putting his brutal past behind him, acting as if he were an integral part of the country's 'democratic transition'.

On the eve of Pinochet's trip to England, he had even become a factor in the Concertación's internal politics. In 1981, Pinochet had made September 11, the date of the military coup in 1973, an official holiday. He and the supporters of the coup held banquets and celebrations, lauding their 'patriotic' seizure of power from the elected government of Salvador Allende in the bloody coup. But since the late 1970s, September 11 had been the date for opponents of the regime to dare to march in the streets, often suffering beatings and imprisonment at the hands of the police and the military. Even after 1990, September 11 remained a controversial date, with repeated confrontations in the streets of the nation's capital. On the twenty-fifth anniversary of the coup, in 1998, thousands of demonstrators were met with large-scale repression by the police, hundreds were arrested, many were treated roughly in custody, a number were injured, and two people were killed.

Since 1990, members of the Concertación had pushed for the abolition of September 11 as a national holiday. But they were stymied in the Senate by right-wing representatives and the appointed senators, who voted against bills to end the holiday. In August 1998, however, Pinochet held private talks with Andrés Zaldívar, a senator aligned with the more conservative sectors of the Christian Democrats, the largest party in the Concertación. The two senators reached an accord to propose legislation eliminating September 11 as a holiday, replacing it with the 'Day of National Unity' on the first Monday in September starting in 1999. This act, called the 'Pinochet–Zaldívar Pact' by the local press, enabled Pinochet to portray himself as the 'great conciliator', a political figure able to rise above the bitter conflicts of the past.[36]

The personal alliance between Pinochet and Zaldívar had repercussions within the ruling coalition. Zaldívar was preparing to run in the Concertación's party primaries against Ricardo Lagos, the Socialist Party candidate. With this pact Zaldívar could paint himself as the candidate who could get things done with the opposition and the ubiquitous Pinochet, unlike Lagos, who had been one of the more outspoken opponents of Pinochet in the 1988 plebiscite. The agreement was thus 'a victory for the Christian Democrats', and Zaldívar's potential triumph as the candidate of the Concertación would help consolidate the *jaula de hierro*, the iron cage that had been put in place by the transition.[37]

Pinochet had remade himself into the 'patriarch of the transition', able to work with politicians from the government coalition and the opposition and leave behind his criminal past. A decade of negotiations with the civilian leaders had honed this image, along with the legal instruments that insulated the protected democracy.

Outside the Concertación, the left and the progressive sectors of Chilean society were largely in a state of demoralization as Pinochet left for London. Families that had suffered the loss of loved ones and those who had survived torture and imprisonment were frustrated in their attempts to find justice, even though many continued to work for it. The Concertación largely ignored calls for justice from the left's political base, focusing their political strategy on accommodation and maintenance of the established political order. Despite some weakening in Pinochet's stature, few believed that justice was possible or that the dictator's senatorial immunity could be stripped, or that he could be tried. Eight years of protected democracy and minimal convictions in human rights cases had stifled expectations, and political analysts proclaimed that Chileans had to reconcile and forget the past – that Chile had to be 'democratized' without justice.

As Pinochet left Chile for London on September 22, 1998, he could look back on the past eight years and pronounce the same words he had used when he left the presidential palace in 1990: 'misión cumplido', mission accomplished.

The power and influence he exercised was reflected in the multiplicity of official hats he wore as he departed. He flew to London as 'senator for life', a position he had held for six months after stepping down as the army's commander in chief. He undertook the trip for personal reasons, to have a bad disc hernia in his back examined, but he travelled with a diplomatic passport, which enabled him to charge the government for the expenses of the trip. The president of Chile, Eduardo Frei, gave Pinochet the title 'Ambassador with a Special Mission' as he went to England. Furthermore, the Chilean military was intent on making this a lucrative trip for the former general, as he was to receive a hefty commission for signing a military arms deal while in London.

6

The entrapment of a dictator

There is some kind of poetic justice and even Shakespearean drama involved in Joan Garcés' survival on September 11, 1973. Historical literature and medieval fiction entertain the notion that as you take over the king's palace, you slay the ruler and his entourage. Family members, key advisers, the dauphin, the chamberlain and anyone who could avenge the ousted king are slaughtered. Joan Garcés, who managed to survive the assault on the Moneda Palace, has come to corroborate the old theory that the usurping prince needs to eliminate all in the palace or they will come back to haunt you.

Augusto Pinochet and his associates may have never read medieval history, but in the aftermath of the coup they certainly did their best to get rid of Allende's cabinet, advisers, loyal military officers and security guards. Most of those who did not die or escape on the day of the coup were imprisoned on Dawson Island, located in the remote and icy lands of southern Chile. Some, like José Toha, who held several high-level ministerial positions under Allende, including Minister of Defence, were tortured and died. But Pinochet's campaign of physical intimidation and elimination was by no means complete, as he himself recognized. Years later, in early 1998, when he was attending a military conference in Quito, Ecuador, he was asked about Garcés' filing of charges against him in Valencia, Spain, for his crimes as head of state. Pinochet arrogantly responded: 'we had him in prison and let him go.' As Garcés says, 'I was never imprisoned by Pinochet but he appears to be expressing some deep Freudian desire to relive those days so he can succeed in capturing and getting rid of me.'[1] This historical mistake would end up costing the usurping prince his freedom, almost exactly a quarter of a century after the destruction of the Moneda Palace in Santiago.

Garcés returned to Spain in 1973 with his dreams shattered, but devoted to the memory of Allende. Just 29 in 1973, he probably would have remained in Chile indefinitely had it not been for the coup. In Spain he set up the Salvador Allende Foundation and wrote a book, *Allende and the Chilean Experience: The Arms of Politics*.

Garcés' volume is a detached account of his experiences during the three years he worked as Allende's adviser. What seems most puzzling about the book is the distance he takes in recalling the last hours of the presidency. Garcés was one of the few who escaped the carnage, yet he writes about the episode almost as if he had not been there. It may have been the pain he carried inside and the attachment he developed toward Allende that made Garcés appear laconic and almost devoid of feelings in the recounting of the moments in which the Chilean experiment in democratic socialism came to an end.

Garcés has undergone a physical mimesis as he approaches the age Allende was when he first met him. Garcés almost looks like the son Allende never had. He sports a moustache the same as Allende's, has a similar broad face and physical profile, and wears glasses on occasion. Garcés is a taciturn and yet modest man, giving the impression that he is always preoccupied with something. He refuses to talk about his central role in bringing Pinochet to justice, and is very reluctant to give interviews to journalists. He says, 'My role is really not very important.'[2]

His modesty is almost out of place; nor does it fit the deed. If it had not been for Garcés' singular determination, to prosecute the case of Antoni Llidó, a Spanish priest tortured and disappeared in Chile in 1974, Judge Baltasar Garzón Real in Madrid would not have requested the extradition of Pinochet for trial in Spain. There were very few Chileans residing in Spain who could press for legal action against Pinochet because at the time of the Chilean coup General Francisco Franco still held on to power in Spain. Most Chileans fleeing their homeland for Europe in 1973 and 1974 wound up in countries like England, the Netherlands and Sweden where social-democratic parties were in office.

Judge Garzón's first efforts in Spain to prosecute former dictators were directed against the Argentine military rulers rather than Pinochet. Argentines always had a much larger presence in Spain than Chileans, primarily because around the turn of the century there was a heavy Spanish migration to Argentina, with many families to this day maintaining dual citizenship. Because the Argentine coup occurred in 1976, a year after Franco's death, thousands of Argentines fled or returned to Spain, giving them a substantial social base to agitate for legal action against the military junta. This explains in large part why in 1996 Judge Baltasar Garzón, who sat on the National Court of Spain, began investigating the Argentine military leaders, just a few months before Garcés filed his case against Pinochet in Valencia.[3]

After Garcés' complaint was filed, it went to the National Court in Madrid where it was assigned not to Garzón but to Judge Manuel Garcia Castellón. Acting in his capacity as an investigative judge, Garcia Castellón almost immediately broadened the case beyond Llido. He compiled evidence on victims of the Pinochet regime not just from Spain, but from Chile and other countries as well. Human rights organizations from Chile like the Association of Family Members of the Detained and Disappeared, and the Association of Family Members of the Politically Executed, became plaintiffs in the case with Joan Garcés acting as their attorney before Garcia Castellón.[4]

Until October of 1998, Garcia Castellón dealt only with charges brought against Pinochet, while Garzón was responsible for investigating the Argentine dictatorship. However, Garzón's investigation soon overlapped with the Pinochet case when he began looking into Operation Condor, the international network to eliminate political opponents that Pinochet and the Chilean secret police set up in conjunction with Argentina and other dictatorships in South America.

Judge Baltasar Garzón takes centre stage in Spain

It was on October 15, 1998 that both judges sent a petition to London requesting the detention of Pinochet there for interrogation. Britain refused the request saying they could only detain Pinochet for extradition, not for questioning. It was then that Garcia Castellón stepped aside, and Garzón alone proceeded to file a request for the detention and extradition of Pinochet from London, using Operation Condor as the bridge for expanding his jurisdiction to take over the entire Pinochet case.[5]

Because Garzón was the judge seeking Pinochet's extradition, he, rather than Garcés, became the most prominent public figure in the unfolding legal drama. It would be hard to imagine two more different people. Garzón is more than a decade younger, having begun his professional career after Franco's death, when Régis Debray and Che Guevara were already figures of the past. Born of humble origins to a father who worked as a peon harvesting olives, Garzón cuts a high profile in Madrid's social circles. Garzón is a brown belt in karate, enjoys fine wines, and likes to tango and go to bullfights. Although Garzón's position as an investigative judge prevents him from granting interviews or talking to the press, it appears that Garzón took on the Pinochet case from Garcia Castellón in part because he does not mind the publicity and pressures that come with high profile cases.[6]

For all their differences, Garzón and Garcés possess the same strong-willed determination to fight for justice and the causes in which they believe. Garzón once declared: 'This is a judge of lost causes.'[7] Appointed to the National Court in 1988, Garzón quickly took on some of the most controversial cases in Spain. In 1990 he began investigating charges that the social-democratic government of Felipe González had set up special hit squads in the Interior Ministry to assassinate members of the militant Basque separatist organization known as ETA.

In 1992 González, at a dinner engagement with Garzón at a restaurant in the historic Plaza Mayor of Madrid, persuaded him to run for parliament as an independent on the governing coalition's slate. If elected Garzón was reportedly promised the post of Minister of Interior. Garzón won his seat and González was returned to power, but Garzón, instead of becoming Interior Minister, was placed in charge of the anti-drug office, a post similar to the head of the Drug Enforcement Agency in the United States. Believing he had been shunted aside and had little influence on government policy, Garzón resigned after about a year in office and returned to his judicial position on the National Court in 1994.[8]

Pinochet and the Iron Lady on the London stage

It is fitting that Amnesty International, the pioneering human rights organization founded in London in 1961, would be a central actor in the pursuit of Pinochet. After the Chilean coup in 1973, Amnesty International became the main organization compiling reports on the crimes of the Pinochet regime and orchestrating international campaigns for the release of political prisoners in his jails.

The head of Amnesty, Andy McEntee, talked to me at length about Amnesty's efforts to bring Pinochet to justice. In the 1990s Amnesty began a sustained effort to find a way to detain and prosecute Pinochet. After abandoning the Chilean presidency in 1990 because he lost the national plebiscite, the Chilean ruler became a frequent visitor to London, often calling on Margaret Thatcher. They had formed a close bond during the war of the Malvinas when Pinochet was the only South American ruler to provide support to Britain in the conflict between Argentina and Great Britain for control of the islands. Pinochet in all of his trips to England never failed to visit and take a box of chocolates to 'the Iron Lady'. Their routine was to have tea at five o'clock and talk about politics. The ex-leaders admire each other and enjoy each other's company.[9]

Pinochet has described Great Britain as 'my favourite country', a view common among members of the Chilean elite, who view themselves as the British of South America. Many of them hold on to the aristocratic airs of old England, including afternoon tea.

The sentimental admiration of the British by the Chilean ruling elite has a long and rather soiled history. Chilean merchants and businessmen have had a prosperous, if subservient, relationship with their British counterparts ever since the early nineteenth century, when Great Britain became the dominant trading partner of Chile. Militarily, the British helped Chile set up its navy, which became one of the most efficient in Latin America. The navy served as an important instrument of Chilean expansionism in the nineteenth century, particularly in the War of the Pacific in 1879 when Chile took over large tracts of territory from Peru and Bolivia, leaving the latter with no outlet to the sea. The British also played a direct role in this war, providing military support, war materials and military knowhow to the Chilean armed forces.[10]

This military help did not come without strings attached. As soon as Chile took possession of the captured territories, English business barons became almost the sole proprietors of its rich nitrate mines.[11] To work their nitrate monopolies, British companies imported thousand of workers from central and southern Chile to labour in the bleak and inhospitable desert in the north of the country. The primitive and exploitative working conditions drove the Chilean workers in the nitrate mines to organize the first trade unions. Soon spreading to other parts of the country, these trade unions became the backbone of the Chilean popular struggle for social and economic equality and were a major pillar in the rise of the Popular Unity coalition.

The most recent chapter of collaboration between Britain and Chile was over the Malvinas, or the Falkland Islands, as the British prefer to call them. In 1982, during the Argentine military dictatorship of Leopoldo Galtieri, economic difficulties and social disarray led the ruling generals to play the nationalism card by occupying the Malvinas, one of the last colonial outposts of Britain in South America. The British declared war on Argentina to retake the islands. As the conflict deepened, all of Latin America denounced the British war effort, with the exception of Pinochet's Chile. The general officially declared Chile neutral in the conflict but provided the British with secret military intelligence and allowed them to use air bases in the south of the country.[12]

The conflict became known as Thatcher's war in Britian. When the British defeated Argentina, Thatcher's domestic popularity skyrocketed. A few weeks after Pinochet's imprisonment in London, Thatcher told a reporter of the *Financial Times* of London that Chile led by General Pinochet was 'a good friend to this country during the Falklands War. By his actions the war was shortened.'[13]

The strong personal relationship between Thatcher and Pinochet explains in large part why the general could visit London at will in the early and mid-1990s with Thatcher's Tories in power. According to Andy McEntee of Amnesty International, when Pinochet visited London in 1994 'we had Amnesty's barrister, Geoffrey Bindman, send a letter to the British Attorney General, alleging that Pinochet should be detained under Britain's 1988 Criminal Justice Act for crimes of torture.'[14] The Attorney General responded that he couldn't prosecute Pinochet until Scotland Yard had carried out an investigation to substantiate the charges. But Scotland Yard did nothing to look into Amnesty's allegations.

In 1995, when Pinochet returned to London, Bindman on behalf of Amnesty International once again notified the Attorney General and Scotland Yard of Pinochet's presence. This time, in an effort to avoid dealing with the case, Scotland Yard told Amnesty that it should undertake its own investigation of Pinochet and come back with the evidence. In 1997 Pinochet returned to London, but he left quickly and nothing could be done.

As McEntee says, 'the problem we faced was how to take away police discretion in determining whether Pinochet should be investigated and arrested'.[15] When a more sympathetic Labour government took power in May 1997, Amnesty began a campaign of contacting key government officials, arguing that the authorities should apply both domestic and international law against Pinochet.

In early October 1998, Joan Garcés once again surfaced as a pivotal figure in the pursuit of Pinochet. He went to London to strategize with McEntee, Bindman and other Amnesty members about how the Spanish and British could collaborate in apprehending the general. They hit upon the Galtieri precedent, a case prosecuted by Judge Garzón in which the Spanish National Court indicted the last military ruler of Argentina and issued an international warrant for his arrest. As a result of this indictment Galtieri has never left Argentina, although he has been prosecuted in the Argentine courts.

In the case of Pinochet, however, the scheme contrived by Garcés and Amnesty was for the Spanish courts to apprehend Pinochet while he was in London. As part of this plan, demonstrations against Pinochet, which had occurred on his previous visits, were called off. 'We didn't want the bird to fly away', declared Vicente Alegría, a Chilean exiled in London who had helped organize many of the previous demonstrations.[16]

Nonetheless, before Pinochet left Chile on September 22 to have back surgery for a herniated disc, some of his own legal advisers had warned him that it would be dangerous to go to London. It was public knowledge that Judges Garcia Castellón and Garzón were both developing legal cases that could affect the former dictator. But Pinochet chose to ignore their warnings, believing that he was untouchable owing to his friendship with Thatcher and the wall of immunity he had built around himself with the legal decrees promulgated by his dictatorship. He also thought he enjoyed diplomatic immunity because he had named himself senator-for-life in the constitution he had imposed on Chile.

'We lost our general'

As McEntee says, once Pinochet arrived in London 'it was a race against the clock' to secure his arrest. Judges Garcia Castellón and Garzón issued their request for an interrogation of Pinochet on October 13, only to have it rejected by the British authorities. Now the danger was that Pinochet would be alerted and flee the country. Indeed, the Chilean embassy in London did suggest that something was afoot and recommended an early departure. But Pinochet was still on heavy medication from his back surgery, and it would have been difficult for the 82-year-old general to leave for at least a few more days.[17] A chartered private plane was an option, but neither Pinochet nor members of his entourage felt it was necessary.

On the morning of Friday, October 16, Garzón sent to London a request for the extradition of Pinochet. A local court in London near the clinic where Pinochet was staying then issued a warrant for his arrest in the afternoon and sent it on to Scotland Yard.

That night, just before the clock struck twelve on Big Ben, Scotland Yard officers entered Pinochet's clinic to present him with the warrant. They were met by two members of his security detail, hand-picked men from the Chilean Special Forces. They were the youngest of the detail, with the more senior guards sleeping in a nearby hotel. The two guards tried to resist the entrance of the Scotland Yard police, but as they moved for their guns, the British pointed their already drawn weapons at them. They were disarmed, and pushed out of the clinic's doors. As the guards ran in desperation towards the hotel of their now aroused compatriots, one of them called on his cell phone: 'We lost him! We lost him! We lost our general!' The other bodyguards emerged from the hotel and ran to the clinic, but it was too late. The British police were stationed at all the entrances, some with machine guns. The Chilean security guards had lost their charge for good.

Most accounts say that inside the clinic Pinochet was so heavily sedated that he could barely do much beyond mumble a few words when he was served with the order for his arrest. Another story that circulated in London, while perhaps untrue, is in keeping with the general's character. It asserts that Pinochet demanded to know on whose orders he was being arrested. A police officer replied: 'Judge Garzón of Spain'. Pinochet then responded: 'ese hijo de la puta comunista' – 'that communist son of a bitch'.[18]

As the news broke that night of Pinochet's arrest, a media hurricane hit London, Chile, and the rest of the world. As Vincente Alegría, notes, 'many of us pinched ourselves when we heard of his arrest to make sure it wasn't a dream. We couldn't believe the man responsible for our worst nightmares was apprehended.' That same night Chilean exiles began to gather in front of the clinic. There are still approximately a thousand Chilean exiles in Great Britain, a large number of them in London. They were joined by hundreds of Britons, and the ongoing demonstrations in front of Pinochet's domicile soon became known as 'the picket of London'.

The large numbers of picketers in front of the clinic constituted a physical as well as a public-relations barrier impeding Pinochet's departure. The clinic was only about 300 yards from the Spanish embassy and it was conceivable that Pinochet could have been secreted away from the clinic with the help of his security personnel. The police who stood guard at the clinic were actually buoyed by the demonstrators and the attention of the media. The police often came over to the picket line, all smiles and even chatting with some of the demonstrators, who would offer them sandwiches, tea and coffee.

'It was a festive atmosphere', according to Jeremy Corbyn, a Labour MP who is also a member of the Commission on Human Rights, and of the Democratic Chile Committee in London. Corbyn's concern with Chile dates back to the early 1970s when he and many other Britons were activists in the international solidarity movement that arose after the coup. Elected to parliament in 1983, Corbyn made several trips to Chile to see first hand the repression and crimes of the Pinochet regime.[19] With the dictator's detention, Corbyn often acted as a go-between with the demonstrators and the police in London, ensuring the development of amicable relations.

The 'Londonazo' in Chile

In Chile, the news of Pinochet's detention arrived that same night via a phone call from the Chilean ambassador in London. Chileans from all walks of life were astonished by the news. Many who heard it from friends or acquaintances thought it was a hoax, and turned on their radios and television to corroborate the unbelievable news: this was not supposed to happen.

The repression of any systematic discussion of the past explains why a social volcano erupted in Chile when news of Pinochet's arrest arrived. It became known as the 'Londonazo'. Chile immediately became a battleground between his supporters and opponents. The anti-Pinochet demonstrators were ecstatic at finally seeing justice served and rushed into the streets chanting 'Carnival, carnival, they took the general prisoner'. They knew that the institutional arrangements of the country had ensured that Pinochet, the symbol of repression, would not be tried at home. If justice came from Spain via England, so be it. Students rejoicing with the news opened champagne bottles in front of Chile's main law school. Families of the disappeared went into the streets with the photos of their disappeared relatives. A concert was held in Santiago where hundreds of thousands of people gathered to listen to musical groups that Pinochet had once banned and exiled.[20]

At the other extreme, infuriated Pinochet supporters went to the upper-class neighbourhood where the English and Spanish embassies are located. Violence flared as they tried to storm the embassies. The government sent the police to stop them. It was the first time in twenty-five years that Pinochet's right-wing supporters felt the hand of police repression. For them, the world had been turned upside down. Many had never seen a police water-cannon in their neighbourhood, only on their televisions when Pinochet sent them into the poor neighbourhoods in the 1980s to repress anti-Pinochet demonstrators. Pinochet's supporters went into a state of shock.

The right-wing mayor of the upper-class district of Providencia, Cristian Labbé, who was also a candidate in the upcoming presidential elections of 1999, ordered the refuse trucks not to pick up the refuse at the Spanish embassy.[21] As the refuse started to accumulate on the sidewalks, Cristina Girardi, the mayor of Cerro Navia, a poor district of Santiago, went personally with her community's refuse trucks to pick it up. With press cameras and microphones surrounding her, she declared to the Spaniards at the embassy: 'If you are willing to take our rubbish [Pinochet], then we will gladly take yours.' It became a national joke.

But more profoundly, the news that Pinochet was detained in London released a whole catharsis of remembering for Chileans. Pinochet's incarceration finally opened up a public debate about what to do with the 'memory of blood' created by the dictatorship and its systematic human rights violations. The issue of the prisoners who disappeared, *los desaparecidos*, was at the centre of the discussions and debates in this new aperture. At the same time, issues concerning the transition to democracy and questions of reconciliation and justice were openly discussed in the public sphere, revealing the failure of the strategies and policies of the years past to heal the impact of the dictatorial regime on Chilean society.[22]

The detention of Pinochet caused multiple problems within the ruling coalition of Eduardo Frei, made up primarily of the Christian Democratic Party and some of the parties and offshoots of the left that had been members of Salvador Allende's coalition. It is public knowledge that the Christian Democratic Party withdrew its support for the Allende government in 1973, and most of its leaders welcomed the coup by Pinochet. Recent secret documents released by the US State Department even reveal that the first democratic president after Pinochet, Patricio Aylwin, wrote a personal letter to Pinochet just days after the coup encouraging him to stay in power as long as necessary.[23]

In light of this ignoble past, it came as no surprise that the Christian Democrats led by President Frei adopted the position of defending Pinochet and arguing that he could not be prosecuted in foreign courts. On the other hand, the coalition partners with roots in the Allende period were torn about how to deal with the Pinochet affair. Some of the people in the government representing these parties had even been imprisoned, tortured or sent into exile by Pinochet.

Among those exiled was the Foreign Minister of Frei's government, José Miguel Insulza of the Socialist Party. Pinochet's supporters in Chile immediately called upon Insulza to resign, saying he was 'biased and incompetent'. On the other hand, members of his own party and the left in general also called on him to resign rather than defend the dictator as Eduardo Frei insisted. Insulza rejected both camps and took up the task of formulating a strategy to bring Pinochet back to Chile.[24] His basic claim was that it was an internal affair and that Chilean sovereignty had been violated. Articles started to appear in the Chilean press suggesting that Insulza was suffering from the Stockholm syndrome, that he had begun to admire his jailer. All of Chile was shaken by the detention of Pinochet. But for the moment it was up to the British courts and politicians to decide the destiny of the dictator held in London.

7

Five hundred days
in the British docket

The detention of Augusto Pinochet in London touched off one of
the most riveting legal battles in contemporary history. For 503 days
Pinochet would remain under house arrest in Britain, the subject of
intense diplomatic, legal and political wrangling involving Spain,
Great Britain, Chile, and to a lesser extent Belgium, France, Italy,
Switzerland, Argentina and the United States. The British government alone spent $17 million in judicial and constabulary expenses
due to the Pinochet affair, while the Chilean state was engulfed in
a political and diplomatic storm that dragged on for more than
sixteen months.[1]

The provisional warrant for Pinochet's arrest from Spain was
simple and straightforward. It alleged that Pinochet 'between 11
September 1973 and 31 December 1983 within the jurisdiction of
the Fifth Central Magistrate of the National Court of Madrid did
murder Spanish citizens in Chile within the jurisdiction of the
Government of Spain'.[2] Within days a second warrant added the
charges of torture and hostage-taking as extraterritorial offences
committed by Pinochet.[3] In terms of processing these charges, the
arresting officers and the local London magistrates that issued the
warrants for Pinochet's arrest acted as arms of the Spanish judicial
system and its magistrate, Justice Baltasar Garzón. This is normal

extradition procedure. When local courts act on extradition requests, they are acting on behalf of foreign courts and their governments.

In the case of Pinochet, his arrest late on Friday night on October 16 meant that while the media stampede unfolded, nothing could be done legally until the courts and government offices opened on Monday morning. The exclusive London firm of Kingsley Napley was retained to defend him. The first step on Monday by Pinochet's lawyers was to petition Jack Straw, the Home Secretary of the Labour government. The Home Secretary has the power to release foreigners or diplomats, irrespective of the courts, based on political and government policy considerations. Pinochet's lawyers argued that Straw should cancel the warrant on the grounds that extraterritorial murder was not an offence in the United Kingdom, and that Pinochet as a former head of state enjoyed immunity from arrest and extradition. Straw, who would be a pivotal figure throughout Pinochet's detention in London, denied the petition. It was widely believed that Straw sympathized with the extradition request because he had been an active participant in solidarity organizations in London in the 1970s that had denounced the military coup in Chile.[4]

The next stop in the legal process was the High Court for England and Wales. Lawyers of the Crown Prosecution Service, who, like the arresting officers, were acting on behalf of the Spanish magistrate, presented the case for Pinochet's extradition. The counter-argument of Pinochet's lawyers was ruthless in its logic: the general enjoyed immunity from prosecution because any murder or torture carried out during his rule was a matter of official state policy.[5]

Ruling on October 28, just twelve days after Pinochet's detention, the High Court agreed with Pinochet's lawyers that the former dictator did indeed enjoy immunity as a former sovereign head of state. Appearing almost reluctant to issue this decision, one of the judges declared: 'unfortunately, history has shown that it has indeed been state policy sometimes to suppress particular groups'.[6] The ruling was no surprise to many exiles and Chileans, who still couldn't believe that Pinochet would ever be tried for his crimes. But there was one important caveat in the High Court's decree: it ordered the continued detention of Pinochet while an appeal was made to the ultimate legal tribunal in Great Britain, the House of Lords.

The House of Lords versus the general

One of the residual but critical powers of the once powerful House of Lords is that it is the ultimate court of appeal for the United Kingdom. At least eleven members of the House of Lords who have held high judicial office or served as practising barristers are selected as Law Lords.[7] In early November five of the Law Lords were chosen to hear the Pinochet case.

Appalled by the shortcomings of the arguments in the High Court of the Crown Prosecution lawyers, who were largely unfamiliar with human rights law, Amnesty International filed a petition to act as a plaintiff in the case before the panel. The Law Lords granted this request and Amnesty sent in a legal team headed by Geoffrey Bindman, a barrister with a long history of involvement in human rights causes. Amnesty and Bindman in turn broadened the list of plaintiffs. The Redress Trust and the Medical Foundation, organizations that had provided treatment for exiled and tortured Chileans in Britain, were brought into the case. Bindman also represented the family of William Beausire, who had disappeared in Chile in 1975 after being arrested, and Sheila Cassidy, a British physician who had been tortured and sexually assaulted while under detention in Chile.[8]

The hearings before the Law Lords began on November 4, 1998. The issue facing the five-member panel was 'the proper interpretation and scope of the immunity enjoyed by a former Head of State from arrest and extradition proceedings in the United Kingdom in respect of acts committed when he was Head of State'.[9] The oral arguments, originally scheduled for two and a half days, took eight court days as four sets of barristers argued their points of view: Pinochet's lawyers led by Clare Montgomery; the Crown Prosecution lawyers; a four-member legal team representing Amnesty and its affiliated plaintiffs; and a neutral jurist, or amicus curiae, appointed by the court.

The deliberations took place in the House of Lords, located in the Houses of Parliament by the River Thames in Westminster. Outside hundreds of demonstrators rallied on St Margaret's Green in front of Parliament, carrying silhouettes representing many of the disappeared and hanging a huge banner on a railing with a painting of a Pinochet-like vampire.[10] The galleries in the courtroom were packed with supporters and opponents of the general. The rendering of the Lords' judgment on November 25, 1998, was a dramatic moment. One by one, in order of seniority, the five judges rose to issue their opinions. The first two judges declared that Pinochet enjoyed immunity and that the case should be dismissed. The next two disagreed, arguing that Pinochet could be extradited and tried for torture and murder as a former head of state. With the vote tied 2 to 2, the audience, including barristers, journalists, activists, and some of the families of the dead and disappeared, held their collective breath as the fifth judge, Lord Hoffman, rose to render his opinion. He proclaimed his support for the extradition of Pinochet. Astonished gasps and muffled cries of joy came from the audience in the courtroom.[11] Never before in peacetime history had a claim of immunity by a former head of state been rejected by a court. Outside on St Margaret's Green the atmosphere was euphoric as people danced, sang and celebrated. The getaway limousine rented to take Pinochet to the airport was returned to its garage while the Chilean air force jet waiting on a nearby Royal Air Force runway departed without the general.[12]

Global reaction was overwhelmingly positive, even from many government leaders. French Prime Minister Lionel Jospin declared: 'It's a surprise, it's a joy, it's bad news for dictators.'[13] However, in Chile pro-Pinochet demonstrators took to the streets to denounce the Lords' decision. The Chilean right wing, given its historic ties to Britain, felt especially betrayed. The conservative House of Lords was not supposed to rule against the general. As Jeremy Corbyn of the Labour Party notes, 'the decision of the Lords reflected the belief that the Pinochet regime went too far with the reign of terror. Even in Thatcher's Tory party, many have been silent about Pinochet, believing that it would be best if he were tried in Spain.'[14]

This judgment by the Lords was by no means the final legal battle in the extradition of Pinochet. After the ruling, the next step was for the Home Secretary to sign off on the extradition ruling. Now public opinion became a factor as the different sides mounted campaigns to influence Jack Straw. He could sign off on the extradition ruling or decide that this was a diplomatic issue rather than a criminal law case and let Pinochet go free.

British public opinion was solidly against Pinochet, with polls showing that around 80 per cent favoured his extradition and prosecution. Pinochet's supporters in Chile hired a public-relations firm and reportedly paid it £200,000 to turn public opinion around.[15] But the momentum was with those campaigning against Pinochet. In London the Chilean/British Ad Hoc Committee for Justice became one of the more important groups lobbying against Pinochet. Comprising largely Chilean exiles and Britons who had participated in the Chilean solidarity movement in the 1970s and 1980s, the Committee orchestrated letter-writing campaigns to members of the Blair cabinet, held press conferences, and brought to London a number of prominent Chileans who had been tortured or imprisoned by Pinochet. One of the leaders of the Committee, Sue Lukes, related:

> This is an astonishing time. It is strange for many of us to have in our country a man who is personally responsible for so much evil. But most surprising and pleasing is the depth and range of support. I find myself on buses having people notice papers I am clutching from our committee and telling me how glad they are that Pinochet is arrested and how much faith it gives them in British justice. I was moved by the responses of teenagers and students who knew nothing about Chile but felt motivated by human rights as an issue and wanted to take a stand on this.

On December 9, 1998 Jack Straw approved the extradition order. As Andy McEntee of Amnesty International noted, 'Public opinion in part pushed Prime Minister Blair to opt for the legal approach. He came into office with a commitment to human rights policies and an ethics-based foreign policy. It would have been backtracking on these stands to allow Pinochet to go free.' McEntee adds: 'Blair only had to take a hands-off policy, one of not interfering with the courts. This allowed his Home Secretary, Jack Straw, to treat Pinochet's extradition as a legal process in which he acts as little more than a rubber stamp in approving the court rulings on Pinochet.'[16]

Straw's extradition order meant that Pinochet had to be arraigned and appear in person in court. On December 11, 1998, Pinochet was brought to the maximum-security court in Belmarsh, about twelve miles southeast of Central London. Pinochet, who had been briefly transferred from the London Clinic to the exclusive Priory Hospital under heavy guard, was released in November and rented a house in suburban Surrey where he remained under arrest. From here, southwest of London and thirty-five miles from Belmarsh, the General was driven to court in a dark green Ford Galaxy, accompanied by a convoy of police vehicles and a helicopter that flew overhead.[17] Rumours had surfaced in the British press in the days prior to Belmarsh that Pinochet partisans at the Chilean embassy were scheming to mount a 'rescue' operation, and the British authorities were taking no chances.

The scene at the courthouse was pure bedlam, with thousands of picketers present, including a contingent of pro-Pinochet demonstrators, many of whom had flown over from Chile. The police separated them into two groups, with the pro-Pinochet demonstrators in front of the courthouse. Jeremy Corbyn, who was with the anti-Pinochet pickets, went to query the police as to why Pinochet's supporters had the more favoured position where the world's media cameras would focus on their banners and placards. The head of the police responded, 'Don't worry, you won't be ignored.'[18] A few minutes later Pinochet's vehicle arrived with a police escort; instead of going to the front entrance, it went around to the side of the building in full view of the anti-Pinochet demonstrators. They triumphantly waved their banners and chanted slogans as the media raced to the side entrance to catch the scene as the former dictator emerged from his vehicle.

Once inside the building and standing before the judge, Pinochet was asked his name and position. Pinochet's response was: 'I am General Pinochet, President of Chile and Commander in Chief of the Armed Forces.' There was an audible gasp in the court, as many were taken aback by Pinochet's use of the present tense to describe his past governmental positions. Pinochet quickly corrected himself, shifting to the past tense, and adding that he was now *senador-vitalicio*, or senator-for-life. Some of those present in the courtroom, like Vicente Alegría, who had been exiled by the military regime, were shaken by Pinochet's statements. 'It was the first time Pinochet was forced to respond publicly for the crimes he committed. It was like hearing a voice from the tomb. The hair on the back of my neck stood up.'[19] Pinochet in a formal statement to the court through an interpreter declared: 'I do not recognize the jurisdiction of any court outside of my country to judge me regarding the lies of Spain. This is all I have to say.'[20]

The general's 'rent-a-mob' in London

After the court scene, Pinochet's supporters who had flown over from Chile proceeded to run their own picket line in front of Parliament. Referred to as the 'rent-a-mob' because many of them had been paid to go to London, they carried placards that read: 'Inglesas piratas, devuelvan nos el tata', or 'the English are pirates, give us back our grandfather.' (*Tata*, or grandfather, is an affectionate term used by many of Pinochet's supporters.) Others shouted more disparaging slogans, like 'Lores, comunistas homosexuales', or 'the Lords, communist homosexuals'.[21]

This behaviour reflected the isolation of the general's supporters and their difficulties in functioning in a democratic atmosphere. Pinochet had destroyed much of civil society and his circle of loyalists had enjoyed total immunity and impunity during his reign of terror. They did not understand that the orders and commands of the general and his associates did not hold in countries like Britain. Their crass slogans were not only acts of desperation after losing total power, but also demonstrated that they had forgotten the civility and rules of democratic society.

However, less than a week after Pinochet's appearance in the Belmarsh court, the world was shocked and Pinochet's supporters were ecstatic when the House of Lords voided the decision of its five-member legal panel. It had come to light that Lord Hoffman, the swing vote on the panel, had served as a director of an Amnesty International fundraising body.[22] Since Amnesty had been a plaintiff in the case, Hoffman had a conflict of interest and his ruling was invalidated.

A month later a new panel of seven Lords was designated to rehear the case for extradition. In this hearing, the Chilean government was allowed to argue, along with Pinochet's attorneys, that he enjoyed diplomatic immunity. Many of Pinochet's foes in London and Chile feared that the 'fix was in', that Pinochet would now be allowed to go free. However, Andy McEntee and Amnesty International remained confident: 'We thought we were going to win, we learned from mistakes we made in our arguments before the first panel of Lords.'[23] Moreover, Nicholas Browne-Wilkenson, the Law Lord who chaired the new panel, made it clear that the case would turn on whether or not the United Nations Convention on Torture – which was incorporated into the 1988 Criminal Justice Act of Great Britain – provided a legal foundation for extraditing a former head of state. This Convention had also been signed by Spain and Chile, and 'double criminality' became an important part of the case for the Law Lords, meaning that any request for extradition had to be based on violations of law recognized in the country carrying out the extradition as well as in the country requesting it.[24]

On the day prior to the Lords' ruling, the Chilean exile organizations in London were authorized to erect a symbolic cemetery on St Margaret's Green in front of Parliament. It was an impressive and sombre site, containing over three thousand white crosses, many with photos attached, representing those who had been murdered or disappeared by the Pinochet regime. This display in London stood in sharp contrast to Chile, where during the previous eight years of 'democratic transition', no such pageant had ever been permitted in front of the Chilean Congress or anywhere else in the country.[25]

On March 24, 1999, the Law Lords ruled 6 to 1 that Pinochet could be extradited to Spain. Once again the Chilean air force jet waiting on the runway had to return to Santiago without the general.[26] However, the new ruling was more limited and narrower than that of the first panel. It declared that Pinochet could only be extradited for crimes committed after the date Parliament approved the Criminal Justice Act in 1988. And just as in the original ruling, the provisions of the United Nations Covenant on Torture meant that only crimes of torture or conspiracy to torture could be the basis for extradition, not summary executions or assassinations. This ruling left standing only three counts brought by Judge Garzón against Pinochet.[27]

However, this did not prevent the addition of new charges of torture and conspiracy to commit torture since 1988. After the ruling Judge Garzón of Spain filed thirty-two additional cases covering the years from 1988 until April 1990, when Pinochet left the Chilean presidency. As one of the charges Garzón included the 1,198 cases of the disappeared victims of the Pinochet regime whose bodies had never been found. His legal argument was that these constituted continuing cases of torture because they had never been resolved, and their families suffered interminably since they did not know the ultimate fate of their disappeared relatives.

Pinochet's legal team, now headed by Michael Kaplan, who called this 'the legal case of the century', proceeded to challenge the validity of the extradition process itself in the British courts.[28] Prior to the court hearing on the process, the right wing in Britain – led by Margaret Thatcher – launched a public campaign to have Pinochet freed, declaring that he was a 'political prisoner' whose rights had been grossly violated. However, in October 1999 a lower court ruled that Pinochet could indeed be extradited under British law. The thirty-four cases of torture filed by Garzón were left standing as a basis for extradition, as well as the thirty-fifth charge, which included all the disappeared cases. What was perhaps most surprising in this ruling was that the magistrate, Ronald Bartle, was known to be a hard-line conservative. He served as a member of the Royal Society of St George, a British nationalist society dedicated to 'England and Englishness', of which Margaret Thatcher was vice-president. In the past Bartle had run for Parliament as a Tory on an anti-immigrant platform, proclaiming that only full British citizens should have access to any housing that enjoyed public support.[29]

Bartle's conservative sympathies may have been overridden by the sheer brutality of the thirty-four cases of torture he heard in court. Of the thirty-four, six died while being tortured in prison. In one of these cases, Pinochet's lawyers actually argued that the torture charge should be dismissed because the man had died too quickly after being arrested to have suffered from torture. The British press and the public were horrified by this macabre legal argument. As Andy McEntee noted, the slogan on a banner used by exile and solidarity pickets who demonstrated every Saturday in front of

Pinochet's mansion in Surrey summed up the sentiment of many Britons: 'There are 35 charges for Pinochet's extradition, and thousands of reasons why he should stand trial.'

Back to the Spanish stage

Joan Garcés, who continued to coordinate the legal team representing the victims of the Pinochet regime in the Spanish courts, declared after Bartle's ruling: 'This case sends a message to aspiring dictators that when they take power by force, sooner or later justice will catch up with them.'[30] At long last, Garcés' quarter-century struggle to bring Pinochet to justice was achieving success and recognition. In Sweden, shortly after Bartle's ruling, Garcés received the Right Livelihood Award, also known as the 'Alternative Nobel Prize'.[31]

The petition in Spain for Pinochet's extradition needs to be understood in the context of that country's traumatic history of civil war and dictatorship going back to the 1930s when Francisco Franco seized power. Franco's fascist regime survived World War II and he remained in power for three more decades. During the civil war and its aftermath, tens of thousands fled from Spain, seeking refuge throughout the world. The Chilean poet Pablo Neruda went to Spain in 1936 to arrange for two thousand refugees to settle in Chile. Members or descendants of these Spanish families, like José Toha, served as officials in the Allende government and participated in the resistance to the Pinochet regime.

Given the similarities between the Pinochet and Franco regimes, it is no surprise that the Chilean general was an admirer of Franco. Pinochet was the only head of state to attend Franco's funeral in 1975. Franco died without ever facing justice for his crimes. Picasso's *Guernica* painting became the aesthetic and symbolic backdrop of Franco's iron-handed rule and Nazi collaboration. But symbols become signs, and signs have shifting meanings. Many Spaniards, including Garcés and Garzón, have transferred their frustration and desires for justice from Franco to Pinochet. The Spanish sociologist Fernando Savater corroborated this view when he told a Chilean newspaper: 'It would have been best if we had prosecuted Francisco Franco. And perhaps, because we did not do it, we are now compensating our desires for justice with Pinochet.'[32] Spanish interest in seeing Pinochet stand trial was also abetted by the cases of Spaniards who were tortured and killed in Chile by Pinochet's regime, particularly Spanish diplomat Carmelo Soria Espinosa, who was picked up and executed in July 1976 while working for the United Nations in Santiago.

This intermingling of Chilean and Spanish histories is central to understanding the political and legal fencing that erupted over Judge Garzón's efforts to have Pinochet stand trial in Spain. Shortly after Pinochet's arrest, his eldest son, Augusto Pinochet Hiriart, went on television to proclaim that he and his father's supporters would mount a campaign to block Spanish imports if the extradition request by Judge Garzón was not voided. Commercial and economic ties between Spain and Chile were significant. In 1997, Chile imported $621 million worth of goods from Spain, while it exported $345 million. But the advocates of Pinochet's trial in Spain realized that Chile would never act on his son's threat. 'Bluff, this is a bluff', declared Joan Garcés, 'Chile depends on foreign investment, and the last thing it would do is question it.'[33]

However, powerful economic figures in Spain who identified with Pinochet continued to lobby on his behalf. Among them was one of the country's richest men, Rodolfo Martin Villa, a militant of the old Franco regime who was also a key backer of the incumbent political party, the conservative Popular Party led by Prime Minister José María Aznar. Martin Villa headed Spain's dominant electrical enterprise, Enersis, which had earlier bought up the Chilean electrical firm Endesa in a transaction that provoked cries of insider favouritism in both countries. Shortly after Pinochet's detention, Martin Villa told the right wing Chilean newspaper *El Mercurio* that if another country had tried to interfere in Spanish affairs like the courts were now intervening in Chile over Pinochet, 'our democracy would not have been successful ... in fact it would have been profoundly disrupted'.[34]

Public opinion polls revealed that over two-thirds of Spaniards did not concur with Martin Villa's views and favoured Pinochet's trial in Spain. But the political castes of Spain by and large sympathized with Pinochet's supporters, and wanted to throw out the extradition request of Baltasar Garzón. Prime Minister Aznar instructed government attorneys to argue against Pinochet's extradition before the National Court of Spain. Just six days after Pinochet's detention in London, the government attorney Pedro Rubira argued in court that the charges should be voided because they were not legitimate 'technical-juridical concerns' of the Spanish courts. Moreover, he declared that they could not be considered to be of a 'genocidal nature' because 'they were not designed to eliminate or displace racial, national or religious groups, but rather had the sole objective of carrying out ideological repression, regardless of profession, employment, economic status, sex or human condition.'[35]

The Spanish Socialist Workers' Party, headed by former prime minister Felipe González, also initially opposed the trial of Pinochet in Spain, asserting that former dictators should be tried in their own countries or before international tribunals set up explicitly for that purpose. The only significant national party in Spain to come out in support of Pinochet's prosecution was the United Left Party, which at the time garnered around 10 per cent of the votes in national elections.

The early opposition of the Socialist Party was linked to the strong personal animosities between Garzón and González, which deepened when Garzón abandoned the government in disgust in 1994. As one political observer notes, 'there is no love lost between Garzón and González'.[36] Relations between them deteriorated even further when Garzón successfully prosecuted the government hit squads set up to eliminate ETA members. González's defeat in the 1995 presidential elections is in part linked to this scandal and the widespread belief that González had endorsed the assassinations. The former president's assertion that judges like Garzón should not enjoy the discretion to prosecute Pinochet also dovetailed with González's belief that Garzón also should not have been prosecuting members of his former government.

But in Spain, due to the liberal constitutional reforms of 1978 adopted after Franco's death, the judiciary has a great deal of autonomy from the government and the country's political processes. When Aznar's government attorneys argued in front of the National Court in October 1998 against bringing Pinochet to Spain, the court threw out these arguments. By a vote of 11 to 0, with one judge absent due to illness, the court ruled that Garzón had the legal competence to request the extradition and trial of Pinochet in Spanish courts. This was a decisive defeat for the Aznar government as well as the Pinochet loyalists in Chile and Spain.

During the five hundred days that Pinochet remained in London, however, the Spanish government never desisted in its efforts to undermine Garzón and the Spanish courts. In August 1999 Aznar even tried to make an end run around Garzón by negotiating with the Chilean government to set up a special judicial panel to review Pinochet's case. The scheme they hit upon was that three judges – one picked by Spain, one by Chile, and the third by both countries – would be empowered to 'arbitrate' the Pinochet case, meaning they would decide whether he should go free or stand trial in a country or tribunal they designated. This proposal caused a political firestorm in Spain. The presidential candidate of the Socialist Party in the 1999 elections, Joaquín Almunia, broke with González's antipathy towards Garzón and argued vigorously against the arbitration tribunal. To set up the panel, the government of Aznar needed parliamentary approval and had to call a meeting of the Council of State, a body that is convened only in extraordinary circumstances. Seeing little political support for this legal gambit, and not wanting to endanger his own re-election bid, Aznar abandoned the negotiations with Chile over the arbitration panel.

The autumn of the patriarch in London

As Pinochet began his second autumn under house arrest in Britain, his prospects for returning to Chile looked bleak. After the first ruling of the House of Lords against him, Pinochet declared: 'I may die in exile, but I will do it for Chile.'[37] Pinochet remained quite scornful of the international efforts to prosecute him even though his stance was contradictory. On one hand, he insisted the case was simply political: 'I am a political prisoner … I take political responsibility for what I did, but not judicially.' But in the same interview in June 1999 with the *Sunday Telegraph* of London he proclaimed: 'I'm not a politician. I'm the head of the army.' He was not, he said,

accountable for his actions: 'I'm absolutely innocent of all charges …
I only answered the call of Chileans who knocked on the doors of
our garrisons asking us to intervene.' As usual, he insisted that he
was the saviour of democracy and the nation: 'We saved the country
from becoming a satellite of the Soviet Union.' Pinochet continually
harked back to the Cold War discourse, ignoring how much the
world had changed since 1989, particularly in Europe.

In Chile Pinochet owned at least three houses, one of them a
mansion with a French-style park, horses and extensive pastures. In
Surrey, Pinochet resided in a closely guarded four-bedroom house
on the Wentworth estate that the Santiago-based Pinochet Foundation rented for £10,000 a month. In the interview he gave to the
Sunday Telegraph he said that the small space he was confined to did
not bother him; that as a soldier, 'I could live on this lawn, with a
tent and a bed and a shower.' Visited by family members and political
supporters from Chile, Pinochet learned to surf the web and even
sent emails to acquaintances in Chile. He also watched a lot of
Spanish-dubbed movies. His favourites were action movies, especially James Bond films like *Octopussy* and *Moonraker*, of which he
had personal copies on one of the shelves in his studio.

By the autumn of 1999, the internment and isolation began to
take its toll on the general. The man who had exiled tens of thousands of Chileans during his reign was now himself experiencing the
bitterness of exile. He became severely depressed and demoralized,
thereby accentuating his physical ailments, which included diabetes,
kidney problems and incontinence. Pinochet's personal physician told
the courts that he had even suffered two minor strokes.

The betrayal of the politicians

The politicians and diplomats, who had been striving for months to
bypass the courts, seized on these reports to begin plotting Pinochet's
return to Chile. The first major step occurred in Rio de Janeiro in
June 1999 in a secret meeting between the British Foreign Secretary,
Robin Cook, and the Spanish Foreign Minister, Abel Matutes. 'I
will not let him die in Britain', promised Cook. 'I will not let him
come to Spain', declared Matutes.[38]

As time would reveal, Pinochet was nowhere near death in the Autumn of 1999, but government officials from Britain, Spain and Chile now focused on playing the 'medical card' to rescue the general from the grip of the courts and the growing web of pro-human-rights rulings. The Chilean Foreign Ministry, headed by José Miguel Insulza, which had argued furiously for almost a year that only Chilean courts could try Pinochet and that his continued detention was damaging relations between Great Britain and Chile, now began to insist that the general's health made his release imperative.

The arrogance of Pinochet at first made it difficult for the Chilean and British authorities to persuade him to take the necessary physical exams. He continued to insist that he was innocent of all charges. He sensed that a release just for medical reasons would not repair the damage that had been done to his international image and stature. But on January 5, 2000, after weeks of badgering by his aides and diplomats, he underwent six hours of tests by four doctors at the Northwick Park hospital in London.[39]

The medical report was sent to the Home Secretary, Jack Straw, who had the power to release the general for medical reasons. The report, which was at first a government secret, did indicate that the general's health had been adversely affected by the two minor strokes. Yet Dr Tomas Palomo, a Spanish physician who reviewed the medical report for Judge Garzón a month later, declared: 'There are no proven arguments that show significant disturbances of his fitness for coordination, remembering, registering, comprehension and under-standing.'[40] While Straw had at one time been an activist in the solidarity movement against Pinochet's reign of terror, he now acted as the consummate politician, intent on ending a legal and human-rights drama that was no longer of interest to the Labour govern-ment. On January 11 he declared that he was 'minded' to halt the extradition process and send the General back to Chile.[41]

This statement caused an outcry among human rights organiza-tions, and Judge Garzón requested a judicial review of Straw's deci-sion and a copy of the medical report. But the Spanish Foreign Office, which had to act as the official courier of any judicial declarations sent to foreign governments, simply refused to forward Garzón's request to Britain. However, the Belgian courts, which after Pinochet's detention in 1998 had also begun to press charges against Pinochet for human rights violations, had their government request a copy of the medical report. Initially Pinochet and his family refused to release the medical reports, asserting that they had been promised 'privacy', but a British court subsequently ruled that the reports had to be turned over to Belgium, as well as to Spain and several other countries in Europe that were requesting Pinochet's extradition.

But the die had been cast by Straw. He had the discretionary power based on his interpretation of the medical reports to release the general and on March 2 ruled that Pinochet should be released for 'humanitarian reasons'. Finally, just over five hundred days after Pinochet's arrest at the London Clinic, a Chilean air force jet flew the General back to Chile in a mission simply dubbed 'Operation Return'.

8

Pinochet's return and
the reckoning in Chile

Five hundred and three days after Pinochet's detention at the London
Clinic, the former general and now senator-for-life returned to Chile.
By all appearances it was a triumphant arrival. A military delegation
led by the head of the army, General Ricardo Izurieta, awaited him
at the airport along with civilian loyalists and leaders of Chile's
right-wing political parties. As Pinochet disembarked in a wheelchair from the Boeing 707 military plane, a band played his favourite martial tunes. Once he touched ground, the ailments that had
secured his release in England seemingly disappeared as he got out
of the wheelchair and walked across the tarmac, waving his crutch
in the air to his assembled supporters. Then he boarded a Puma
helicopter to fly to the military hospital for a physical checkup in
Providencia, an upper-class suburb of Santiago. There over five
thousand wildly cheering supporters greeted him, waving banners
and flags while singing the national anthem. After a physical exam,
Pinochet retired to his country estate, south of Santiago, with his
family and personal entourage.[1]

However, the enthusiastic reception by his supporters was decep-
tive. The Chile Pinochet returned to was not the same Chile he had
left sixteen and a half months before. As Elias Padilla, a university
sociologist and a former president of Amnesty International in Chile,

notes: 'We finally felt free to discuss and say things that were considered taboo even after years of civilian rule. It was as if an oppressive shroud had been lifted from the country.'[2] The hostility of large sectors of the population to his return was palpable in Santiago. The government called for calm, fearing violence as thousands of opponents demonstrated against his arrival in the capital. The area around the military hospital itself was the scene of an intense military operation, with army and police sharpshooters stationed on the roofs of the surrounding buildings to ensure that no attempts were made on Pinochet's life.

The main threats to Pinochet, however, proved to be legal rather than physical. Just over a week after Pinochet's arrival, Ricardo Lagos was inaugurated as the first Socialist president of Chile since Salvador Allende. In a public address from the balcony of the presidential palace, Lagos declared that Chileans 'will always remember the traitors who bombed the palace' on September 11, 1973, leading to the death of Allende, and to Pinochet's takeover. As he spoke the packed plaza in front of Lagos chanted 'juicio a Pinochet', or 'trial for Pinochet'.

Along with the clamour for Pinochet's prosecution came a drive to revitalize Chile's civic and governmental institutions. The day after his inauguration Lagos gave his first major policy address to an even larger crowd on the steps of the popular Belles Artes museum, next to the Mapocho river in Santiago where bodies had floated in the early months of the Pinochet regime. There, Lagos declared that the 'authoritarian enclaves' of the constitution written by Pinochet must be eliminated and that his government would complete the 'transition' from the dictatorship to a full-fledged democracy.

During the presidential campaign, Lagos, as well as his right-wing opponent, Joaquín Lavin, had largely ignored the issue of Pinochet, calling only for his return to Chile. Both insisted that Chileans should try Pinochet for any crimes he had committed, although few thought he would ever stand trial at home because of immunity laws and the legal system he had put in place before leaving office in 1990. Lagos's position reflected that of the centre-left coalition government of Eduardo Frei, which did not want to offend a military that still exercised considerable power in Chile.

Concerned that politicians in the Lagos government might back-slide in their new commitment to pursue him, the human rights movement in Chile campaigned aggressively against Pinochet, demanding his prosecution and that of all other officials of the military regime who were responsible for human rights violations. A week after the inauguration, on the night of March 18 under a bright moon, more than 50,000 people attended a concert at Santiago's National Stadium to raise funds for a memorial centre dedicated to the victims of the dictatorship. Sponsored by the Organization of the Families of the Detained and Disappeared, the crowd in attendance at the concert was composed overwhelmingly of people in their teens and twenties, who chanted and jeered at every mention of Pinochet. Also at the concert were high-ranking ministers of the Lagos government, who appeared to enjoy the gathering as much as the youth, sometimes rising to chant and even dance to anti-Pinochet lyrics.[3]

After the inauguration ceremonies, Lagos in his early days in office made few comments on the prosecution of Pinochet, largely limiting himself to saying that 'the judicial process must take its course' and that the executive branch would not interfere. However, as Lagos was keenly aware, no judicial system functions in a vacuum. Pinochet was easily the most despised figure in Chile, with polls showing that upwards of 70 per cent wanted to see him stand trial. And as José Bengoa, the rector of a private university in Santiago and a noted political analyst, stated: 'Failure to prosecute Pinochet would impair the integrity of the court system and the justices who are trying to show they are no longer the pawns of Pinochet.'[4]

The legal groundwork for prosecuting Pinochet had been laid well before his return to Chile. Indeed the first charges against him in Chile had been filed over nine months before the general left for London, in early January 1998. Then Gladys Marin, the head of the Chilean Communist Party, went to court to charge Pinochet with the murder of her husband and four other leaders of the Communist Party in 1976. And at the end of the month, on January 28, charges were brought against Pinochet for one of those who died in the Caravan of Death, the special military mission designated by Pinochet shortly after the coup, in September and October 1973.[5]

Juan Guzmán: the judge who trapped Pinochet

To hear the charges against Pinochet, Judge Juan Guzmán Tapia of the Appeals Court of Santiago was selected in a judicial lottery. Under Chilean law, which draws on the Napoleonic system, judges serve as prosecutors. When charges are brought against someone, it is a judge who reviews the evidence brought by the plaintiffs and their lawyers and then decides whether or not an indictment and trial are warranted. Also under Chilean law, all related charges brought against a particular individual are heard by the same judge selected to hear the initial charge.

The cases brought against Pinochet in January 1998 initially attracted little attention. Virtually all observers of Chile's judicial system, opponents as well as sympathizers of Pinochet, believed that the charges would be dropped because of the Amnesty Law. Decreed in 1978 by Monica Madariaga, the Minister of Justice and a relative of Pinochet, the law exonerated anyone who committed politically related crimes between the day of the coup and March 10, 1978.[6] Technically, the amnesty law applied to crimes by the regime's opponents as well as those of the military government. Some sixty-nine political opponents of the regime were released from prison, but this was actually a fig leaf for the military, as the principal beneficiaries were the members of the military and security services who had murdered or disappeared thousands of people. Subsequently, when cases were brought in civilian courts for human rights abuses, the cases were handed over to the military system of justice where the amnesty law was immediately applied.[7]

In 1986, the Amnesty Law was challenged in a civilian court by Ana Luisa González, whose 17-year-old son, the president of his high-school student association, was abducted and disappeared by the Caravan of Death. González argued that the Amnesty Law did not apply to cases of abduction because until the victim or his remains were found the crimes were ongoing. The military courts promptly claimed jurisdiction and applied the Amnesty Law.[8] But the principle she argued for survived and was later resurrected by Judge Guzmán.

Initially Juan Guzmán appeared to be an unlikely figure to take on Augusto Pinochet. A social conservative of aristocratic origins, Guzmán ruled in favour of banning in Chile *The Last Temptation of Christ*, a controversial film directed by Martin Scorsese. In his youthful years, Guzmán was not involved in protest politics; nor did he participate in any of the Chilean political movements. Having completed his law degree at the conservative Catholic University of Chile, he went to Paris for an advanced degree at the Sorbonne. After marrying a French woman who picked him up while hitchhiking, he returned to Chile in 1970, just as Salvador Allende was elected the first Socialist president of Chile.

Guzmán requested a local judicial appointment, which required the approval of the new government. Allende, knowing Guzmán's father, a renowned Chilean writer, decided to interview Guzmán for the post. The new president reportedly asked him, 'You don't agree with our political beliefs do you?' Guzmán responded, 'That is right, I don't.' Expecting Allende would insist he join one of the political parties that backed the government, he heard instead Allende say: 'I will appoint you a judge if you swear never to abuse the poor.' Astounded, Guzmán said: 'I swear it.'[9]

When Pinochet and the Chilean armed forces violently overthrew Allende on September 11, 1973, Guzmán supported the coup, believing 'it was going to be a moment of re-establishing order'. It was not until much later that he began to understand 'the crimes, torture, detention, and persecution' that were committed. In 1976, he first became concerned with the number of 'habeas corpus' suits brought by family members of victims who had disappeared or died. In 1978, he was appointed to a criminal court in Santiago. In the court records he found 'hundreds of photographs of people, poor people, poor women that had been simply shot in the streets.'[10]

Although unnerved by these and subsequent experiences, he never openly opposed the Pinochet regime. Nor did he support the Catholic Church's patriarch in Santiago, Cardinal Raúl Silva Henríquez, who led the human rights movement against the dictatorship. Guzmán has never felt comfortable with the changes in the Catholic Church that came with Vatican II and the theology of liberation, saying that the Church 'lost a great part of its mystery and the power it had ... including the rituality and mysticism'. Only today does he admit in a somewhat joking, self-deprecating manner, 'I am starting to understand the new system of how mass is being done and why mass is done in the vernacular languages, but I do prefer the other way.'[11]

Guzmán's first real judicial break with the regime came at the very end of Pinochet's rule in 1990 when he was selected by lottery along with another civilian judge and three military-appointed judges to preside over a martial law case involving an ex-intelligence officer accused of killing a union leader. With Guzmán's swing vote, the special tribunal ruled 3 to 2 to convict the officer and sentenced him to ten years in prison.

Eight years later Guzmán took charge of the most controversial judicial case in Chilean history, just as Pinochet was ending his twenty-five year tenure as head of the army and assuming the post of senator-for-life. Guzmán maintains that even if Pinochet hadn't subsequently been detained in London for seventeen months before returning to Chile, 'I would have continued just like a train, something that I started that I had to continue. I had a large amount of evidence in this case, over eight volumes of material.' Guzmán asserts that well before Pinochet's detention in London, in Chile 'we had evolved as judges, I myself evolved'. Guzmán believes that 'international opinion was something of a recognition, a moral support, that made us realize that we are in the era of human rights.' It worked in tandem with the judicial process in Chile, but did not determine what happened there.

While Pinochet was detained in London, Guzmán did indeed make significant progress in prosecuting the case of the Caravan of Death. On June 10, 1999, Guzmán ordered the indictment of five leaders of the Caravan of Death, including the general Pinochet had placed in charge of the Caravan, Sergio Arellano Stark. It was in this case that Guzmán first used the innovative legal argument that the Amnesty Law did not apply in the cases of disappeared persons because these were ongoing crimes. Arellano Stark and the other indicted officers contested this interpretation, but Guzmán's position was subsequently upheld by the Chilean Supreme Court.[12] By the time Pinochet returned to Chile on March 3, 2000, a total of fifty-nine charges had been filed against him in Guzmán's court.[13]

Guzmán faced a major obstacle to indicting Pinochet, in that he enjoyed parliamentary immunity from prosecution as a senator-for-life. The courts of Chile, however, have the power to lift this immunity if serious crimes are involved. This is precisely what Judge Guzmán proceeded to argue. On March 6, 2000, just three days after Pinochet returned, Guzmán filed a petition in the Santiago Appeals Court to strip Pinochet of his immunity.

In May 2000, just prior to the Appeals Court's ruling, over a hundred generals visited Pinochet's residence to express their 'solidarity'. A few days later, the military chiefs held a well-publicized meeting in a restaurant designed to intimidate the courts and to make known their indignation over the legal procedures being undertaken against Pinochet. However, President Lagos was adept at keeping the military off-balance. The day after the gathering in the restaurant Lagos castigated the military, declaring: 'We aren't stupid, we know what they were trying to do yesterday. It is not necessary for the armed forces to demonstrate that they stand behind someone, because their duty is to stand behind the president of Chile.'[14]

On June 5, the Court of Appeals in Santiago voted 13 to 9 to strip the former dictator of his parliamentary immunity. When the Appeals Court formally announced its decision, the head of the army, General Izurieta, limited himself to proclaiming: 'Pinochet is an example of heroic sacrifice', who 'awaits the judgement of history, and not that of his contemporaries'.[15] All eyes now turned to the country's Supreme Court, where Pinochet's attorneys immediately appealed the ruling.

On August 8, 2000, the Supreme Court voted 14 to 6 to lift Pinochet's immunity. About two hundred people assembled in front of Pinochet's residence in Santiago to lament the decision, while thousands of opponents of the dictator demonstrated throughout the streets of the capital in what many described as a 'carnival-like atmosphere'. Champagne flowed freely, balloons were released into the air, while some sang 'Adios General', a song released by a popular Chilean musical group. Many assembled around the National Stadium, where Pinochet had imprisoned and tortured thousands of people in the days immediately after the coup. Others marched on the presidential palace and gathered in the Constitutional Plaza near the statue of Salvador Allende. Internationally, the decision was greeted with widespread acclaim. Amnesty International declared 'justice has triumphed', while Joan Garcés stated: 'this means a head of state does not enjoy immunity for crimes against humanity.' The following day Pinochet denounced the decision of the court, and proclaimed that he would defend himself. Still determined to go after his old enemies, he declared he was 'indignant at seeing banners of the Communist Party in the Constitutional Plaza'.[16]

The Supreme Court decision meant that Guzmán could now proceed with the arraignment and indictment of Augusto Pinochet. As part of this process, Chilean law required that Pinochet be formally interrogated concerning the charges he faced and subjected to a mental examination to decide if he were competent to stand trial.

The first legal battleground was over the nature of the examinations Pinochet was to undergo. The Chilean penal code is quite specific, stating that anyone over 70 years old is to go through mental examinations to determine if they are 'crazy or demented'. There is no requirement for more extensive exams to diagnose physical ailments. However, the lawyers for Pinochet immediately filed a petition for a series of physical tests. The hope of the defence was that they would get Pinochet off with the 'London scenario', meaning that sympathetic doctors would examine the former general and then rule that his health was too poor for him to stand trial.

Simultaneously, Pinochet's legal and political advisers decided to mount a broader campaign to pressure the country's judicial and political system to exempt him from indictment and trial. An organization composed mainly of retired military officers, 'Chile, Mi Patria', called for a 'political solution', arguing that the judicial system could not understand the historic context that required military intervention to save the country from 'Marxism'. Pinochet also assumed a more public role in trying to rouse support for his cause. A couple of weeks after the lifting of his parliamentary immunity he participated in a public act at the Pinochet Foundation, commemorating the soldiers 'who died in combat and terrorist acts' from 1973 to 1990. A high-ranking general from the army attended the event, putting the Lagos government on alert that the military intended to continue supporting Pinochet.

Lagos's betrayal

Days later, on August 29, 2000, President Lagos had a private dinner with the head of the army, General Izurieta. The details of their conversation have not been revealed, but after the meeting relations between the military and the Lagos government improved significantly. Subsequent events indicate that a quid pro quo was worked out: in exchange for the military's commitment to lower its profile on behalf of Pinochet, the Lagos government would agree to lobby the courts for extensive physical examinations of the former dictator that would exempt him from further prosecution. At about the same time, the highest-ranking official in the government, the Minister of Interior, José Miguel Insulza, declared that Pinochet should be exempted from prosecution for health reasons, and that Pinochet 'will not be sent to prison'.[17]

Lagos had apparently come to the conclusion that the continued prosecution of Pinochet would only further agitate the military and paralyse an economy that was dominated by right-wing business interests that were upset with the prosecution of the man who had bestowed so many economic favours on them. In fact Lagos tipped his hand in early October 2000, when in a gathering of the leaders of the major business associations at his residence he declared that he knew they were preoccupied with the Pinochet case and that the proceedings against him would 'end well and quickly'.[18]

The only problem for Lagos's new stance was that Judge Guzmán and the human rights organizations did not concur. Two people affiliated with the government approached Guzmán in an effort to get him to alter his rulings in the Pinochet case. First a representative of the cabinet asked him to expand the scope of the mental examinations. Guzmán's curt response was: 'Look young man, I'm going to do as my conscience tells me. Goodbye.' In fact Guzmán hardened his position and moved more aggressively in the Pinochet case. On December 1, 2000 he ordered that Pinochet should be legally processed and indicted, before the examinations had even taken place. Within hours someone from the Lagos administration tried to get him to drop the indictment. Guzmán was incensed, and told him: 'You should know that you cannot interfere with a judge's decision. It is very improper what you have done. Thank you very much. Goodbye.'[19]

Guzmán's decision to indict Pinochet provoked a political uproar in Chile. Lagos was out of the country attending the inauguration of Vincente Fox as president of Mexico. Upon hearing of the indictment, General Izurieta went to tell the Minister of Interior, José Miguel Insulza, who also served as acting vice-president, that the indictment of Pinochet could not stand. Furthermore Izurieta declared that the Chilean armed forces were going to call a meeting of the Council of National Security (Conesa), an institution imposed on the country by the Pinochet regime so the military could exercise influence over civilian governments. There are eight seats on the council, four from the military (the heads of the army, navy, air force and national police) and four civilians (the president, the head of the Supreme Court, the president of the Senate, and the Controller).

Insulza was in constant communication with Lagos in Mexico; together they finally managed to convince the military to postpone the convening of Conesa until Lagos returned on December 5. Shortly after he arrived, Lagos held an extended meeting with the heads of the armed forces. Lagos argued that Conesa should not be convened because it would represent a blatant interference in the country's judicial process. The military commanders initially refused to back off, but, realizing that they did not have a majority on the council, agreed to a compromise proposal put forth by Lagos: Conesa would be convened once the issue of the indictment of Pinochet was resolved in the courts.

Pinochet's lawyers, of course, wasted no time in appealing Guzmán's indictment to the Supreme Court. They argued that Pinochet could not be arraigned and indicted because no examinations had taken place and because Pinochet had not been formally interrogated, as required by Chilean law. Guzmán's position was that the tests did not have to occur until after Pinochet was arraigned, and that he had already interrogated Pinochet while he was in London. (Guzmán in 1999 had sent the general a letter concerning the crimes he was alleged to have committed. Pinochet refused to respond directly, but declared in comments to the press in London that he was not guilty of any of the charges filed against him. Guzmán argued that this fulfilled the interrogation requirements.[20])

On December 11, 2000, the court struck down Guzmán's indictment of Pinochet. But it declared that Guzmán could proceed with a new indictment once he had conducted a direct interrogation of Pinochet. Regarding the examinations, the court made it clear that only mental tests were required, that there was no legal requirement for physical examinations. The Council of National Security was subsequently convened in early January by Lagos. No resolutions came out of the meeting and the case of Pinochet was not directly discussed, although the general theme of human rights was broached.[21] While the heads of the military left the meeting demanding a 'political solution' to the Pinochet affair, the Lagos government declared the next day that 'it was a positive meeting' because the military 'accepted the autonomy of the judicial system' and supported 'national unity'.[22] Lagos had successfully defused the military challenge over Pinochet's indictment.

Pinochet: hiding under the military's skirts

The month of January 2001 proved to be decisive in the Pinochet affair. Guzmán set the dates of January 7 and 8 for the medical examinations and January 9 for the interrogation. Pinochet's representatives, his lawyers and his family, issued brusque statements that Pinochet would 'not follow the court orders'. The general retreated to his ranch at Los Boldos near the Pacific Ocean with his bodyguards, apparently intent on resisting any legal efforts to arrest or indict him, which Guzmán could order if Pinochet failed to show up. One of the attorneys pressing the charges for the Caravan of Death, Hugo Gutierrez, declared sarcastically: 'The first son of our country has demonstrated he is bereft of courage and dignity. He is trying to hide under the military's skirts.'[23]

On the eve of the physical, General Izurieta went to Pinochet's ranch. It was subsequently revealed that Izurieta told the former dictator 'to respect the law.' Izurieta was in a position to enforce this order, as the army had recently altered the composition of the detail assigned to provide security to Pinochet, replacing committed loyalists of the former general with soldiers responsible to the army's high command. Pinochet's oldest daughter subsequently denounced Izurieta for this manoeuvre, declaring that 'he wants to carry on with God and the Devil', and that 'he doesn't represent the views of the entire army'.[24]

Pinochet did not show up for the medical examination on the scheduled date. But shortly after Izurieta's visit to the ranch, a spokesman for Pinochet announced that he 'would respect the law'. Judge Guzmán, recognizing that the former general now intended to comply with the court orders, set new dates for the physicals on January 10–12 and scheduled the interrogation for January 23.

Izurieta's decision to compel Pinochet to submit to the legal process was based not only on his collaborationist efforts with the Lagos government, but also on the reality that the military was subject to increasing public scrutiny and hostility. On January 7, the same day as Pinochet was to appear for his originally scheduled mental examinations, the Chilean military released a list of 180 people who were 'disappeared' during military rule. Six months before, the military had agreed to try to determine the location of the remains of as many people as possible out of the more than 1,100 people who were formally listed as disappeared. This was part of an accord between the military, the government, and sectors of civil society called the 'Mesa de Diálogo', or the Table of Dialogue. The military hoped that by finding the remains of the disappeared, former and even active officers who might be charged with 'ongoing crimes' could be exonerated under the Amnesty Law.[25]

Yet the military's hopes of evading prosecution by providing information on some of the disappeared victims failed abysmally. The public was aghast as the military for the first time acknowledged its direct responsibility in disappearing and murdering opponents of the Pinochet regime. The macabre details of many deaths were revealed in the report. Some victims were 'thrown in the ocean from helicopters', others were interred in 'mine pits', and still others were tossed in deep holes dug in military forts near their execution sites. Independent of the report, an officer involved in dumping people in the ocean declared 'we split their stomachs open while they were alive to stop them from floating'.[26]

Public outrage grew even stronger as it became known that much of the information provided in the report on the disappeared was false. Six bodies were reportedly buried at a location not far from Santiago. But after a thorough excavation of the area, only two bones were found and they did not belong to any of the victims. Carmen Hertz, a prosecuting attorney for the Caravan of Death whose husband numbered among the disappeared, declared, 'the information provided is a fraud'.[27] According to the military report, her husband was dumped in the ocean one day after he was detained. This was contradicted by witnesses who reported seeing him alive several days after his detention.

Due to the public revulsion, even the two major right-wing parties began to distance themselves from Pinochet in hopes that they would not suffer losses in the upcoming congressional elections at the end of the year. And some on the left, such as the editorialists of the periodicals *La Firme* and *Punto Final*, pointed out that it was not just military officers who were responsible for the deaths of thousands of Chileans: many civilian ministers and vice-ministers were also involved, at the very least in covering up and denying the existence of a network of state-sponsored terror.[28]

The examination of Pinochet at the state-run medical institute in Santiago was neurological as well as mental, to determine if his cerebral capacities had been affected by minor strokes he had suffered. Four state-appointed medical experts conducted the tests, with the presence of two additional doctors, one selected by the defence and one by the prosecuting attorneys. Pinochet was obviously not 'demented or crazy' during the exams. He joked with the medical experts, telling an examining neurologist who was exiled during the dictatorship: 'you are not like your two aunts [supporters of the military regime], who were very pretty and nice'.[29]

In their report, the examining physicians concluded that the general did not suffer from any serious mental impairments. However, the tests did reveal 'vascular dementia' related to the strokes. Pinochet's attorney's promptly proceeded to argue that this dementia meant that he could not stand trial. As Carmen Hertz, one of the prosecuting attorneys, responded: 'Pinochet with two light strokes is more than capable of handling himself in court.'[30]

The next critical event was the interrogation scheduled for January 23. It took place at the general's elaborate residence in Deshesa, an exclusive area on the eastern side of Santiago. Guzmán was forced to use the maids' entrance. Some say that this was not an intended slight, but an effort to shield Guzmán from the press. Guzmán even had tea with Pinochet's wife Lucia when a laptop computer and a printer brought to record the session did not function properly and had to be repaired. Pinochet did not rise to greet Guzmán, and sat in his armchair throughout the entire session, dressed in his customary brown suit with a blue tie and a pearl clasp.[31]

Prior to the interrogation, some of Pinochet's attorneys had argued that the general should not respond to Guzmán's questions or that he should declare that he didn't remember anything, in order to give the impression that he suffered from severe dementia. However, according to one of the attorneys present, because of 'the personality of the general' Pinochet decided to respond to the questions. He could not accept the idea of being characterized as 'demented'. In his answers to Guzmán's questions regarding the Caravan of Death, Pinochet claimed he 'never ordered anybody to be executed or disappeared', that he had only sent General Arellano Stark on the mission 'to accelerate the judicial process'.[32] He refrained from blaming Arellano Stark for any of the atrocities committed by the Caravan. When queried as to why he did not order an investigation once he heard reports of the executions and disappearances in the wake of the Caravan, he said that this was not his responsibility; it depended on the local military commander of the region. These statements concurred with those made by Arellano Stark, who was already under indictment.

The claims of Pinochet and Arellano Stark were sharply contradicted the very next day by retired general Joaquín Lagos, the military officer who was in charge of the mining region of Chile when the Caravan of Death carried out many of its summary executions there.

In a dramatic statement on national television, General Lagos (no relation to President Lagos) declared that when the Caravan arrived in his zone and began to take prisoners out to be executed he had gone to Arellano Stark and asked him to explain his actions. Arellano Stark had responded: 'I am in charge', stating that he 'was the official designated to ... intervene and undertake any necessary actions'. General Lagos later confronted Pinochet with information on those executed and 'the cadavers that were pulverized' by Arellano Stark's Caravan, but Pinochet had refused to disown Arellano Stark's actions. Lagos a year later was forced into early retirement by Pinochet.[33]

On the day Lagos appeared on television the attorneys for the defence and the prosecution filed their petitions with Judge Guzmán. As was expected, the defence argued that the general could not stand trial for health reasons, while the prosecution insisted that he should be immediately charged and indicted. Guzmán left Santiago for the remainder of the week, going to his house on the beach to prepare his decision on the fate of Pinochet.

The indictment of the dictator

On Monday, January 29, 2001, on a bright summer day, three years after the first charges were filed against Pinochet for the Caravan of Death, Judge Guzmán decreed that Pinochet should stand trial and be placed under house arrest. As word spread throughout Santiago in the morning that Guzmán was about to issue his orders, hundreds of demonstrators gathered in front of the court to hear the decision. Many carried pictures of family members who were killed or disappeared by the regime. Among the more notable were pictures of Victor Jara, the popular Chilean folk singer who was executed after he had his hands broken while playing the guitar in prison. Pictures of Carlos Prats were also displayed, the general whom Pinochet replaced as head of the Chilean armed forces shortly before the military coup, and who was later assassinated by DINA operatives while living in exile in Argentina.[34]

The demonstrators chanted 'no amnesty, no impunity, the blood of our people cannot be negotiated', alluding to efforts by some of the country's politicians to exempt Pinochet from trial. The crowd also chanted 'Allende, Allende, you are with us now.' On the day of the coup, Allende in his final address to the nation had declared 'I am certain … the cowardliness and the treachery [of the coup leaders] will be punished.'[35]

Carmen Hertz, one of the lawyers who led the effort to prosecute Pinochet, declared 'This is an historic moment, not only for the families of the victims, but for all of Chile.' Hertz added that the orders issued by Guzmán 'are an expression of justice and reparation for the tens of thousands of victims of the military dictatorship, not only those who were murdered and disappeared, but also for those who were tortured or forced into exile'.[36] Roberto Garretón, a prominent attorney who had handled human rights cases in Chilean courts since 1974, proclaimed:

> This day will go down in history as a turning point. The human rights movement has persevered. It has succeeded in indicting a dictator who wrote his own constitution and decreed his own amnesty. After leaving office he was protected by politicians who have lied to the Chilean people and the world, asserting that we lived in a democracy and that everyone wanted to forget about the past. Judge Guzmán and the human rights movement have given us justice and the truth. They have changed Chile and the world.[37]

Even though the internal political and juridical terrain had shifted considerably with the indictment of Pinochet, his defence lawyers had by no means exhausted their legal options. They immediately appealed the indictment, arguing that it should be thrown out on legal grounds as well as for health reasons. Just days after the indictment, the leaders of Chile's two major right-wing parties, the Independent Democratic Union and the National Renovation Party, went to visit Pinochet at his residence where he was under house arrest. The leaders were visibly concerned about the adverse political fallout from the long process leading up to his indictment after he returned to Chile and the effect it might have on their political fortunes. Pinochet, in recognition of their concerns, told them: 'Don't become involved with my case or worry about me. I'll defend myself alone.'[38]

The general was as astute as ever in his belief that he could manipulate the political and judicial system of Chile. In March an Appeals Court ruled that Pinochet could not be charged as an accomplice in the murders of the Caravan of Death, but that he would have to stand trial for covering up the crimes committed by the Caravan. Although the charges were not as severe, they nonetheless meant that the general could still be subjected to a trial and a significant sentence. And even if he were exonerated of the cover-up charges relating to the Caravan, he faced more than two hundred other charges that had been filed against him. This meant Pinochet could spend the remainder of his life in and out of courts with the threat of incarceration continually hanging over his head. And with each indictment he would be placed under house arrest.

From then on Pinochet's lawyers locked into the legal strategy of arguing that the general could not stand trial for health and mental reasons. In particular they insisted that Pinochet's vascular dementia rendered him unable to defend himself in court. This argument was taken up by the Sixth Court of Appeals in Santiago. Pinochet now appeared to have decided that he would go along with his lawyers' advice and use the medical pretext to try to avoid standing trial.

In the coming months, Pinochet made repeated visits to the military hospital, visits that were permitted under the terms of house arrest. And when legal clerks went to his residence to take his fingerprints and mug-shots as required by law for the Caravan charges, Pinochet's personal physician refused to let them in, asserting that the general's very life would 'be endangered' if he had to be subjected to this process.

Just days before the anticipated Appeals Court ruling in July 2001 Pinochet checked into the military hospital yet again. But this time it was for little more than a dental visit, as the general had a minor gum infection. However, the newspapers gave the impression that this was a significant medical crisis. As *La Tercera*, one of the country's leading newspapers, noted under banner headlines, the general, after suffering from 'disorientation', and 'marked changes in blood pressure', was 'urgently admitted to the military hospital yesterday and underwent a facial surgical intervention'.[39] The paper went on to report that Pinochet would 'remain in the hospital to receive intravenous antibiotics', and that his vital signs would be 'closely monitored', especially for problems related to his diabetes.

Pinochet's grand evasion: crazy and demented

The alleged medical crisis ended the next day with Pinochet's discharge from the hospital. But then on the eve of the ruling by the Appeals Court, a rumour was leaked that Pinochet had died. The rumour was almost immediately discredited, but not until after the major media in Chile had reported the story, giving the impression that the general was at death's door.

The health ruse worked. On July 9, a cold winter day in Santiago, the Appeals Court ruled by a vote of 2 to 1 to suspend the Caravan case against Pinochet for health reasons. The ruling had no basis in existing Chilean law. As Carmen Hertz, one of the prosecuting attorneys, stated:

> I have read the majority ruling a number of times and it is incoherent. They couldn't use Chilean legal standards. Chilean statutes are very clear that one can be excused from prosecution only if one is mentally incompetent or insane. There was no basis for such a ruling regarding Pinochet so they dreamt up a mish mash of illogical statements that make no sense.[40]

Why did the Appeals Court make this ruling? As Carmen Hertz states:

> The entire political and social establishment in Chile wanted an end to the Pinochet case. The newspapers and the media are overwhelmingly right-wing, and of course virtually all of the business leaders are supporters of Pinochet. The Lagos government also abandoned its pledge not to interfere in the courts in the Pinochet case. Government officials made it clear they wanted an end to the Pinochet process. The judicial system of Chile, like that of many other countries, responded to these political pressures and declared, without foundation, that Pinochet was not fit to stand trial for mental and health reasons.[41]

Hernan Quezada, a legal expert on international law who worked in the Ministry of Foreign Relations, went even further in his criticism of the government's role. 'Lagos did not want to rile up the military, and if Pinochet stood trial the government's cordial relations with General Izurieta and the military high command would have been disrupted.'[42] On July 7, two days before the ruling, Lagos went out of his way to show his concern for the military's interests. At the home of the civilian Defence Minister Lagos met with the heads of the Chilean armed forces. There were no statements or communiqués issued at the end of the meeting, but it was clear to all that Lagos by meeting with the military was throwing his weight behind a court ruling that would exempt Pinochet from trial.[43]

However, in spite of the intervention of the establishment of Chile on behalf of Pinochet, the prosecutions of other military and civilian officials who had committed human rights crimes continued unabated. On the very day that Pinochet was exempted from trial, Judge Guzmán indicted five former military officials for the human rights abuses committed in the 1970s at the clandestine torture centre Villa Grimalda. And on the same date, parliamentary deputy Andres Palma and families of the disappeared announced that they had proof that some of the victims the military claimed they had no information on in the Mesa de Diálogo had actually been thrown down mine shafts alive.[44]

A year later, on July 1, 2002, the Chilean Supreme Court upheld the decision of the Appeals Court. Pinochet would never have to go to jail for his crimes as dictator of Chile. However, the dictator had to suffer yet another humiliation as a result of this final ruling. Because he was still officially a 'senator-for-life', his opponents in Congress made it clear that anyone officially declared 'crazy or demented' could not conceivably hold on to his post in the Senate. A movement began immediately in Congress to have him thrown out. But Pinochet, fearful that he would lose his pension and other privileges as an ex-president if he were voted out of office, decided to resign voluntarily, 'negotiating' his final pact with the head of the Senate, Andrés Zaldívar, who had been so helpful to him in bygone years as a leader of the conservative wing of the Christian Democratic Party.[45]

Pinochet first called Zaldívar to offer his resignation, asserting that he was not 'crazy or demented'. He then called upon another collaborator who had been lobbying for his exemption from prosecution, Cardinal Errazuriz of Santiago. Pinochet asked the cardinal to take his letter of resignation personally to the Senate. The letter reads like many of his statements, before and after his years as dictator, filled with historical distortions and lies, refusing to recognize any of the atrocities he committed. The very first sentence asserts that he overthrew Allende 'to defend our sovereignty, national security, and the peace of our people'. He goes on to claim he 'made tremendous personal sacrifices, all for the welfare and happiness of our citizens'.[46] Pinochet to the end remained a sociopath, a person capable only of doing and saying what served his narrow self-interests, regardless of the death and tremendous suffering inflicted on others.

On the day when Zaldívar formally presented his resignation to the senators and deputies, mass demonstrations erupted both inside and outside of the congressional building. Deputy Fidel Espinoza of the Socialist Party, whose father was executed by the military regime in December 1973, held up a large placard on the floor of congress proclaiming: 'Pinochet killed my father.' A riot immediately broke out in the congressional gallery and on the floor. Espinoza declared: 'I represent the sentiments of thousands of Chileans who suffered the death or disappearance of loved ones.'[47]

The hounded dictator in his lair

After his resignation had been tendered, Pinochet apparently felt that he was on a roll, that the good old days had returned. He decided to take a vacation in Iquique, his favourite port city in northern Chile, where he had spent many enjoyable years as a younger officer. But he failed to take account of the fact that the Caravan of Death in October 1973 had buried some of the bodies of the executed in the desert near Iquique. The city was riven with deep-seated resentment against the former dictator, and protests in Iquique began before he arrived to take up residence at an apartment complex. Even before he left Santiago, the trip appeared ill-fated, as some of his guards suffered a serious car accident on their way to Iquique to prepare for his visit. After his arrival some residents in the building made it clear they didn't want him around. Then some of his uninjured security guards brusquely apprehended two teenagers and a young man who were carrying a pressure pump gun near a beach site Pinochet intended to visit and had them thrown in jail. The youths and their parents held a press conference to protest their treatment and threatened legal action. Finally Pinochet was forced to terminate his Iquique jaunt abruptly and flee back to his heavily fortified compounds in Santiago.[48]

Meanwhile Joan Garcés in Spain made it clear that if Pinochet ever dares set foot out of Chile again he will be apprehended by the Spanish courts. A legal memo circulated globally by Garcés just two days after the Chilean Supreme Court's ruling states that 'Pinochet remains a fugitive of justice' before the National Court of Spain and that 'Pinochet is charged with the crimes of genocide, terrorism and torture.' The Spanish judicial order for his 'apprehension by Interpol remains in effect'. The memo goes on to note that according to eight eminent medical physicians retained by the National Court, 'Pinochet is in fit mental condition to stand trial.'[49] In his remaining years, Pinochet will remain a hounded and detested man, even as he seeks solace behind the walls of his closely guarded residences in Chile.

There is no doubt that the long legal process starting with Pinochet's arrest in London and continuing with the efforts to try him in Chile dramatically transformed his historical legacy and even altered the transition process. Although Pinochet has avoided a trial, he has become a completely discredited figure in Chile. As Carmen Hertz noted, well before his resignation from the Senate, while he was under indictment: 'He is a political cadaver.' Roberto Garretón declared: 'On his birthday on November 25, 2001, for the first time since 1973, only his family celebrated.'[50] No political figures of any importance wished him well or came to visit him at his residence. Under Chilean law, Pinochet could not vote in the parliamentary elections in mid-December 2001 because of his criminal indictment. The news media did not mention his name on the day of the elections: it was as if he had ceased to exist on the political scene.

Even the Chilean army was transformed by the Pinochet affair. On January 6, 2003, the new commander in chief of the army, General Juan Emilio Cheyre, declared that the military dictatorship's 'violations of human rights had no justification'. He called on the courts to continue prosecuting all those who had committed crimes, including those in the military; this would be the only way for Chile to 'achieve social peace'.[51] Cheyre represents a new generation of military officials who look to the legacy of Generals René Schneider and Carlos Prats, former heads of the Chilean Army who upheld the country's constitution and were assassinated for their beliefs.

Some political observers in Chile began talking of 'the Garzón–Guzmán syndrome' as a number of judges started pursuing the perpetrators of human rights violations with the same intensity and determination as Judges Baltasar Garzón of Spain and Juan Guzmán of Chile.[52] Judge Guzmán himself acknowledged that a 'Pandora's Box has been opened with the prosecution of Pinochet. There are now six judges in Santiago alone dedicated to human rights issues who are taking over some of the cases I began work on.' Guzmán adds, in an almost joking manner, 'a few of these judges are even more tenacious than me in the pursuit of justice for the victims of human rights abuses. Many individuals once considered untouchable are now being prosecuted.'[53]

Perhaps the best personal statement on the importance of the Pinochet affair is provided by Pedro Pablo Gac Becerra, whose father was disappeared by the military in a provincial Chilean town when Pedro was only 5 years old:

> The victors of yesterday are today the defeated.... It is strange that a son of one of the victims should say this, but it is the truth. What has happened to the fascist project that inspired the criminals? Absolutely nothing, not even the army today dares to celebrate what were once called 'the glories of the country.'... The military regime and its leader have ceased being the light that once illuminated the path of the right. Today for the right this past is nothing more than a bothersome memory, to be discarded and abandoned in the backyard of history.

Gac goes on to point out that as of January 2003, over two hundred people are either imprisoned or under indictment for crimes committed during the years of the Pinochet regime.[54]

Roberto Garretón aptly summed up the importance of the Pinochet affair from a Chilean human rights perspective:

His arrest in London on October 16, 1998 changed everything. It dramatically altered the transition process in Chile, largely removing the dark shadow of the dictator. The military came to his aid, but as the prosecution of Pinochet unfolded, even the leading military officials were forced to retreat from the political scene, limiting their actions to lobbying on behalf of Pinochet, which also cost them dearly in terms of public esteem. Perhaps even more importantly the Pinochet affair altered the course of international law. It led directly to indictments and prosecutions of a number of military and political leaders around the globe who had committed atrocious human rights violations.[55]

The quest for justice continues in Chile and abroad.

CONCLUSION

State terrorism versus
the globalization of justice

Placed in historical perspective, the Pinochet affair – the series of
events extending from the detention of Pinochet and the rulings
against him by the House of Lords to the lifting of his parliamentary
immunity when he returned to Chile and his indictment by Chilean
courts – represents a surprising and remarkable victory for the international human rights community. In the end Pinochet avoided trial
and imprisonment by manipulating claims of declining health and
advanced age. But the legal rulings against him were never overturned and he continues to be sought by courts around the world,
with extradition requests pending in several countries. Most importantly the principle of 'universal jurisdiction' was effectively encoded
in international law, meaning that judges and courts in one country
can apprehend and try a former head of state from another country
for crimes against humanity.

   To comprehend fully its significance, the Pinochet affair needs to
be situated in a global context. 'Globalization' is a term often applied
to the discussion of economic issues and the expansion of multinational corporate interests. However, the Pinochet affair demonstrates that globalization has come to affect virtually all arenas of
human activity, including politics, culture, human rights and the
domain of justice. Indeed, in a world where national boundaries are

becoming ever more porous, human rights have become a critical concern shaping international relations and the political discourse between countries and societies.[1]

In the case of Pinochet, his apprehension represented the culmination of years of patient and ardent work by an international community of human rights activists and lawyers in Spain, Britain, Chile, the United States and many other countries. As such his arrest stands as a high water mark in a human rights movement that attained global resonance in the 1970s, became a major issue in international diplomacy and politics in the 1980s, and then emerged as a touchstone that the Western powers sought to manipulate – often in a hypocritical manner – to reorganize the world under their aegis with the end of the Cold War. In a global context the Pinochet affair is also a case study in how the human rights movement has been shaped by and responds to issues of state and international terrorism. It is an uncanny historical coincidence that the attacks on the World Trade Center and the Pentagon on September 11, 2001 occurred exactly twenty-eight years after General Augusto Pinochet toppled the elected government of Socialist president Salvador Allende in Chile. Each September 11 unleashed a chain of events and issues that are of critical importance to understanding how terrorism and the human rights movement are intertwined.

The bloody coup in Chile on September 11, 1973 stunned the world. In the wake of the repression imposed on the Chilean people in the days and months after the coup, a human rights movement appeared both in Chile and internationally that called for an end to the state terrorism of the Pinochet regime. The global scope of the human rights movement also received impetus from the regime's actions beyond the borders of Chile. Prior to the attack on the Pentagon on September 11, 2001, the most sensational international terrorist operation in the US capital occurred on September 21, 1976. On that day a team of operatives recruited by the Pinochet regime detonated a car bomb just blocks from the White House, killing a leading opponent of the regime, Orlando Letelier, and his colleague Ronni Moffitt.

These assassinations were linked to the first international terrorist network in the western hemisphere, known as Operation Condor.

Begun in 1974 at the instigation of the Chilean secret police, the DINA, Operation Condor was a sinister cabal composed of the intelligence services of at least six South American countries that collaborated in tracking, kidnapping and assassinating political opponents. Based on documents divulged under the Chile Declassification Project during the last years of the Clinton administration, it is now recognized that the CIA knew about these international terrorist activities and may have abetted them.

The Chilean secret police, often with the assistance of other Condor partners, carried out a number of international terrorist operations. On September 30, 1974, retired general Carlos Prats, whom Pinochet replaced as head of the Chilean military shortly before the 1973 coup, was killed by a car bomb while living in exile in Buenos Aires, Argentina. In Rome in 1975, DINA operatives attacked and seriously maimed Chilean Christian Democratic politician Bernardo Leighton and his wife.

Papers found in Paraguayan archives in the 1990s reveal that Operation Condor was also linked to the assassination of a Brazilian general and two Uruguayan parliamentarians, as well as to scores of lesser-known political activists. After the murders of Letelier and Moffitt in Washington DC, the CIA appears to have concluded that Condor was a rogue operation and may have tried to contain its activities. However, the network of southern cone military and intelligence operations continued to act throughout Latin America at least until the early 1980s, sometimes in concert with US covert activities. Chilean and Argentine military units assisted the dictator Anastasio Somoza in Nicaragua and helped set up death squads in El Salvador. Argentine units also aided and supervised Honduran military death squads that began operating in the early 1980s with the direct assistance and collaboration of the CIA.[2]

In Chile the severe repression of political parties and of much of civil society meant that in the early years of the military regime only religious organizations were in a position to challenge the regime's severe violations of human rights. However, by the late 1970s secular human rights organizations had established themselves in Chile as well as in other southern cone countries, particularly Argentina. From the start this human rights movement drew strength from its ties to international human rights organizations in Western Europe and the United States. This international network mounted campaigns to prod the governments in Western countries to apply political and economic sanctions against the regimes in the southern cone. It is the strength of this movement that led Jimmy Carter in 1977 at the inception of his presidency to proclaim that human rights would be 'the soul' of his foreign policy.

In historical retrospective Carter's human rights policy can be viewed as an exercise in political relativism, if not opportunism. In the Middle East and much of Asia, the United States virtually ignored the issue of human rights, while in the case of the Soviet Union and Eastern Europe US charges of human rights violations were mainly acts of posturing as the US government tried to score ideological points against its Cold War adversaries. However, in Latin America there were some advances, as US military and economic assistance was curtailed due to human rights abuses. The pro-human-rights discourse emanating from the United States also helped embolden international institutions like the Organization of American States and the United Nations.

State terrorism and the United States

The Reagan administration came into office in 1981 determined to undo the human rights agenda enunciated by Carter. The early 1980s in fact witnessed the consolidation of state terrorism as a de facto policy of the United States government. In practice this meant that the Reagan administration stopped pressuring repressive regimes like Chile's over human rights abuses, and even invited senior Chilean military officials to Washington DC.

Perhaps the most momentous foreign policy initiative of the Reagan administration was its decision to embark on a policy of supporting so-called 'freedom fighters'. Clandestine and military resources were mobilized on a global scale to support right-wing political organizations and militias to wage war against revolutionary governments in countries as diverse as Angola, Mozambique, Afghanistan and Nicaragua. Here again the events of September 11, 2001 are linked to this earlier period as the mujahidin guerrillas in Afghanistan became the largest recipients of US counter-revolutionary military assistance. Afghanistan was devastated by a war in the 1980s in which the United States provided billions of dollars in armaments. Once Soviet soldiers departed and the socialist government was overthrown, the United States abandoned the country. Afghanistan soon became a land of battling warlords and Islamic fundamentalists.

In the case of Nicaragua, the Reagan administration waged a war against the revolutionary Sandinista government by mobilizing thousands of former soldiers of dictator Anastasio Somoza's repressive National Guard. Using bases in Honduras to strike across the border, they inflicted atrocities on the civilian population that far exceeded any charges of human rights abuses the United States levelled against the Sandinistas. In 1984 the United States employed special operations forces (similar to those used in Afghanistan in 2001) to launch raids and set fire to oil storage depots in Puerto Corinto, Nicaragua's busiest port facility. As a result of these attacks, the Sandinista government filed charges against the United States in the World Court at the Hague for aggression and violation of the United Nations covenant. After the court accepted the Nicaraguan suit and ruled against the United States, the Reagan administration withdrew from the World Court, refusing to acknowledge or accept any of its rulings.

While scorning international law and supporting counter-revolutionary movements around the world, the Reagan administration in the mid-1980s made a U-turn in its policy of unswerving support for authoritarian regimes. Due to the growing radicalization of opposition movements in countries like Chile, the administration began to worry that these regimes might be toppled and replaced by revolutionary governments, as had occurred in Nicaragua when the Sandinistas overthrew Somoza. This explains Reagan's support for the opponents of Pinochet in the plebiscite in 1988, as well as US manoeuvring against dictators like Ferdinand Marcos in the Philippines and 'Baby Doc' Duvalier in Haiti.

The end of the Cold War and human rights

The world entered a new era in the 1990s with the fall of the Berlin Wall, the ousting of national liberation movements like the Sandinistas in Nicaragua, the implosion of the Soviet Union, and the departure from office of dictators like Pinochet. Francis Fukuyama has called this new age the 'end of history', meaning that market-oriented democracies have become the ascendant and desired form of governance throughout the world.

The end of the Cold War undoubtedly changed the world and the focus of inter-state rivalry, particularly for the Western world. Capitalism had triumphed globally and the leading powers along with their dominant elites recognized that their interests were intertwined. Any conflicts among them, like World Wars I and II, would be inherently self-destructive. Moreover, a greater opening emerged for taking up human rights issues. As Roberto Garretón notes:

> The tit for tat between the Soviet Union and the United States, the unending trade off over which of their allies would or would not be castigated for human rights abuses, had come to an end. The deadlock was broken. There was now a broader concern with human rights and humanitarian issues.[3]

In 1991 former UN secretary general Javier Pérez de Cuéllar probably put the most optimistic spin on this new era when he stated: 'We are clearly witnessing what is probably an irresistible shift in public attitudes toward the belief that the defense of the oppressed in the name of morality should prevail over frontiers and legal documents.'[4]

This did not mean that big power interventions and regional conflagrations ended, especially in the Third World and in areas of former Communist rule. However, the orchestration and rationale for these interventions did shift as Western Europe and the United States began to employ humanitarian and human rights rhetoric in their quest for a 'New World Order'. The latter term was first used by George Bush Senior as he called for a grand coalition to expel Saddam Hussein's invading Iraqi army from Kuwait. Although the coalition stopped short of ousting Hussein in Baghdad, Bush did declare a no-fly zone for Iraqi airplanes over parts of the country, allegedly to prevent Hussein from repressing religious and ethnic groups like the Kurds and the Shiite Muslims. In 1991 Bush also sent US troops into Somalia, this time in what appeared to be a more humanitarian intervention aimed at feeding the Somalis and imposing order on the country's warring factions.

Bill Clinton during his eight years in office repeatedly employed the discourse of human rights and humanitarianism as an integral part of his call for the development of 'market democracies'. At first, however, it appeared that his commitment to humanitarian concerns was even shallower than Bush's. When eighteen US soldiers were shot and dragged through the streets of Somalia, Clinton hastily withdrew the US military contingent. Then, when a genocidal war broke out in Rwanda in 1994, the Clinton administration dallied, allowing tens of thousands of Tutsi to be massacred by the Hutu, the dominant ethnic group.[5] Belatedly a French mission was sent to Rwanda, with US and UN backing; it did little.

However, there were advances in international law during the Clinton years in the pursuance and prosecution of those who had committed gross violations of human rights. In 1993 a war crimes tribunal was set up for Yugoslavia by the UN Security Council. The Yugoslav confederation had begun to break up in 1992; as the Croatians and Bosnians tried to establish their own republics, Serbian militias, often with assistance from the Yugoslav military dominated by Serbian officers, embarked on a practice of ethnic cleansing. Territorial slices of the new republics fell under Serbian control as systematic terror, looting and rape were used by the militias to eliminate and drive out non-Serbs. When other groups in the former Yugoslavian republics, particularly the Croats, also engaged in ethnic cleansing, the Yugoslav International Tribunal began issuing indictments against the leaders involved in these atrocities as well.[6]

In 1994 the UN Security Council approved another resolution setting up a tribunal for Rwanda. In this case, however, its mandate was not as broad as that of the Yugoslav tribunal. In Rwanda there was a set time period for the tribunal's operations, and indictments were issued only against those involved in the massacre. There was no legal jurisdiction for pursuing others in Rwanda who might have committed human rights abuses, including the Tutsi.[7]

The first major intervention by the Clinton administration in the name of humanitarianism and human rights occurred in Haiti. In 1991 Haitian military leaders, many of whom had once backed the bloody rule of the Duvalier family, overthrew the democratically elected government of Jean-Bertrand Aristide. Many popular organizations in Haiti, like the National Popular Assembly, believe that the Bush administration and the CIA were behind the coup, although their complicity has never been proven. It is, however, widely recognized that after the coup US operatives supported leaders of FRAPH, a paramilitary organization that terrorized supporters of Aristide, slaughtering hundreds of innocent individuals in raids on local communities. The head of FRAPH, Emmanuel 'Toto' Constant, was on the payroll of the CIA.[8]

During the Clinton administration, however, the Haitian military regime came to be recognized as an unmitigated disaster for US interests. Brutal repression was the regime's only means of holding on to power, as it had no internal legitimacy. With the imposition of international trade sanctions, Haiti's already devastated economy continued to deteriorate, and as a result thousands of Haitians flooded to US shores, provoking an immigration crisis.[9] The regime was isolated internationally, and under these conditions the Clinton administration, with the backing of the United Nations and the Organization of American States, called for the restoration of Aristide. Under threat of an outright invasion in mid-1994 the Haitian military finally agreed to relinquish power. In September 1994, US troops peacefully occupied the country, bringing back Aristide and ensuring a relatively tranquil transition that included the dismantling of FRAPH.

This was the first US occupation of a Latin American country that mitigated human rights abuses and restored an authentic democracy. However, after the invasion the United States did little to bring to justice those who had engaged in systematic violations of human rights. Indeed, as part of the deal allowing US troops to enter Haiti without resistance, the key military leaders, including members of FRAPH, were allowed to leave the country and seek refuge abroad, with some of them going to the United States.

US intervention in Haiti also demonstrated the contradiction between the interests of economic globalization and the consolidation of authentic democratic institutions. Aristide, once back in power, was compelled to accept much of the US agenda, including the privatization of public enterprises and the acceptance of IMF-imposed neoliberal policies. Most of the radical democratic reforms Aristide promised upon taking office in 1991 were never implemented. As a result Lavalas, the popular movement founded by Aristide, veered from its progressive platform. Under Aristide and his hand-picked successor, René Preval, many committed leaders of Lavalas broke with the movement. Both presidents, including a re-elected Aristide in 2001, became consumed with the demands placed on them by international interests while trying to consolidate their own hold on power by creating and catering to an elite group of supporters at home.

After the intervention in Haiti, the Clinton administration, along with most of the Western European states, shifted their focus to Yugoslavia. The intervention of the dominant powers in Yugoslavia soon demonstrated that while the issue of human rights had become a major factor in international relations, 'humanitarian interventions' would be orchestrated primarily to advance the interests of the dominant nation-states. While the United States and Western Europe called for an end to genocide and 'ethnic cleansing', their primary concern was to impose social and economic stability on the region. This concern led to the Dayton Accords, a pact with the Devil, since the main regional power broker they relied upon to implement the accords was Slobodan Milošević, the president of what remained of the Yugoslav republic. The Dayton agreement did virtually nothing to bring peace to the region or to stop ethnic cleansing. The Serb militias, Milošević, and the strong-arm ruler of Croatia, Franjo Tudjman, continued to violate the fundamental rights of the peoples of the former Yugoslav republics.[10]

However, while the big powers were conducting their interventions in the name of humanitarianism, an ever-expanding number of non-governmental organizations became involved in the promotion of human rights. Indeed, the very human rights parlance used by governments had reinforced a broader popular advocacy and acceptance of the importance of human rights in international relations. As Mary Kaldor points out, civil society on a global level became engaged in human rights issues. For Kaldor civil society consists 'of groups, individuals and institutions which are independent of the state and of state boundaries, but which are, at the same time pre-occupied with public affairs.' Kaldor adds: 'To be part of civil society implies a shared commitment to common human values and, in this sense, the concept of global civil society might be equated with the notion of a global human rights culture.'[11]

The ascent of a global civil society concerned with atrocities and issues of torture and genocide provided the broad ambience needed for human rights organizations, lawyers and jurists to argue and advance human rights cases in the courts in the 1990s. This is the backdrop to understanding why the Pinochet affair exploded on the international scene in 1998.

Pinochet and advances in international law

The arrest of Pinochet shifted the terms of the international debate over human rights and human rights interventions while represent-ing the cause célèbre of a human rights movement that acted inde-pendently of the state and state interests. Joan Garcés, the Spanish lawyer who first took the Pinochet case to an obscure judge in Valencia in 1996, and members of Amnesty International who helped orchestrate Pinochet's arrest in London, were part of this growing movement based in civil society that insisted justice has no borders. Then the rulings by the British House of Lords that Pinochet could be extradited to Spain to stand trial reflected just how deeply the consciousness of civil society had penetrated into the hallowed halls of one of the oldest tribunals in the world.

Following the ruling against Pinochet, other national leaders who had engaged in state-sponsored terrorism were pursued and some were indicted. Judge Garzón, who requested the extradition of Pinochet, also ordered the arrest of Argentine military officers who murdered or disappeared upwards of 30,000 people in that country's 'dirty war' from 1976 to 1983. Perhaps the most interesting case in regard to Argentina is that of Ricardo Miguel Cavallo, who went to Mexico after the Argentine military abandoned power and became director of Mexico's national motor-vehicle registry. When Garzón requested the extradition of Cavallo to stand trial in Spain for his crimes against humanity, a Mexican judge ordered his detention and approved the extradition request.

Pinochet's arrest also affected other countries and continents. In Africa, a Senegalese court indicted the former dictator of Chad, Hissène Habré, placing him under house arrest in 1999 for the torture and deaths of hundreds of victims. Dutch courts prosecuted former Suriname dictator Desi Bouterse on charges of torture.[12] Even US officials began to collaborate with requests for the prosecution of human rights offenders. When Haitian courts tried and convicted *in absentia* former military officers for human rights abuses, the US Immigration and Naturalization Service (INS) detained Carl Dorelien, a former colonel of the Haitian Army living in the United States, who had participated in summary executions and gross violations of human rights in Haiti. While the US government did nothing to bring Emmanuel Constant to justice, allowing him to continue residing in the United States, the Clinton administration began to collaborate with the legal efforts to prosecute Pinochet, ordering the declassification of US documents relating to his years in power.

In the wake of the Pinochet affair, human rights organizations began campaigns to bring other gross violators of human rights to justice. Human Rights Watch, for example, called for the arrest of Uganda's Idi Amin, residing in Saudi Arabia; Ethiopia's Mengistu Haile Mariam in Zimbabwe; Paraguay's Alfredo Stroessner in Brazil; and Haiti's Emmanuel 'Toto' Constant in the United States.[13] Perhaps the most fascinating consequences of the Pinochet affair were the calls for the arrest of Henry Kissinger for his involvement in genocidal activities in countries ranging from Cambodia and East Timor to Chile. French and Chilean courts issued orders for the interrogation of Kissinger relating to Operation Condor and the murder of US journalist Charles Horman in Chile in 1973. Small wonder that Kissinger wrote an article in *Foreign Affairs* decrying the use of the principle of 'universal jurisdiction' to apprehend human rights violators.[14]

A critical event in the advance of human rights law occurred in August 1998, two months before the arrest of Pinochet, when 120 nations signed a treaty in Rome calling for an International Criminal

Court (ICC). The court would have the power to prosecute 'the most serious crimes of international concern' – such as genocide, crimes against humanity and war crimes – when domestic criminal justice systems failed to act. The ICC would also have jurisdiction over the crime of aggression and state terrorism. The United States was among seven countries in Rome that voted against the treaty, on the grounds that its military officials should be exempt from prosecution by the ICC.

However, less than a year after the ICC treaty and Pinochet's arrest, the launching of the NATO war against Yugoslavia demonstrated that the dominant powers, allegedly in the name of human rights, would engage in military actions that violated international law and take a heavy toll on civilian populations. When Milošević tightened his grip on Kosovo, a province of the Yugoslav Republic, and embarked on a sustained military campaign against the Kosovo Liberation Army (KLA), the Clinton administration mobilized the NATO alliance. Unlike the intervention in Haiti, the United Nations did not pass a resolution supporting the war against Yugoslavia. The NATO intervention even violated the NATO charter, as it only permits defensive actions if any NATO country is directly attacked.

A secondary but troubling aspect of the Yugoslav war was that it provoked divisions within the human rights community. Most human rights advocates and organizations were adamantly opposed to the intervention. As Noam Chomsky argued, this was a war in which 'the aggressors have kicked aside the UN, opening a new era where might is right'.[15] Robin Blackburn pointed out in detail that the war caused a greater human catastrophe due to aerial bombings and the subsequent ethnic cleansing of Serbians in Kosovo by KLA elements than the actions Milošević and the Yugoslav military had carried out.[16]

Others, who had previously supported human rights causes, made what could be called a Faustian pact by endorsing the NATO war against Yugoslavia, arguing that intervention by the big powers had to be accepted as the only option at the current historical juncture. At the official level, the vociferous endorsement of the war by German Foreign Minister Joschka Fischer of the Green Party represented a betrayal of the principles of non-intervention that he and his party had stood for in the past. Fred Halliday, a progressive professor in International Relations at the London School of Economics, wrote that it is not sufficient to rely on the Pinochet precedent or the establishment of the ICC, that the NATO intervention could be justified because there needed to 'be an overlap between self-interest and humanitarian action'.[17] For Halliday the principal issue was whether the Yugoslav intervention made pragmatic sense.

Within months after the end of the Yugoslav war, Milošević lost a presidential re-election bid, was imprisoned in Belgrade, and was then whisked away to stand trial before the Yugoslav Tribunal in the Hague for his crimes against humanity. In a certain sense, the Yugoslav war had played upon the two countervailing tendencies that had emerged in the struggle in the 1990s over how to deal with human rights abuses.

On the one hand is the globalist school that advocates the use of international tribunals, extradition treaties and the apprehension of human rights violators by police and by limited international security force. The Pinochet affair as well as the extradition of Milošević to the Hague reflected this tendency.

On the other hand, the NATO war against Yugoslavia demonstrated the increasing determination of the dominant powers to violate international treaties and to pursue their own narrow interests by using the façade and rhetoric of humanitarianism and human rights. The world's only superpower, the United States, is the most blatant example of this tendency, often deciding unilaterally how to pursue its particular interests and then mobilizing any international support it can find to support its actions. In its waning days in office, the Clinton administration made a diplomatic nod to the globalist school by conditionally signing the ICC treaty, but it also stated that it would not ratify the accord unless US military officials were exempt from prosecution, an exemption that most other signatories of the treaty refused to approve.

George W. Bush, like Ronald Reagan exactly two decades before, came into office bent on tossing out the limited concessions to human rights concerns made by the preceding administration. Bush proclaimed that he would follow what was essentially a unilateralist agenda, even if that meant violating international treaties and widely accepted human rights norms. In its early months in office the Bush administration declared that it would not ratify the ICC, that it would tear up the Anti-Ballistic Missile Treaty, and that the Kyoto Accords on curtailing greenhouse gas emissions were unacceptable. Then, in the aftermath of the attacks on the World Trade Center and the Pentagon on September 11, 2001, the Bush administration used the event and the subsequent war against al-Qaeda to violate fundamental civil liberties and human rights at home and abroad. Like many advocates of a world based on law rather than violence, Judge Baltasar Garzón decried the US war in Afghanistan, proclaiming that 'lasting peace and freedom can be achieved only with legality, justice, respect for diversity, defense of human rights and measured and fair responses.'[18] Within the United States, thousands of immigrants were detained and held for months with no hearings or right to due process. On behalf of the administration, Attorney General John Ashcroft announced that the United States would use special US military tribunals to try, and even execute, members of al-Qaeda and the Taliban. Many captured prisoners in Afghanistan were sent to the US military base in Guantánamo, Cuba, where they were interrogated and held under abusive conditions with no rights. This situation was so appalling that the OAS Inter-American Commission on Human Rights, which normally bows to US interests, ruled that the Bush administration was required by the Geneva Convention to file formal charges against the hundreds of Taliban and al-Qaeda detainees at Guantánamo Bay.[19]

Yet even in the midst of the so called 'war against terror', judges around the world remain determined to see that international justice is carried out. In mid-February 2003, Belgium's highest court ruled that Prime Minister Ariel Sharon of Israel could be prosecuted in Belgian courts for the 1982 massacres of Palestinian refugees in occupied Lebanon while Sharon was Minister of Defence of Israel. Although the court ruled that Sharon could not be prosecuted until he left office as prime minister, it did decree that proceedings could begin against Amos Yaron, the former head of the Israeli Army in 1982, for 'crimes against humanity'.[20]

The war in Iraq presented new and difficult challenges for the human rights movement. Clearly the US-led invasion flouted a series

of international covenants and treaties, including the very charter of
the United Nations, which does not allow for 'pre-emptive' wars.
Iraqi citizens attempted to use the same Belgian laws that were used
to prosecute the Israelis to file suit against the US commander of the
invasion, Tommy Franks. They charged that troops under his command stood idly by while hospitals in Baghdad were looted, while
other US soldiers fired on ambulances that were carrying wounded
civilians. The Bush administration reacted angrily, threatening the
Belgian government with 'diplomatic consequences' if it allowed the
case to go forward.[21]

Then, when US Secretary of Defense Donald Rumsfeld attended
a meeting at NATO headquarters in Brussels in June 2003, he
threatened to end US financing for new NATO facilities and to
move the headquarters to another country if the Belgian government
did not intervene to suspend the court cases.[22] Undoubtedly, as we
achieve some distance from the war, and perhaps a 'regime change'
in the United States, investigations will be held and charges brought
against the US invaders of Iraq in other countries for their human
rights abuses and lies about the war, perhaps even in US courts.

The struggle is joined. The years to come will focus on the great
divide over basic human rights that became pronounced after September 11, 2001. On the one side stands an arrogant unilateralist
clique in the United States that engages in state terrorism and human
rights abuses while tearing up international treaties and paying lip
service to human rights. On the other is a global movement determined to advance a broad conception of human rights and human
dignity by using human rights law, extradition treaties and limited
policing activities. It is fundamentally a struggle over where globalization will take us, whether the powerful economic and political
interests of the world headed by reactionary US leaders will create
a new world order that relies on great power intervention and state
terrorism, or whether a globalist perspective from below based on
a more just and egalitarian conception of the world will gain
ascendancy.

Notes

Introduction

1. There was to a certain extent a third option for Allende, the possibility
that a coup attempt would be frustrated and he would be able to get rid
of the rebellious officers while maintaining Chile's democratic institutions. Early on September 11, Allende initially entertained some hope
that this might be the case. General José María Sepúlveda, the head of
the Chilean national police (the Carabineros), along with a small
contingent of officers, came to the palace to defend the government.
But when Allende asked them for a report on loyal sectors of the military, they admitted that they were cut off even from the national police
forces and that the authority of Sepúlveda had been effectively usurped
by General Cesar Mendoza, the eighth ranking officer of the Carabineros.
Other loyal officers, like Admiral Raúl Montero, the head of the Navy,
were arrested before they could leave their houses on the morning of
the 11th. Patricia Verdugo, *Interferencia Secreta: 11 de Septiembre de 1973*,
8th edn, Editorial Sudamericana Chilena, Santiago 1998, pp. 43, 52–3.

2. For an extended analysis of the collapse of socialism in Chile and Latin
America, see Roger Burbach, 'Socialism is Dead, Long Live Socialism',
NACLA Report on the Americas, November–December 1997.

Chapter 1

Special thanks to Claudio Duran for his assistance in working on an
early draft of this chapter in 1999.

1. Hugh O'Shaughnessy, *Pinochet: The Politics of Torture*, New York University Press, New York 2000, pp. 73, 159–60.

2. Brian Loveman, *Chile: The Legacy of Hispanic Capitalism*, Oxford University Press, New York 1988, pp. 47, 56, 103.

3. Even Judge Juan Guzmán, who is of aristocratic origins and has studied Chilean history, acknowledged in a wide-ranging interview that the military 'have always been instructed by the plutocracy – the wealthy class.... The army has been used many times.' See Roger Burbach 'The Man Who Brought General Pinochet to Justice: Interview with Chilean Judge Juan Guzmán', transcript of interview with Guzmán, January 2001.

4. Seymour M. Hersh, *The Price of Power: Kissinger in the Nixon White House*, Summit Books, New York 1983, p. 259.

5. Interview with Joan Garcés, June 1999.

6. William Blum, *The CIA: A Forgotten History. US Global Interventions since World War II*, Zed Books, London 1986, p. 232.

7. Pamela Constable and Arturo Valenzuela, *A Nation of Enemies: Chile under Pinochet*, W.W. Norton, New York 1991, p. 23.

8. Blum, *The CIA*, p. 235.

9. Hersh, *The Price of Power*, p. 268.

10. Ibid., pp. 269, 274.

11. Loveman, *Chile*, p. 295.

12. Hersh, *The Price of Power*, p. 284.

13. Blum, *The CIA*, p. 243.

14. Hersh, *The Price of Power*, pp. 294–5.

15. 'Carter and the Generals, Human Rights in the Southern Cone', *NACLA Report on the Americas*, vol. 3, no. 1, March–April 1979, p. 37.

16. See NACLA, *New Chile*, North American Congress on Latin America, Berkeley 1972.

17. For a description of the policies and programmes of the Popular Unity government by many of its participants, see J. Ann Zammit, ed., *The Chilean Road to Socialism*, proceedings of an ODEPLAN–IDS Round Table, March 1972, Institute of Development Studies, University of Sussex, 1973.

18. See Elizabeth Farnsworth, Richard Feinberg and Eric Leenson, 'Chile: Facing the Blockade', *NACLA's Latin America and Empire Report*, vol. 7, no. 1, January, 1973.

19. Michael Fleet, *The Rise and Fall of Chilean Christian Democracy*, Princeton University Press, Princeton 1985, pp. 165–7.

20. Blum, *The CIA*, p. 241.

21. Mónica González, *La conjura, los mil y un días del golpe*, Ediciones B Chile, Santiago 2000, pp. 311, 321, 325.

22. Patricia Verdugo, *Interferencia Secreta, 11 de Septiembre de 1973*, 8th edn, Editorial Sudamericana Chilena, Santiago 1998, p. 35.

23. Ibid., p. 65.
24. Ibid., pp. 67–9.
25. Ibid., p. 59.
26. Ibid., pp. 107–8.
27. Ibid., p. 112.
28. Ibid., p. 132.
29. González, *La conjura*, pp. 364, 370.

Chapter 2

1. Mónica González, *La conjura, los mil y un días del golpe*, Ediciones B Chile, Santiago 2000, p. 405.
2. Pablo Azócar, *Pinochet: epitafio para un tirano*, Editorial Cuarto Propio, Santiago 1999, p. 131.
3. Eduardo Deves, 'Las cuatro vidas de Augusto Pinochet', unpublished manuscript, Santiago, pp. 8–11.
4. Azócar, *Pinochet*, p. 48
5. Ian Kershaw, *Hitler, 1889–1936: Hubris*, W.W. Norton, New York 1999, pp. 11–13.
6. Raquel Correa and Elizabeth Subercaseaux, *Ego Sum*, Editorial Planeta Chilena, Santiago 1986, p. 39.
7. Kershaw, *Hitler*, p. xxv.
8. Deves, 'Las cuatro vidas de Augusto Pinochet', pp. 26–7.
9. Ibid., p. 33.
10. Correa and Subercaseaux, *Ego Sum*, pp. 49–50.
11. Azócar, *Pinochet*, p. 87.
12. *The Columbian Encyclopedia*, 6th edn, 2001, www.bartleby.com/65/ib/Ibanezde.html.
13. Azócar, *Pinochet*, p. 59.
14. Correa and Subercaseaux, *Ego Sum*, p. 53.
15. Andy Beckett, *Pinochet in Piccadilly: Britain and Chile's Hidden History*, Faber & Faber, London 2002, p. 224.
16. Correa and Subercaseaux, *Ego Sum*, p. 52.
17. Stated in 'The Pinochet Case', documentary film directed by Patricio Guzmán.
18. *Encyclopedia of World History*, 'Chile, 1932–45', Bartleby.com, online 2001 edition. www.bartleby.com/67/2247.html.
19. Carmelo Furci, *The Chilean Communist Party and the Road to Socialism*, Zed Books, London 1984, pp. 27, 33.
20. Azócar, *Pinochet*, p. 69, 73. Interview with Patricia Lutz, December 2002.
21. Interview with Patricia Lutz, December 2002.
22. Interview with Federico Willoughby, April 2002.

23. Interview with Patricia Lutz, December 2002; interview with Francisco Para, December 2002.

24. Patricia Lutz often went to the Pinochet home to baby-sit the Pinochet's youngest daughter, Jacqueline, who was named after Jacqueline Kennedy. Lutz is writing an unauthorized biography of Pinochet. Patricia Lutz in *Mujer a Mujer* (weekly magazine published in Santiago), May 18, 2002. See also Patricia Lutz, *Años de Viento Sucio*, Editorial Planeta Sur, Santiago 1999.

25. Interview with Federico Willoughby, April 2002.

26. *Mujer a Mujer*, May 18, 2002.

27. Based on an evaluation arrived at after extensive interviews concerning Pinochet's character, and discussions with my sister, Ann Burbach, who holds a doctorate in psychology.

28. Interview with Eduardo Deves, December 2002. See also Hugh O'Shaughnessy, *Pinochet: The Politics of Torture*, New York University Press, New York 2000, p. 24.

29. Manuel Araya Villegas, *Biografía de su Excelencia el Presidente de la República y miembros de la Honorable Junta de Gobierno. Perfiles de Honor*, Teltrapre, Santiago 1984, p. 197.

30. Interview with Patricia Lutz, December 2002.

31. Augusto Pinochet Ugarte, *Camino recorrido: memorias de un soldado*, Vol. 1, Instituto Geográfico Militar de Chile, Santiago 1990, p. 118.

32. Araya Villegas, *Biografía*, p. 201.

33. Pinochet, *Camino recorrido*, Vol. 1, p. 121.

34. Interview with Patricia Lutz, December 2002.

35. Augusto Pinochet Ugarte, *The Crucial Day, September 11, 1973*, English edn, Editorial Renacimiento, Santiago 1982, p. 39.

36. O'Shaughnessy, *Pinochet*, p. 26.

37. Augusto Pinochet Ugarte, *Síntesis geográfica de la República de Chile*, Instituto Geográfico Militar de Chile, Santiago 1963.

38. Augusto Pinochet Ugarte, *Geopolítica*, 3rd edn, Editorial Andrés Bello, Santiago 1977, pp. 23, 59, 61.

39. Azócar, *Pinochet*, pp. 152–3.

40. Ibid., p. 157.

41. Deves, 'Las cuatro vidas de Augusto Pinochet', p. 91; based on 1969 Iquique newspaper reports and statements made by Pinochet to the press.

42. Pinochet, *Camino recorrido*, Vol. 1, p. 194.

43. Deves, 'Las cuatro vidas de Augusto Pinochet', p. 91; quotes from 1969 Iquique newspaper stories.

44. Pinochet, *Camino recorrido*, Vol. 1, p. 195.

45. http://icarito.tercera.cl/biografias/1958–1999/bios/schneider.htm.

46. According to the Church Select Committee Intelligence Hearings, 1975, there is a dispute over the CIA role in the assault and whether it wanted

to kidnap or assassinate him.

47. Deves, 'Las cuatro vidas de Augusto Pinochet', p. 92; quote from 1969 Iquique newspaper stories.
48. González, *La conjura*, p. 119.
49. Deves, 'Las cuatro vidas de Augusto Pinochet', p. 93.2; as quoted in the newspaper *Puro Chile*, December 5, 1971.
50. Ibid., p. 93.3.
51. The 'crucial day' refers to September 11, 1973.
52. Pinochet, *The Crucial Day*, pp. 73, 75.
53. See González, *La conjura*. A basic thesis of her book is that Pinochet deeply resented the early coup plotters, and methodically proceeded to eliminate virtually all of them, either physically or by removing them from his government.
54. González, *La conjura*, pp. 159–61.
55. Azócar, *Pinochet*, p. 103.
56. Ibid., pp. 92–3.
57. I witnessed this demonstration while living in Santiago in August 1973, just a few houses away from the Prats' residence.
58. González, *La conjura*, p. 256.
59. Ibid., p. 305.
60. Ibid., p. 311.
61. Pinochet, *The Crucial Day*, p. 120.
62. Gonzalo Vial, *Pinochet: la biografía*, Vol. 1, Empresa El Mercurio, Santiago 2002, pp. 215–16.

Chapter 3

1. Maria Eugenia Oyarzun, *Conversaciones inéditas, Augusto Pinochet: diálogos con su historia*, Editorial Sudamericana Chilena, Santiago 1999, p. 143.
2. During the aftermath of the coup I witnessed much of the anti-communist hysteria that swept the country, although I was fortunate not to be detained or imprisoned. In addition to Teruggi, my good friend Charles Horman also died.
3. Interview with Mónica González, December 2002.
4. Maria Olivia Monekeberg, *El saqueo de los grupos económicos al Estado Chileno*, Ediciones B Chile, Santiago 2001, p. 260.
5. Seymour M. Hersh, *The Price of Power: Kissinger in the Nixon White House*, Summit Books, New York 1983, p. 260.
6. Gonzalo Vial, *Pinochet: la biografía*, Vol. 1, Empresa El Mercurio, Santiago 2002, p. 222.
7. Patricia Lutz, *Mujer a Mujer*, May 18, 2002.
8. Gonzalo Vial, *Pinochet*, Vol. 1, p. 223.
9. Ibid.

10. The word *pericos* is a demeaning term in Chile, indicating someone who talks a lot of nonsense while trying to display his plumage.
11. Paz Rojas, Viviana Uribe, Maria Eugenia Rojas, Iris Largo, Isabel Ropert and Víctor Espinoza, *Páginas en Blanco: El 11 de Septiembre en La Moneda*, Ediciones B Chile, Santiago 2001, pp. 40–41, 51, 54, 59.
12. Ibid., pp. 41, 45–7, 56–7.
13. Interview with Paz Rojas, December 2002. See also Paz Rojas et.al., *Páginas en Blanco*, p. 49.
14. Interview with Paz Rojas, December 2002.
15. Interview with Patricia Lutz, December 2002.
16. Ibid.
17. Patricia Verdugo, *La Caravana de la Muerte: pruebas a la vista*, Editorial Sudamericana Chilena, Santiago 2000, p. 16.
18. Vial, *Pinochet*, Vol. 1, p. 234.
19. Mónica González, *La conjura, los mil y un días del golpe*, Ediciones B Chile, S.A., Santiago 2000, p. 431.
20. Ibid. pp. 432–3.
21. Vial, *Pinochet*, Vol. 1, p. 235.
22. Carlos Huneeus, *El régimen de Pinochet*, Editorial Sudamericana Chilena, Santiago 2000, p. 105.
23. Vial, *Pinochet*, Vol. 1, p. 236.
24. Huneeus, *El régimen de Pinochet*, p. 108.
25. It should be noted that DINA only existed for less than four of those sixteen years. See Elías Padilla Ballesteros, *La memoria y el olvido: detenidos desaparecidos en Chile*, Ediciones Orígenes, Santiago 1995, p. 54.
26. Gonzalo Vial, in his two-volume study of Pinochet, records many of DINA's and the dictator's crimes. But Vial attempts to place Pinochet alongside the great leaders of the past by arguing that 'men who modify history are by "nature extraordinarily large" figures, … of enormous qualities, and (not uncommonly) of profound ethic failures'. Vial then proceeds to place Pinochet in the pantheon of past Chilean leaders 'like O'Higgins, José Miguel Carrera, Portales, Arturo Alessandri…' (Vial, *Pinochet*, Vol. 2, pp. 731–2, and jacket of Volume 2.) It is patently absurd for Vial to discuss Pinochet alongside Bernardo O'Higgins, the great liberator of Chile, a man who had his demons but never engaged in barbaric practices like those of Pinochet and Contreras. Carrera's troops in 1820 did ravage a town in Argentina, but this occurred in the midst of a cruel war for independence in which both sides committed atrocities. Many other Chilean presidents had flaws and committed abuses, but all of them pale in comparison to the crimes of the Pinochet era.
27. Hugh O'Shaughnessy, *Pinochet: The Politics of Torture*, New York University Press, New York 2000, p. 123.
28. Interview with Edmundo Lebrecht, former MIR member, December 2002.

29. Ascanio Caballo, Manuel Salazar and Oscar Sepúlveda, *La historia oculta del régimen militar: memoria de una época, 1973–1988*, Editorial Grijalbo, Santiago 1997, p. 47.
30. González, *La conjura*, p. 473.
31. Caballo et al., *La historia oculta*, p. 60.
32. González, *La conjura*, p. 455.
33. Caballo et al., *La historia oculta*, pp. 31–2.
34. González, *La conjura*, p. 469.
35. Huneeus, *El régimen de Pinochet*, p. 107.
36. I spoke with Letelier in Washington shortly before his death. Later, FBI agents who were intent on finding a 'leftist connection' to the assassination interrogated friends of mine who worked in news and solidarity organizations.
37. Vial, *Pinochet*, Vol. 1, p. 250.

Chapter 4

1. See National Security Archive, Department of State, Chilean Executions, November 16, 1973.
2. See Jonathan Power, *Amnesty International: The Human Rights Story*, Pergamon Press, Oxford and New York 1981.
3. Ibid., p. 23.
4. Mark Ensalaco, *Chile under Pinochet: Uncovering the Truth*, University of Pennsylvania Press, Philadelphia 2000, p. 100.
5. Ibid., p. 105.
6. Elizabeth Quay Hutchinson and Patricio Orellana, *El movimiento de derechos humanos en Chile, 1973–1990*, Centro de Estudios Políticos Latinoamericanos Simón Bolívar (CEPLA), Santiago 1991, p. 93.
7. See the FASIC website: www.fasic.org.
8. Brian H. Smith, 'Old Allies, New Enemies: The Catholic Church as Opposition to Military Rule in Chile, 1973–1979', in J. Samuel Valenzuela and Arturo Valenzuela, eds, *Military Rule in Chile: Dictatorship and Oppositions*, Johns Hopkins University Press, Baltimore 1986, p. 284.
9. Hutchinson and Orellana, *El movimiento*, p. 94.
10. Ascanio Caballo, Manuel Salazar and Oscar Sepúlveda, *La historia oculta del régimen militar: memoria de una época, 1973–1988*, Editorial Grijalbo, Santiago 1997, p. 19.
11. Lars Schoultz, *Human Rights and the United States Policy in Latin America*, Princeton University Press, Princeton 1981, p. 12.
12. Margaret E. Keck and Kathryn Sikkink, *Activists Beyond Borders: Advocacy Networks in International Politics*, Cornell University Press, Ithaca NY, 1998, p. 91–92.
13. See for example 'Chile: The Story Behind the Coup', *NACLA's Latin*

America and Empire Report, vol. 7, no. 8, October 1973.

14. Hutchinson and Orellana, *El movimiento*, p. 40.
15. Keck and Sikkink, *Activists Beyond Borders*, p. 11.
16. Ibid. p. 104.
17. Schoultz, *Human Rights*, p. 106.
18. Ibid., pp. 52–3.
19. Caballo et al., *La historia oculta*, p. 111.
20. This story of the relocation of the Church's human rights work is based on an interview with Fernando Zegers, who worked as a lawyer for Copachi, the Vicariate, and later CODEPU. A chapter could be written alone on Fernando's human rights work on behalf of victims of the Pinochet regime, and on the sacrifices and threats to his own life that he incurred as a result of his work. Interestingly, Fernando's lineage in Chile dates back to Juan Francisco Zegers, the first foreign minister of Chile, whom Bernardo O'Higgins brought over from France to set up the ministry. Fernando's interviews and discussions with me were invaluable in composing this chapter and other parts of the book.
21. Hutchinson and Orellana, *El movimiento*, p. 9.
22. Schoultz, *Human Rights*, p. 113.
23. Ensalaco, *Chile under Pinochet*, p. 161.
24. Lucy Komisar, 'Kissinger Encouraged Chile's Brutal Repression, New Documents Show', *Albion Monitor*, March 8, 1999.
25. Schoultz, *Human Rights*, p. 4.
26. Cited in Hutchinson and Orellana, *El movimiento*, p. 101.
27. Ibid., p. 97.
28. Ibid.
29. Ensalaco, *Chile under Pinochet*, pp. 164–5.
30. Caballo et al., *La historia oculta*, p. 161.
31. Ensalaco, *Chile under Pinochet*, p. 169.
32. Cited in Hutchinson and Orellana, *El movimiento*, p. 48.
33. Interview with Fernando Zegers, April 2002.
34. Hutchinson and Orellana, *El movimiento*, pp. 105–6.
35. Interview with Fernando Zegers, January 2001.
36. Hutchinson and Orellana, *El movimiento*, p. 107.
37. Ibid., p. 40.
38. Ensalaco, *Chile under Pinochet*, p.136.
39. Cathy Lisa Schneider, *Shantytown Protest in Pinochet's Chile*, Temple University Press, Philadelphia 1995, pp. 173–5.
40. See Jeanne Kirkpatrick, *Dictatorships and Double Standards*, Simon & Schuster, New York 1982.
41. Ensalaco, *Chile under Pinochet*, p. 163.
42. Schneider, *Shantytown Protest*, pp. 176–80.
43. Ensalaco, *Chile under Pinochet*, p. 137.
44. Ibid., 139–41.

NOTES 169

45. Cited in William I. Robinson, *Promoting Polyarchy: Globalization, US Intervention, and Hegemony*, Cambridge University Press, Cambridge 1996, p. 168.
46. Ensalaco, *Chile under Pinochet*, p. 175.
47. See Robinson, *Promoting Polyarchy*.
48. Ibid., p. 187.
49. Ibid., p. 190.
50. Ibid., pp. 180–81.
51. Pinochet's comportment during this attack revealed the cowardly behaviour that he had displayed on other occasions, albeit in a less dramatic fashion. A number of sources report that when the first gunfire erupted Pinochet threw himself on the floor of the Mercedes Benz he was riding in and had his bodyguards lie on top of him. He totally ignored the fate of his 9-year-old grandson who was in the car with him. In fact it was the grandson who threw open the curtains inside the Mercedes so that the chauffeur could use the rear-view mirror to back the car up and avoid further assaults, thereby saving the lives of those in the vehicle. (The exterior mirror on the driver's side of the car had been rendered unusable because of the initial attack.) Pinochet later proclaimed that at the time of the assault he had a vision of the Virgin Mary, who had come to save him. Account based in part on interview with Edmundo Lebrecht, former MIR member, December 2002. See also Patricia Verdugo and Carmen Hertz, *Operación Siglo XX*, Las Ediciones del Ornitorrinco, Santiago 1990, p. 164.
52. Schneider, *Shantytown Protest*, p. 187.
53. Hutchinson and Orellana, *El movimiento*, p. 113.
54. Ibid., p. 113.

Chapter 5

1. Mary Helen Spooner, *Soldiers in a Narrow Land: The Pinochet Regime in Chile*, University of California Press, Los Angeles and Berkeley 1994, p. 241.
2. Pablo Azócar, *Pinochet: epitafio para un tirano*, Editorial Cuarto Propio, Santiago 1999.
3. Based on the account of Roger Burbach, who was among the demonstrators in the aftermath of the plebiscite.
4. Rafael Otano, *Crónica de la transición*, Editorial Planeta Chilena, Santiago 1995, p. 74.
5. Pamela Constable and Arturo Valenzuela, *A Nation of Enemies: Chile under Pinochet*, W.W. Norton, New York 1991, p. 312.
6. Constitución Política de la República de Chile de 1980, Article 5 (1980).
7. Constable and Valenzuela, *A Nation of Enemies*, p. 318.

8. Peter M. Siavelis, *The President and Congress in Post Authoritarian Chile, Institutional Constraints to Democratic Consolidation*, Pennsylvania State University Press, University Park 2000, p. 33.

9. Constable and Valenzuela, *A Nation of Enemies*, p. 316.

10. According to Alexander Wilde, these and other 'ceremonies of reconciliation' were planned in the early years of the Aylwin administration to 'heal the wounds of the country's traumatic past'. Wilde charted the many charged moments during the 1990s that reminded the public of the previous decades of political conflict, arguing that as the decade progressed the transitional governments dropped their focus on expressive politics in exchange for forging agreements among political elites. See Alexander Wilde, 'Irruptions of Memory: Expressive Politics in Chile's Transition to Democracy', *Journal of Latin American Studies*, no. 31, 1999, pp. 473–500.

11. Patricia Verdugo, *Chile, Pinochet, and the Caravan of Death*, North–South Center Press, University of Miami, Coral Gables, FL 2001, p. 185.

12. Tomas Moulián, *Chile actual: anatomía de un mito*, Lom Ediciones, Santiago 1997, pp. 47–8.

13. 'Raúl Rettig: Lawyer Who Exposed the Crimes of Pinochet's Chile', *Guardian*, May 5, 2000.

14. David Weissbrodt and Paul W. Fraser, 'Book Review: Report of the Chilean National Commission on Truth and Reconciliation', *Human Rights Quarterly*, 1992, p. 603.

15. For an excellent commentary on the Rettig Report see Elías Padilla Ballesteros, *La memoria y el olvido: detenidos desaparecidos en Chile*, Ediciones Orígenes, Santiago 1995.

16. This bargain, or *pacto* – maintaining stability by fostering an elite-focused reconciliation – was one struck by Chilean political elites throughout history after periods of political instability and civil conflict. Corporación de Promoción y Defensa de los Derechos del Pueblo (CODEPU), *El irrenunciable camino de la justicia: Pinochet y la Mesa de Diálogo*, Serie Opinión y Perspectivas, No. 6, Santiago 2000, p. 42. See also Jorge Mera, 'Chile: Truth and Justice under the Democratic Government' in Naomi Roht-Arriaza, *Impunity and Human Rights in International Law and Practice*, Oxford University Press, New York 1995, pp. 174–5.

17. Elizabeth Lira and Brian Loveman, *Las suaves cenizas del olvido: La vía chilena de Reconciliación, 1814–1932*, DIBAM/LOM, Santiago 1999.

18. Human rights lawyers primarily presented cases about events that occurred after March 10, 1978, when the amnesty law didn't apply, to avoid dismissals. Under the Pinochet regime judges who found military officers culpable even after the period of the amnesty were generally declared incompetent and cases were referred to military courts, which dismissed them.

19. Gregory Weeks, 'Waiting for Cincinnatus: The Role of Pinochet in

Postauthoritarian Chile', paper prepared for presentation at the meeting of the Latin American Studies Association, Miami, March 2000, p. 11.

20. Felipe Portales, *Chile: una democracia tutelada*, Editorial Sudamericana Chilena, Santiago 2000, p. 234.
21. Human Rights Watch, 'Why Chile Won't Prosecute Pinochet', New York, November 11, 1998.
22. Mera, 'Chile: Truth and Justice', p. 181.
23. US Rep. Maurice Hinchey (D–NY) quoted in the *Washington Post*, 'House Democrats Urge Pinochet's Indictment', December 19, 2000.
24. Portales, *Chile: una democracia tutelada*, pp. 320–21.
25. Ibid., pp. 329, 335–6.
26. CODEPU, *Tortura durante la transición a la democracia: el trabajo de CODEPU en el período*. Serie Retrospectiva y Reflexión, No. 4, Santiago, June 1999.
27. Historically, the economic elites have been the real power in the country, despite Chile's democratic tradition. In a 2001 interview, Judge Juan Guzmán noted that the military in Chile 'have always been instructed by the plutocracy – the wealthy class.… The army has been used many times.' Roger Burbach, 'The Man Who Brought General Pinochet to Justice: Interview with Chilean Judge Juan Guzmán', quotation from transcript of interview with Guzmán, January 2001.
28. See Kenneth M. Roberts, *Deepening Democracy? The Modern Left and Social Movements in Chile and Peru*, Stanford University Press, Stanford, CA 1998.
29. R. Lucía Sepúlveda, 'Aylwin mató a la revista análisis', SERPAL (Servicio de Prensa Alternativa), January 21, 2003, carried in Boletín Piensa Chile, www.piensachile.com. See also Juan Pablo Cárdenas, *Contigo en la distancia*: crónicas diplomáticas, Cuarto Propio, Santiago 1998.
30. Otano, *Crónica de la transición*, p. 85.
31. Brian Turner, 'Judicial Protection of Human Rights in Latin America: Heroism and Pragmatism', in Mark Gibney and Stanislaw Frankowski, eds, *Judicial Protection of Human Rights: Myth or Reality?*, Praeger, Westport, CT 1999, p. 97.
32. 'Supreme Court Applies Geneva Conventions for the Disappeared', *El Mercurio*, September 11, 1998.
33. In addition, the Internet made censorship more difficult to sustain. In 1998, an investigative journalist, Alejandra Matus, published the *Black Book of Justice*. In it she criticizes judges during the dictatorship for ignoring human rights abuses. The book was censored, Matus left the country after threats and sedition charges were brought against her, and her publishers were arrested. Even so, the book continued to be read by Chileans because it was put on a non-Chilean website.
34. See CODEPU, *Foro de derechos humanos de la cumbre de los pueblos de América*, April 14–17, 1998, Lom Ediciones, Santiago 1998.

35. Agence France Presse, March 7, 1998.
36. 'Pinochet: The Great Conciliator', *NACLA Report on the Americas*, vol. 32, no. 2, September–October 1998, p. 5.
37. Ibid.

Chapter 6

Special thanks to Claudio Duran for his assistance in working on an early draft of this chapter in 1999.

1. Interview with Joan Garcés, June 1999.
2. Ibid.
3. Norbert Bermúdez and Juan Gasparini, *El testigo secreto: el Juez Garzón contra la impunidad en Argentina y Chile*, Javier Vergara Editor, Madrid 1999, pp. 15–17. Also based on interview with Carlos Slepoy, Argentine lawyer representing the Argentine victims before Judge Garzón, July 1999.
4. Interview with Joan Garcés, June 1999.
5. Ibid.
6. Bermúdez and Gasparini, *El testigo secreto*, pp. 20–22.
7. Ibid., p. 18.
8. 'Baltasar Garzón: Perfil de un Controvertido Juez', *Diario Estratégica*, Santiago, October 26, 1998. Also interview with Carlos Iriart, press secretary of Argentine Association in Spain, Madrid, July 1999.
9. Juan Francisco Coloane R., *Britannia y un general*, Lom Ediciones, Santiago 2000, pp. 58–61.
10. Andy Beckett, *Pinochet in Piccadilly: Britain and Chile's Hidden History*, Faber & Faber, London 2002, pp. 44–55.
11. Ibid., pp. 56–9.
12. Hugh O'Shaughnessy, *Pinochet: The Politics of Torture*, New York University Press, New York 2000, p. 4.
13. Beckett, *Pinochet in Piccadilly*, p. 230.
14. Interview with Andy McEntee, June 1999.
15. Ibid.
16. Interview with Vicente Alegría, July 1999.
17. Beckett, *Pinochet in Piccadilly*, p. 225.
18. Based on interviews in London with Andy McEntee, Vicente Alegría and Jeremy Corbyn, June and July 1999.
19. Interview with Jeremy Corbyn, June 1999.
20. Reports by Claudio Duran based on telephone conversations with family and friends in Chile in 1998 and 1999.
21. Pablo Azócar, *Pinochet: epitafio para un tirano*, Editorial Cuarto Propio, Santiago 1999, p. 42.
22. Interview with Elías Padilla, March 2000.

23. National Security Archive, Documents on Chile. See CIA, State, NSC
Documents Declassified on Chile, June 30, 1999.
24. Azócar, *Pinochet*, pp. 23–4.

Chapter 7

1. Juan Francisco Coloane R., *Britannia y un general*, Lom Ediciones, Santiago 2000, p. 163.
2. See Reed Brody, 'The Case of Augusto Pinochet', in Reed Brody and
Michael Ratner, eds, *The Pinochet Papers: The Case of Augusto Pinochet in
Spain and Britain*, Kluwer Law International, The Hague, London and
Boston 2000, p. 61.
3. Ibid.; see Document 10: The Second Provisional Arrest Warrant 222,
October 1998, pp. 67–9.
4. Interview with Jeremy Corbyn, July 1999.
5. Frances Webber, 'Justice and the General: People vs. Pinochet', *Race &
Class*, vol. 41, no. 4, 2000, Institute of Race Relations, p. 52.
6. Brody, 'The Case of Augusto Pinochet', p. 9.
7. At the time of the Pinochet case there were nineteen Law Lords. See
Online *Oxford Dictionary of Law*.
8. Webber, 'Justice and the General'. p. 53.
9. Brody, 'The Case of Augusto Pinochet', p. 9.
10. Webber, 'Justice and the General'. p. 54.
11. Brody, 'The Case of Augusto Pinochet', p. 10.
12. Webber, 'Justice and the General'. p. 54.
13. Brody, 'The Case of Augusto Pinochet', p. 10.
14. Interview with Jeremy Corbyn, June 1999.
15. Coloane, *Britannia y un general*, p. 174.
16. Interview with Andy McEntee, June 1999.
17. Coloane, *Britannia y un general*, p. 153.
18. Interview with Jeremy Corbyn, July 1999.
19. Interview with Vicente Alegría, July 1999.
20. Coloane, *Britannia y un general*, p. 154.
21. Interview with Vicente Alegría, July 1999.
22. 'Pinochet Law Lord Linked to Amnesty, *Guardian*, December 8, 1998.
23. Interview with Andy McEntee, July 1999.
24. Michael Ratner, 'The Lords Decision in Pinochet III', in Brody and
Ratner, eds, *The Pinochet Papers*, p. 39.
25. Coloane, *Britannia y un general*, p. 182.
26. 'La Jula de Oro', *El País*, March 25, 1999.
27. Clare Dyer, 'Pinochet Fails in Latest Bid to Fight Off Extradition',
Guardian, May 28, 1999.
28. Telephone interview with Michael Kaplan in London, July 1999.

29. *Guardian*, October 1, 1999.
30. Interview with Joan Garcés, November 1999.
31. See web page of Transnational Institute, www.tni.org/campaigns/
pinochet/watch/watch0810.htm.
32. *La Tercera*, October 25, 1998.
33. Fernando Mas, *De Nuremberg a Madrid: historia íntima de un juicio*, Grijalbo,
Buenos Aires 1999, p. 258.
34. Ibid., p. 262.
35. Ibid., p. 260.
36. Interview with Carlos Iriart, July 1999.
37. Coloane, *Britannia y un general*, p. 173.
38. 'The Long Road From Surrey to Santiago', *Guardian*, March 3, 2000.
39. Ibid.
40. Email from Joan Garcés, March 8, 2001.
41. In the second Blair government after the June 2001 elections Straw was
rewarded for his diplomatic manoeuvring to get Pinochet out of Great
Britain by being appointed to the post of Foreign Secretary. In 2002
and 2003 he acted as Blair's right hand man in pushing for war with
Iraq.

Chapter 8

1. Roger Burbach, 'Pinochet's Trial and Tribulations', *Connection to the
Americas*, The Resource Center of the Americas, Minneapolis, MN,
April 2000.
2. Interview with Elias Padilla, March 2000.
3. I witnessed this event in Chile in March 2000, attending the concert as
well as the Lagos inauguration.
4. Interview with José Bengoa, March 2000.
5. Corporación de Promoción y Defensa de los Derechos del Pueblo,
(CODEPU), *El irrenunciable camino de la justicia: Pinochet y la Mesa de
Diálogo*, Serie Opinión y Perspectivas, No. 6, Santiago 2000, p. 58. See
also Patricia Verdugo, *La Caravana de la Muerte: pruebas a la vista*, Editorial Sudamericana Chilena, Santiago 2000, p. 18.
6. Mónica Madariaga is an example of the civilians who are clearly impli-
cated in the crimes of the Pinochet era, but who have managed to
escape prosecution. Well aware of the pervasive human rights abuses of
DINA, Madariaga as Minister of Justice and Pinochet's cousin was also
a close personal confidante of the general throughout the 1970s. But in
the mid-1980s she finally opted to begin questioning some of the new
abuses of the regime, just as the Reagan administration was beginning
to turn against Pinochet. Because of this she was compelled to resign
her final post, ambassador to the Organization of American States.

Pinochet refused to talk to her for years. Recently, however, after opposing his prosecution in Europe as well as in Chile, she has renewed her friendship with Pinochet. She refused my requests to be interviewed, asking at one point over the telephone if I was willing to pay her to talk with me.

7. 'The Legal Case Against Chile's Ex-Dictator is Getting Stronger all the Time', *Guardian*, August 10, 2000.
8. Ibid.
9. Interview with Juan Guzmán, January 2001.
10. Ibid.
11. Ibid.
12. 'El hombre que cerco a Pinochet', *Que Pasa*, May 27, 2000.
13. CODEPU, *El irrenunciable camino de la justicia*, p. 58.
14. *La Tercera*, May 30, 2000.
15. *La Tercera*, June 7, 2000.
16. *La Tercera*, August 9, 2000. See also *El Mostrador*, August 8 and 9, 2000.
17. Insulza also served as Minister of Foreign Relations during the government of Eduardo Frei and led the diplomatic charge to bring Pinochet home from England, insisting on repeated occasions that Pinochet would be fairly tried in Chile. Now he became the leading official in the Lagos government arguing that Pinochet should not be tried.
18. *La Tercera*, October 12, 2000.
19. Interview with Juan Guzmán, January 2001.
20. Ibid.
21. *La Tercera*, January 2, 2001.
22. *La Tercera*, January 3, 2001.
23. *El Mostrador*, January 7, 2001.
24. *La Tercera*, January 12, 2001.
25. Roger Burbach, 'Military Horrors Shake Chile's Controlled Democracy', Redress Information and Analysis, January 24, 2001, www.redress.btinternet.co.uk.
26. *La Firme*, Santiago, January 2001.
27. Carmen Hertz is a remarkable example of the new women of Chile who dedicated their lives to resisting the dictatorship and have led the struggle for truth and justice. A warm, vibrant and elegant woman in her fifties, she has demonstrated enormous strength and resilience in the face of adversity. She was fresh out of law school and living with her husband, Carlos Berger, and their infant son in northern Chile when the coup occurred. Carlos, who worked at a radio station, was detained and then executed in October 1973. She was soon forced to flee abroad, to Buenos Aires, Caracas and Paris, finally returning to Chile in 1977. She immediately threw herself into human rights work, and in 1985 was the first lawyer to file charges against Arellano Stark for his role in the Caravan of Death. The charges were thrown out in

fifteen days, but in 1999 she filed new charges against Pinochet as well as Stark and became a central figure in the legal team that stripped Pinochet of his parliamentary immunity and successfully indicted him in January 2001. Burbach, 'Military Horrors'.

28. Burbach, 'Military Horrors'.
29. Ibid.
30. Interview with Carmen Hertz, January 2001.
31. *La Tercera*, January 24, 2001.
32. Ibid.
33. Roger Burbach, 'Pinochet in the Docket', Pacific News Service, January 31, 2001.
34. Ibid.
35. Ibid.
36. Ibid. Also interview with Carmen Hertz, January 2001.
37. Interview with Roberto Garretón, January 2001.
38. *La Nación*, February 2, 2001.
39. *La Tercera*, July 2, 2001.
40. Interview with Carmen Hertz, December 2001.
41. Ibid.
42. Interview with Hernan Quezada, December 2001.
43. *La Tercera*, July 8, 2001.
44. *La Tercera*, July 9, 2001.
45. 'Los tres pactos de Zaldívar que han salvado a Pinochet', *Primera Línea*, July 5, 2002. See also Roger Burbach, 'Pinochet Mocks Justice in Chile: "No Truce" Declares Human Rights Movement', Redress Information and Analysis, July 14, 2002, www.redress.btinternet.co.uk/rburbach10.htm.
46. 'Texto completo: la carta de Pinochet al Senado', *Primera Línea*, July 5, 2002.
47. *Primera Línea*, July 9, 2002.
48. *El Mostrador*, July 16 and 17, 2002.
49. 'Caso Pinochet en España', email by Joan Garcés, July 3, 2002.
50. Interview with Roberto Garretón, December 2001.
51. *Primera Línea*, January 6, 2003.
52. Interview with Juan Pablo Cárdenas, December 2002. Also interview with Tomas Moulían, December 2002.
53. Interview with Juan Guzmán, December 2002.
54. Pedro Pablo Gac Becerra, 'Hace 29 Años, en un Día como Hoy, La Caravana de la Muerte paso por Quillota', Resumen Numero 851, January 22, 2003, PolíticaConoSur@GruposYahoo.com
55. Interview with Roberto Garretón, April 2002.

Conclusion

1. For a discussion of the relationship of the Pinochet Affair to historic socialism, the new social movements and globalization in the Americas, see Roger Burbach, *Globalization and Postmodern Politics: From Zapatistas to High Tech Robber Barons*, Pluto Press, London 2001, pp. 105–15.
2. Lucy Komisar, 'Into the Murky Depths of Operation Condor', *Los Angeles Times*, November 1, 1999.
3. Interview with Roberto Garretón, December 2001.
4. David Rieff, 'A New Age of Liberal Imperialism?', in Jeffrey N. Wasserstrom, Lynn Hunt and Marilyn B. Young, eds, *Human Rights and Revolutions*, Rowman & Littlefield, Lanham, MD 2000, p. 177.
5. See Samantha Power, 'Bystanders to Genocide', *Atlantic Monthly*, September 2001.
6. Interview with Roberto Garretón, April 2002.
7. Ibid.
8. 'Lying Down with Dogs', *Time*, October 17, 1994.
9. 'Haiti, Economic Trends and Outlook', US Department of Commerce, National Trade Data Bank, Online Paper, September 3, 1999.
10. Mary Kaldor, 'Transnational Civil Society', in Tim Dunne and Nicholas J. Wheeler, eds, *Human Rights in Global Politics*, Cambridge University Press, Cambridge 1999, pp. 202–5.
11. Ibid., p. 210.
12. David Sugarman, 'From Unimaginable to Possible: Spain, Pinochet and the Judicialisation of Power', *Journal of Spanish Cultural Studies*, March 2002, p. 115.
13. Human Rights Watch, *1999 Human Rights World Report*, Online Report.
14. Henry Kissinger, 'The Pitfalls of Universal Jurisdiction', *Foreign Affairs*, Fall 2001.
15. Noam Chomsky, *The New Military Humanism: Lessons From Kosovo*, Common Courage Press, Monroe, ME 1999.
16. See Robin Blackburn, 'Kosovo: The War of NATO Expansion', in Wasserstrom et al., eds, *Human Rights and Revolutions*.
17. Fred Halliday, *Irish Times*, April 1, 1999.
18. Baltasar Garzón, 'The West Shares the Blame', in Roger Burbach and Ben Clarke, eds, *September 11 and the US War*, City Lights Books, San Francisco 2002.
19. *New York Times*, March 14, 2002.
20. *New York Times*, February 13, 2003.
21. Justin Webb, 'White House Threatens Belgium over War Crimes Prosecution' BBC, April 29, 2003.
22. *New York Times*, June 12, 2003.

Bibliography

Amnesty International. 'Chile, An Inescapable Obligation: Bringing to Justice Those Responsible for Crimes Against Humanity Committed Under Military Rule', October 1998.

Araya Villegas, Manuel. *Biografía de su Excelencia el Presidente de la República y miembros de la Honorable Junta de Gobierno. Perfiles de Honor*, Santiago, Teltrapre, 1984.

Azócar, Pablo. *Pinochet: epitafio para un tirano*, Santiago, Editorial Cuarto Propio, 1999.

Beckett, Andy. *Pinochet in Piccadilly: Britain and Chile's Hidden History*, London, Faber & Faber, 2002.

Bermúdez, Norberto and Juan Gasparini. *El testigo secreto: el Juez Garzón contra la impunidad en Argentina y Chile*, Madrid, Javier Vergara Editor, 1999.

Blackburn, Robin. 'Kosovo: The War of NATO Expansion', in Jeffrey N. Wasserstrom et al., eds, *Human Rights and Revolutions*, Lanham MD, Rowman & Littlefield, 2000.

Blum, William. *The CIA: A Forgotten History. US Global Interventions Since World War II*, London, Zed Books, 1986.

Brody, Reed and Michael Ratner, eds. *The Pinochet Papers: The Case of Augusto Pinochet in Spain and Britain*, The Hague, London and Boston, Kluwer Law International, 2000.

Burbach, Roger. *Globalization and Postmodern Politics: From Zapatistas to High Tech Robber Barons*, London, Pluto Press, 2001.

———. 'The Man Who Brought General Pinochet to Justice: Interview with Chilean Judge Juan Guzmán', complete transcript, January 2001.

———. 'Military Horrors Shake Chile's Controlled Democracy', Redress Information and Analysis, 24 January 2001, www.redress.btinternet.co.uk.

———. 'Pinochet in the Docket', Pacific News Service, 31 January 2001.

———. 'Pinochet Mocks Justice in Chile: "No Truce" Declares Human Rights Movement', Redress Information and Analysis, 14 July 2002, www.redress.btinternet.co.uk/rburbach10.htm.

Caballo, Ascanio, Manuel Salazar and Oscar Sepúlveda. *La historia oculta del régimen militar, memoria de una época, 1973–1988*, Santiago, Editorial Grijalbo, 1997.

Cárdenas, Juan Pablo. *Contigo en la distancia: crónicas diplomáticas*, Santiago, Cuarto Propio, 1998.

Chomsky, Noam. *The New Military Humanism: Lessons From Kosovo*, Monroe ME, Common Courage Press, 1999.

Coloane R., Juan Francisco, *Britannia y un general*, Santiago, Lom Ediciones, 2000.

Constitución Política de la República de Chile de 1980. Article 5.

Corporación de Promoción y Defensa de los Derechos del Pueblo, (CODEPU). Foro de Derechos Humanos de la Cumbre de los Pueblos de America, 14–17 April 1998, Santiago, Lom Ediciones, 1998.

———. *El irrenunciable camino de la justicia: Pinochet y la mesa de diálogo*, Serie Opinión y Perspectivas, No. 6, Santiago 2000.

———. *Tortura durante la transición a la democracia. El trabajo de CODEPU en el período*. Serie Retrospectiva y Reflexión, No. 4., Santiago, June 1999.

Columbian Encyclopedia, Online Version, 6th Edition, 2001.

Constable, Pamela and Arturo Valenzuela. *A Nation of Enemies: Chile Under Pinochet*, New York, W.W. Norton, 1991.

Correa, Raquel and Elizabeth Subercaseaux. *Ego Sum*, Santiago, Editorial Planeta Chilena, 1986.

Deves, Eduardo. 'Las cuatro vidas de Augusto Pinochet', unpublished manuscript, Santiago.

Encyclopedia of World History. 'Chile, 1932–45', Bartleby.com, Online 2001 edn, www.bartleby.com/67/2247.html.

Fleet, Michael. *The Rise and Fall of Chilean Christian Democracy*, Princeton NJ, Princeton University Press, 1985.

Gac Becerra, Pedro Pablo. 'Hace 29 años, en un día como hoy, La Caravana de la Muerte paso por quillota', Resumen Número 851, January 22, 2003, PolíticaConoSur@GruposYahoo.com

Garcés, Joan E. *Allende y la experiencia Chilena: las armas de la política*, Barcelona, Editorial Ariel, 1976.

Ensalaco, Mark. *Chile Under Pinochet: Uncovering the Truth*, Philadelphia, University of Pennsylvania Press, 2000.

Fundación de Ayuda Social de las Iglesias Cristianas (FASIC). Fasic, La Institución, www.fasic.org/institu/institucion.htm

Furci, Carmelo. *The Chilean Communist Party and the Road to Socialism*, London, Zed Books, 1984.

Garzón, Baltazar. 'The West Shares the Blame', in Roger Burbach and Ben Clarke, eds, *September 11 and the US War*, San Francisco, City Lights Books, 2002.

González, Mónica. *La conjura, los mil y un días del golpe*, Santiago, Ediciones B Chile, 2000.

Guzmán, Patricio. 'The Pinochet Case', Documentary Film, 2002.

Halliday, Fred. *Irish Times*, April 1, 1999.

Hersh, Seymour M. *The Price of Power: Kissinger in the Nixon White House*, New York, Summit Books, 1983.

Human Rights Watch. 'Why Chile Won't Prosecute Pinochet', New York, 11 November 1998.

————. *1999 Human Rights World Report*, Online Report.

Huneeus, Carlos, *El régimen de Pinochet*, Santiago, Editorial Sudamericana Chilena, 2000.

Hutchinson, Elizabeth Quay, and Patricio Orellana. *El movimiento de derechos humanos en Chile, 1973–1990*, Santiago, Centro de Estudios Políticos Latinoamericanos Simón Bolívar (CEPLA), 1991.

Kaldor, Mary. 'Transnational Civil Society', in Tim Dunne and Nicholas J. Wheeler, eds, *Human Rights in Global Politics*, Cambridge and New York, Cambridge University Press, 1999.

Keck, Margaret E. and Kathryn Sikkink. *Activists Beyond Borders: Advocacy Networks in International Politics*, Ithaca NY, Cornell University Press, 1998.

Kershaw, Ian. *Hitler, 1889–1936: Hubris*, New York, W.W. Norton, 1999.

Kirkpatrick, Jeanne. *Dictatorships and Double Standards*, New York, Simon & Schuster, 1982.

Kissinger, Henry, 'The Pitfalls of Universal Jurisdiction', *Foreign Affairs*, Fall 2001.

Komisar, Lucy. 'Into the Murky Depths of Operation Condor', *Los Angeles Times*, November 1, 1999.

————. 'Kissinger Encouraged Chile's Brutal Repression, New Documents Show', *Albion Monitor*, 8 March 1999.

Lira, Elizabeth and Brian Loveman. *Las suaves cenizas del olvido: La vía chilena de Reconciliación, 1814–1932*, Santiago, DIBAM/LOM, 1999.

Loveman, Brian, *Chile: The Legacy of Hispanic Capitalism*, New York, Oxford University Press, 1988.

Lutz, Patricia. *Años de vientos sucios*, Santiago, Editorial Planeta Sur, 1999.

————. 'Biografía "No Autorizada" de Pinochet', interview with Jimena Córdova, *Mujer a Mujer*, 18 May 2002, Santiago.

Mas, Fernando, *De Nuremberg a Madrid: Historia Íntima de un Juicio*, Grijalbo, Buenos Aires, 1999.

Martin, Elizabeth A., ed., *Oxford Dictionary of Law*, Oxford University Press, eBook Online, 2002.

Mera, Jorge, 'Chile: Truth and Justice under the Democratic Government' in Naomi Roht-Arriaza, ed., *Impunity and Human Rights in International Law and Practice*, Oxford University Press, New York 1995.

Monekeberg, Maria Olivia. *El saqueo de los grupos económicos al estado Chileno*, Santiago, Ediciones B Chile, 2001.

Moulían, Tomas. *Chile actual: anatomía de un mito*, Santiago, Lom Ediciones, 1997.

NACLA (North American Congress on Latin America). *New Chile*, Berkeley, 1972.

NACLA's Latin America and Empire Report, 'Chile: Facing the Blockade', by Elizabeth Farnsworth, Richard Feinberg and Eric Leenson, vol. 7, no. 1, January 1973.

NACLA's Latin America and Empire Report, 'Chile: The Story Behind the Coup', vol. 7, no. 8, October 1973.

NACLA Report on the Americas, 'Carter and the Generals, Human Rights in the Southern Cone', vol. 3, no. 1, March–April 1979.

NACLA Report on the Americas, 'Pinochet: The Great Conciliator', vol. 32, no. 2, September–October 1998.

National Security Archive. Declassified Documents on Chile. See National Security Archive online documents on Chile, www.gwu.edu/~nsarchiv/latin_america/chile.htm..

O'Shaughnessy, Hugh. *Pinochet: The Politics of Torture*, New York University Press, New York, 2000.

Otano, Rafael, *Crónica de la transición*, Santiago, Editorial Planeta Chilena, 1995.

Oyarzun, María Eugenia. *Conversaciones Inéditas, Augusto Pinochet: Diálogos con su Historia*, Santiago, Editorial Sudamericana Chilena, 1999.

Padilla Ballesteros, Elías. *La memoria y el olvido, detenidos desaparecidos en Chile*, Santiago, Ediciones Orígenes, 1995.

Pinochet Ugarte, Augusto. *Camino recorrido: memorias de un soldado*, Santiago, Instituto Geográfico Militar de Chile, 1990.

———. *The Crucial Day, September 11, 1973*, English edn, Santiago, Editorial Renacimiento, 1982.

———. *Geopolítica*, 3rd edn, Santiago, Editorial Andrés Bello, 1977.

———. *Síntesis geográfica de la República de Chile*, Santiago, Instituto Geográfico Militar de Chile, 1963.

Portales, Felipe. *Chile: una democracia tutelada*, Santiago, Editorial Sudamericana Chilena, 2000.

Power, Jonathan. *Amnesty International, The Human Rights Story*, Oxford and New York, Pergamon Press, 1981.

Power, Samantha. 'Bystanders to Genocide', *Atlantic Monthly*, September 2001.

Rieff, David. 'A New Age of Liberal Imperialism?', in Jeffrey N. Wasserstrom, Lynn Hunt and Marilyn B. Young, eds, *Human Rights and Revolutions*, Rowman & Littlefield, Lanham, MD 2000.

Roberts, Kenneth M. *Deepening Democracy? The Modern Left and Social Movements in Chile and Peru*, Stanford CA, Stanford University Press, 1998.

Robinson, William I. *Promoting Polyarchy: Globalization, US Intervention, and Hegemony*, Cambridge, Cambridge University Press, 1996.

Rojas, Paz, Viviana Uribe, María Eugenia Rojas, Iris Largo, Isabel Ropert and Víctor Espinoza. *Páginas en blanco: el 11 de Septiembre en La Moneda*, Santiago, Ediciones B Chile, 2001.

Schneider, Cathy Lisa. *Shantytown Protest in Pinochet's Chile*, Philadelphia, Temple University Press, 1995.

Schoultz, Lars, *Human Rights and the United States Policy in Latin America*, Princeton NJ, Princeton University Press, 1981.

Sepúlveda R., Lucía. 'Aylwin mató a la revista análisis', SERPAL, Servicio de Prensa Alternativa, 21 January 2003, in *Boletín Piensa Chile*, www. piensachile.com.

Siavelis, Peter M. *The President and Congress in Post Authoritarian Chile, Institutional Constraints to Democratic Consolidation*, University Park PA, Pennsylvania State University Press, 2000.

Smith, Brian H., 'Old Allies, New Enemies: The Catholic Church as Opposition to Military Rule in Chile, 1973–1979', in J. Samuel Valenzuela and Arturo Valenzuela, eds, *Military Rule in Chile: Dictatorship and Oppositions*, Baltimore MD, Johns Hopkins University Press, 1986.

Spooner, Mary Helen. *Soldiers in a Narrow Land: The Pinochet Regime in Chile*. Los Angeles and Berkeley, University of California Press, 1994.

Sugarman, David, 'From Unimaginable to Possible: Spain, Pinochet and the Judicialisation of Power', *Journal of Spanish Cultural Studies*, March, 2002.

Time. 'Lying Down with Dogs', 17 October 1994.

US Department of Commerce. National Trade Data Bank, 'Haiti, Economic Trends and Outlook', online paper, 3 September 1999.

US Senate Intelligence Committee. *Covert Action in Chile, 1963–73*, Washington DC, US Government Printing Office, 18 December 1975.

Verdugo, Patricia. *La Caravana de la Muerte: pruebas a la vista*, Santiago, Editorial Sudamericana Chilena, 2000.

———. *Chile, Pinochet, and the Caravan of Death*, University of Miami, North–South Center Press, 2001.

———. *Interferencia secreta, 11 de Septiembre de 1973*, Santiago, Editorial Sudamericana Chilena, 1998.

Verdugo, Patricia and Carmen Hertz. *Operación Siglo XX*, Santiago, Las Ediciones del Ornitorrinco, 1990.

Vial, Gonzalo. *Pinochet: La Biografía*, 2 vols, Santiago, Empresa El Mercurio, 2002.

Webber, Frances. 'Justice and the General: People vs. Pinochet', *Race & Class*, vol. 41, no. 4, 2000, London, Institute of Race Relations, pp. 43–57.

Weeks, Gregory. 'Waiting for Cincinnatus: The Role of Pinochet in Postauthoritarian Chile', paper prepared for presentation at the meeting of the Latin American Studies Association, Miami, March 2000.

Wilde, Alexander. 'Irruptions of Memory: Expressive Politics in Chile's Transition to Democracy', *Journal of Latin American Studies*, no. 31, 1999, pp. 473–500.

Zammit, J. Ann, ed. *The Chilean Road to Socialism*, Proceedings of an ODEPLAN–IDS Round Table, March 1972, Institute of Development Studies, University of Sussex, 1973.

Newspapers, magazines and news services

Agence France Presse
Diario Estratégica, Santiago
La Firme, Santiago
Guardian, London
Irish Times
El Mercurio, Santiago, Chile
El Mostrador, Online News Service, Santiago
La Nación, Santiago
New York Times
Pacific News Service, San Francisco, California
El País, Madrid
Primera Línea, Online News Service, Santiago
La Segunda, Santiago
Sunday Telegraph, London
Time
Washington Post

Index

Aznar, Prime Minister José Maria,
117–18, 119

Balmaceda, José Manuel, 21
Bartle, Ronald, 115
Beausire, William, 109
Benenson, Peter, 56–7
Bengoa, José, 125
Bindman, Geoffrey, 101
Pinochet's extradition and, 109
Blair, Prime Minister Tony, extradition
of Pinochet and, 111
boinazo, 84–5
Bonilla, General Oscar
death of, 53
DINA and, 52–3
Bouterse, Desi, international law and,
156
Bush, George (senior), 151
Bush, George W., human rights and,
158–9

Cáceres, Carlos, 79
Caravan of Death, 48–9, 125, 126, 142
Prosecutions and, 128, 133
Carter, Jimmy, 64–5
human rights and, 149
Cassidy, Sheila, 109
Castillo Velasco, Jaime, 67
Castro, Fidel, in Chile, 35
Cavallo, Ricardo Miguel, international
law and, 155–6
Cheyre, General Juan Emilio, 143–4
Chile Declassification Project, 148
Chile Mi Patria, 130
Chilean/British Ad Hoc Committee
for Justice, 111
Chomsky, Noam, 157
Christian Democratic Party
arrest of Pinochet and, 105–6
Communist Party and, 44
September 11 holiday and, 93
churches, role in human rights work,
59–60, 61
CIA, 45
FRAPH and, 153
General Viaux and, 33–4
Operation Condor and, 148
propaganda against Allende, 11–13
September 11 coup and, 15
Clinton, President Bill, 152

CNI (National Centre of Information),
65
founding of, 55
CNT (National Workers' Command),
73
CODEJU (Commission de Derechos
Juveniles), 68
CODEPU (Committee for the
Defence of the Rights of the
People), 47, 68
Amnesty law and, 86
Cold War, end of, and human rights,
150–55
Comando Conjunto, MIR and, 51–2
Comando de No, 77–8
Comités Anti-Represivos, 75
Comisión Chilena de Derechos
Humanos, founding of, 67–8
Communists
growing campaign against, 28,
43–5
Nixon and, 12
resurgence of, 70
CONAR (National Committee to
Assist Refugees), 58–9
Concertación, 81
formation of, 79
political activity and, 87–8
September 11 holiday and, 92–3
CONESA (Council of National
Security), 80, 132
Contreras, Lieutenant Colonel (later
General) Manuel, 60
assassinations in Washington and,
85–6
as head of DINA, 49–55
Cook, Robin, 120
Copachi (Comité de Cooperación para
la Paz en Chile), 59–60
Corbyn, Jeremy, 104, 110, 112
Cuban Revolution (1959), 8–9

Dayton Accords, 154
Debray, Régis, 9
democratic socialism, death of in
Chile, 2
Derian, Patricia, 65
desaparecido, see disappeared
desencanto, period of, 87
Desmond, Cosmas, 57
Día de la Raza, 7

Titles of related interest from Zed Books

Rogue State: A Guide to the World's Only Superpower
Updated Edition
William Blum

'After reading *Rogue State*, it is impossible to hang fast to the comforting illusion that the "American Way" is some kind of enlightenment.' – Will Self in the *New Statesman*

    Hb ISBN 1 84277 220 1 £36.95
    Pb ISBN 1 84277 221 X £ 9.99

Killing Hope: US Military and CIA Interventions Since World War II
William Blum

'Far and away the best book on the topic.' – Noam Chomsky

    Hb ISBN 1 84277 368 2 £50.00
    Pb ISBN 1 84277 369 0 £12.99

Bitter Dawn: East Timor – A People's Story
Irena Cristalis

'The author's knowledge, understanding and love of the country shine from every page. This will surely become the definitive account of East Timor's most traumatic years.' – Fergal Keane, BBC Special Correspondent

    Hb ISBN 1 84277 144 2 £49.95 $69.95
    Pb ISBN 1 84277 145 0 £14.95 $25.00

Apartheid Israel: Possibilities for the Struggle Within
Uri Davis

'a devastating critique of Israel's internal apartheid system and by extension the entire ideology of political Zionism.' – Hisham Sharabi

    Hb ISBN 1 84277 338 0 £49.95 $75.00
    Pb ISBN 1 84277 339 9 £14.95 $22.50

Living Silence: Burma under Military Rule
Christina Fink

'*Living Silence* is particularly valuable for its study of the psychological effects of military rule on the people of Burma.' – Aung San Suu Kyi

    Hb ISBN 1 85649 925 1 £49.95 $69.95
    Pb ISBN 1 85649 926 X £14.95 $19.95

Syria: Neither Bread nor Freedom
Alan George

'This searing documentary takes the reader on a chilling tour inside Syrian politics, the actions of a courageous civil society, and the reactions by abusive power holders. It is an astounding record and at the same time a disturbingly beautiful book.' – Lotte Leicht, Brussels Director, Human Rights Watch

 Hb ISBN 1 84277 212 0 £39.95 $65.00
 Pb ISBN 1 84277 213 9 £13.95 $22.50

The Future of Revolutions: Rethinking Radical Change in the Age of Globalization
Edited by John Foran

'A long fascinating conversation about whether revolution is still a relevant concept with which to analyse the contemporary world, and if so, under what conditions they might occur.' – Immanuel Wallerstein, Yale University

 Hb ISBN 1 84277 032 2 £49.95 $75.00
 Pb ISBN 1 84277 033 0 £15.95 $25.00

The Economist's Tale: A Consultant Encounters Hunger and the World Bank
Peter Griffiths

'Unputdownable – as thrilling as any thriller.... I've never read an account of the life of an economic consultant which came anywhere near it in the vividness of the observation or the pace of the action.' – Clive Dewey, Emeritus Reader in Economic History, University of Leicester

 Hb ISBN 1 84277 184 1 £49.95 $69.95
 Pb ISBN 1 84277 185 X £15.95 $25.00

Another American Century? The United States and the World since 9/11
Nicholas Guyatt

'A provocative book that provides an illuminating point of departure for future discussions about how to make the world more just and equitable and what responsibilities the United States should assume in such efforts.' – *Millennium Journal*

 Hb ISBN 1 84277 428 X £36.95 $55.00
 Pb ISBN 1 84277 429 8 £ 9.99 $17.50

Mexico under Siege: Popular Resistance to Presidential Despotism
Donald Hodges and Ross Gandy

'Offers a comprehensive introduction to the Mexican revolutionary tradition and thus should be read by all US activists seeking a more international perspective.... This book has no parallel in English or Spanish.' – *New*

Formulation, June 2002
  Hb ISBN 1 84277 124 8   £45.00 $69.95
  Pb ISBN 1 84277 125 6   £14.95 $25.00

*Armed Actors in Latin America: Organised Violence and State Failure
in Latin America*
Edited by Kees Koonings and Dirk Kruijt

In this volume, Latin Americanist scholars explore the recent evidence relating
to the ways in which partial state failure in the continent is interacting with
organized violence of a new type, thereby undermining the process of democratic consolidation that has characterized Latin America over the past two
decades.
  Hb ISBN 1 84277 444 1   £49.95 $65.00
  Pb ISBN 1 84277 445 X   £16.95 $27.50

*Societies of Fear: The Legacy of Civil War, Violence and Terror in
Latin America*
Edited by Kees Koonings and Dirk Kruijt

This superb collection examines the ongoing legacy of past conflict, violence
and terror in the countries of South and Central America. How deep-rooted
in the historical experience of these societies is this legacy? In particular,
could it continue to thwart economic recovery, social justice and democratic
consensus and stability?
  Hb ISBN 1 85649 766 6   £49.95 $65.00
  Pb ISBN 1 85649 767 4   £16.95 $27.50

*Political Armies: The Military and Nation Building in the
Age of Democracy*
Edited by Kees Koonings and Dirk Kruijt

'*Political Armies* lays bare the important truth about civil-military relations in
the post-cold war world' – Johanna Mendelson Forman, Research Professor,
American University, Washington, DC
  Hb ISBN 1 85649 979 0   £49.95 $75.00
  Pb ISBN 1 85649 980 4   £16.95 $29.95

Running Guns: The Global Black Market in Small Arms
Edited by Lora Lumpe

'This book provides a wealth of analysis and outlines concrete steps that
governments must take if they are serious about shutting down the traffic in
small arms.' – Jody Williams, International Campaign to Ban Landmines and
Nobel Peace Laureate
  Hb ISBN 1 85649 872 7   £49.95 $69.95
  Pb ISBN 1 85649 873 5   £15.95 $27.50

A People Betrayed: The Role of the West in Rwanda's Genocide
Linda Melvern

'Quite extraordinary: precise, and yet overwhelming; a fine balance in the face of depravity … Linda Melvern has written an extraordinary account of the Rwanda genocide, and the shocking failure of the West to lift a finger.… What Melvern demonstrates so powerfully is that where Western geopolitical interests are absent, Western morality and 'civilised' concerns are nowhere to be found.… A brave and compelling book.' – Professor Richard Falk, Center of International Studies, Princeton University

    Hb ISBN 1 85649 830 1 £49.95 $69.95
    Pb ISBN 1 85649 831 X £14.95 $19.95

The Congo from Leopold to Kabila: A People's History
Georges Nzongola-Ntalaja

'Georges Nzongola-Ntalaja is one among those very few intellectuals who possess the background, the knowledge, the commitment and the vantage point from which to assess the historical possibilities for contemporary Congo.' – Mahmood Mamdani, Herbert Lehman Professor of Government, Columbia University

    Hb ISBN 1 84277 052 7 £45.00 $69.95
    Pb ISBN 1 84277 053 5 £14.95 $25.00

Continent of Mothers, Continent of Hope: Understanding and Promoting Development in Africa Today
Torild Skard

'This is a book from the front-line in the defence of children in West Africa. And as you read, it grows on you.' – Stephen Lewis, UN Special Envoy for HIV/AIDS in Africa, former Deputy Executive Director of UNICEF

    Hb ISBN 1 84277 106 X £45.00 $65.00
    Pb ISBN 1 84277 107 8 £14.95 $22.50

Primitive Rebels or Revolutionary Modernizers? The Kurdish Nationalist Movement in Turkey
Paul J. White

'This is the best scholarly analysis yet written on the PKK. It will be difficult in future to understand the great importance of the "Kurdish question" in the Middle East and global politics without reading White's book.' – Professor Robert Olson, University of Kentucky

    Hb ISBN 1 85649 821 2 £49.95 $69.95
    Pb ISBN 1 85649 822 0 £15.95 $25.00